Exam Ref AZ-300
Microsoft Azure Architect
Technologies

Mike Pfeiffer

Derek Schauland

Nicole Stevens

Tim Warner

Exam Ref AZ-300 Microsoft Azure Architect Technologies

Published with the authorization of Microsoft Corporation by:
Pearson Education, Inc.

ISBN-13: 978-0-13-580254-0
ISBN-10: 0-13-580254-7

Library of Congress Control Number: 2019948461

1 2019

TRADEMARKS

Microsoft and the trademarks listed at *http://www.microsoft.com* on the "Trademarks" webpage are trademarks of the Microsoft group of companies. All other marks are property of their respective owners.

WARNING AND DISCLAIMER

Every effort has been made to make this book as complete and as accurate as possible, but no warranty or fitness is implied. The information provided is on an "as is" basis. The authors, the publisher, and Microsoft Corporation shall have neither liability nor responsibility to any person or entity with respect to any loss or damages arising from the information contained in this book or from the use of the programs accompanying it.

SPECIAL SALES

For information about buying this title in bulk quantities, or for special sales opportunities (which may include electronic versions; custom cover designs; and content particular to your business, training goals, marketing focus, or branding interests), please contact our corporate sales department at corpsales@pearsoned.com or (800) 382-3419.

For government sales inquiries, please contact governmentsales@pearsoned.com.

For questions about sales outside the U.S., please contact intlcs@pearson.com.

CREDITS

EDITOR-IN-CHIEF
Brett Bartow

ACQUISITIONS EDITOR
Loretta Yates

ASSISTANT EDITOR
Charvi Arora

DEVELOPMENT EDITOR
Songlin Qiu

MANAGING EDITOR
Sandra Schroeder

SENIOR PROJECT EDITOR
Tracey Croom

COPY EDITOR
Charlotte Kughen

INDEXER
Ken Johnson

PROOFREADER
Donna Mulder

TECHNICAL EDITOR
Thomas Palathra

EDITORIAL ASSISTANT
Cindy Teeters

COVER DESIGNER
Twist Creative, Seattle

COMPOSITOR
codeMantra

Contents at a glance

Contents

Chapter 5   Develop for the cloud and for Azure Storage   217

Acknowledgments

Thank you to Loretta for inviting me to become a Microsoft Press author; that was a career-long dream you helped me realize! Thanks to my co-authors—Mike, Derek, and Nicole—for making this book so much easier to complete. Thanks to Charvi for your project management. Thanks to the Microsoft Azure product teams for working so diligently to deliver such an excellent public cloud platform. Last, but certainly not least, thanks to all my students, without whom I would not have such a rewarding career.

—TIM WARNER

Working on this book has been a great experience and has taught me a lot about the cloud. I would like to thank my coauthors for the opportunity to work on this project. I also thank my wife Laura (and my co-workers) for allowing me time to devote to getting this completed. While books are a good deal of work, they always manage to teach me things and leave me better off than when I entered the project; for that I am eternally grateful.

—DEREK SCHAULAND

I'm grateful for the opportunity to contribute to this book project. I'd like to thank my wife, Abby, and my daughter, Isabel, for putting up with my crazy schedule! Love you guys. I'd also like to thank my co-authors Derek Schauland, Nicole Stevens, and Tim Warner for their determination and work ethic. You guys are amazing.

—MIKE PFEIFFER

Huge thanks to Mike Pfeiffer for sending this awesome opportunity my way and dragging me so far beyond my comfort zone I can't see it. To the editors from Pearson, Loretta Yates and Charvi Arora, for their support, and Qui Songlin and Thomas Palathra for deciphering my ramblings and quirky English colloquialisms. To my friends, who always make me smile while supplying a Costa or beer as needed. To my parents, who instilled in me the work ethic and drive needed to get projects like this over the line. And finally, to my amazing family, who fill our house with laughter. In particular, my boys Jack and Harry, whose energy, creativity and passion inspire and motivate me every day.

—NICOLE STEVENS

About the Authors

 TIM WARNER is a Microsoft Certified Azure Solutions Architect with more than 20 years of experience working with the Microsoft technology stack. Tim teaches Microsoft Azure courses for Pluralsight and O'Reilly Live Online Training, and he's based in Nashville, Tennessee. Contact Tim via Twitter (@TechTrainerTim) or his website, TechTrainerTim.com.

 DEREK SCHAULAND is an IT professional with 20 years' experience. He currently specializes in cloud technologies. He spent 10 years of his career as a Microsoft MVP, first in file system storage and then in cloud and datacenter management.

In addition to writing about cloud technologies, he has co-authored two other books and countless articles and blogs. Outside of the technology space, he enjoys barbecuing with family and friends.

 MIKE PFEIFFER is a 20-year tech industry veteran who's worked for some of the largest technology companies in the world, including Microsoft and Amazon Web Services (AWS). He's the founder and chief technologist at CloudSkills.io, a cloud consulting and training firm. Mike is an author for Pluralsight, international conference speaker, Microsoft Azure MVP, and host of the CloudSkills.fm podcast.

 NICOLE STEVENS is technical director of an independent software venture (ISV) in the United Kingdom, which provides on-premises and hosted solutions across a variety of technologies and sectors. She has spent more than 20 years working within software development, starting out as an Oracle DBA to troubleshoot performance, design, and integration issues for large enterprises across EMEA. Switching to an ISV start-up brought fresh challenges, with a role spanning IT professional, technical consultancy, technical pre-sales, and software development. Nicole is currently driving adoption of Microsoft cloud services across the business, and her primary focus is the re-architecture of legacy software solutions for customers in the cloud.

Introduction

The purpose of the AZ-300 certification exam is to test your understanding of Microsoft Azure solutions architecture. The exam validates your ability to recognize which Azure services compose a particular solution and your ability to perform service configuration. Like the AZ-300 certification exam, this book is geared toward giving you a broad understanding of Azure itself, of the common services and components in Azure, and of Azure solutions architecture.

While we've made every effort possible to make the information in this book accurate, Azure is rapidly evolving, and there's a chance that some of the screens in the Azure portal are slightly different now than they were when this book was written. It's also possible that other minor changes have taken place, such as name changes in features and so on.

This book covers every major topic area found on the exam, but it does not cover every exam question. Only the Microsoft exam team has access to the exam questions, and Microsoft regularly adds new questions to the exam, making it impossible to cover specific questions. You should consider this book a supplement to your relevant real-world experience and other study materials. If you encounter a topic in this book that you do not feel completely comfortable with, use the "Need more review?" links in the text to find more information and take the time to research and study the topic. Great information is available in the Microsoft Azure documentation (*https://docs.microsoft.com/azure*) and Microsoft Learn (*https://microsoft.com/learn*).

Organization of this book

This book is organized by the "Skills measured" list published for the AZ-300 certification exam. The "Skills measured" list is available for each exam on the Microsoft Worldwide Learning website at *https://aka.ms/examlist*. Each chapter in this book corresponds to a major topic area in the list, and the technical tasks in each topic area determine a chapter's organization. If an exam covers six major topic areas, for example, the corresponding book contains six chapters.

Microsoft certifications

Microsoft certifications distinguish you by proving your command of a broad set of skills and experience with current Microsoft products and technologies. The exams and corresponding certifications are developed to validate your mastery of critical competencies as you design and develop, or implement and support, solutions with Microsoft products and technologies both with on-premises solutions and in the cloud. Certification brings a variety of benefits to the individual and to employers and organizations.

> **MORE INFO** **ALL MICROSOFT CERTIFICATIONS**
>
> For information about Microsoft certifications, including a full list of available certifications, go to *http://www.microsoft.com/learn*.

Quick access to online references

Throughout this book are addresses to webpages that the authors recommend you visit for more information. Some of these addresses (also known as Uniform Resource Locators, or URLs) can be painstaking to type into a web browser, so we've compiled all of them into a single list that readers of the print edition can refer to while they read.

Download the list at *https://MicrosoftPressStore.com/ExamRefAZ300/downloads*.

The URLs are organized by chapter and heading. Every time you come across a URL in the book, find the hyperlink in the list to go directly to the webpage.

Errata, updates, and book support

We've made every effort to ensure the accuracy of this book and its companion content. You can access updates to this book—in the form of a list of submitted errata and their related corrections—at

https://MicrosoftPressStore.com/ExamRefAZ300/errata.

If you discover an error that is not already listed, please submit it to us at the same page.

For additional book support and information, please visit *https://MicrosoftPressStore.com/Support*.

Please note that product support for Microsoft Azure is not offered through the previous addresses. For help with Microsoft Azure, go to *https://timw.info/azsupport*.

Stay in touch

Let's keep the conversation going! We're on Twitter: *http://twitter.com/MicrosoftPress*.

Important: How to use this book to study for the exam

Certification exams validate your on-the-job experience and product knowledge. To gauge your readiness to take an exam, use this Exam Ref to help you check your understanding of the skills tested by the exam. Determine the topics you know well and the areas in which you need more experience. To help you refresh your skills in specific areas, we have also provided "Need more review?" pointers, which direct you to more in-depth information outside the book.

The Exam Ref is not a substitute for hands-on experience. This book is not designed to teach you new skills.

We recommend that you round out your exam preparation by using a combination of available study materials and courses. Learn more about available classroom training and find free online courses and live events at http://microsoft.com/learn. Microsoft Official Practice Tests are available for many exams at http://aka.ms/practicetests.

This book is organized by the "Skills measured" list published for the exam. The "Skills measured" list for each exam is available on the Microsoft Learn website: http://aka.ms/examlist.

Note that this Exam Ref is based on this publicly available information and the author's experience. To safeguard the integrity of the exam, authors do not have access to the exam questions.

## CHAPTER 1

Deploy and configure infrastructure

If you already work as a Microsoft Azure cloud solutions architect (CSA), you might wonder why the AZ-300 certification exam requires that you demonstrate how to perform resource deployment and configuration tasks. After all, isn't the CSA role normally associated with designing solutions and then handing them off to the professionals who will implement them?

Although that may be the case in the real world, you still can expect to see performance-based lab items on your AZ-300 exam. These items involve making a Remote Desktop Protocol (RDP) connection to a Microsoft-managed Azure subscription directly from within your exam session. In each lab, you're required to complete a series of deployment or configuration tasks by using the Azure portal.

> **IMPORTANT**
> ### *Have you read page xiv?*
> It contains valuable information regarding the skills you need to pass the Microsoft AZ-300 certification exam.

The goal for this chapter is to make sure you know how to do all the work that comprises this objective domain. Remember that the Azure Solution Architect certification is an expert-level title, so we expect that you already have at least intermediate-level Azure configuration abilities.

Skills covered in this chapter:

- Skill 1.1: Analyze resource utilization and consumption
- Skill 1.2: Create and configure storage accounts
- Skill 1.3: Create and configure a virtual machine for Windows and Linux
- Skill 1.4: Automate the deployment of virtual machines
- Skill 1.5: Implement solutions that use virtual machines
- Skill 1.6: Create connectivity between virtual networks
- Skill 1.7: Implement and manage Azure virtual networking
- Skill 1.8: Manage Azure Active Directory
- Skill 1.9: Implement and manage hybrid identities

Skill 1.1: Analyze resource utilization and consumption

We'll start by reviewing how to check your Azure resource utilization. Your customers will be nearly universally concerned with monitoring their monthly spend and finding opportunities for optimization. Troubleshooting is another great reason to enable diagnostic settings on all your resources.

> **This skill covers how to:**
> - Configure diagnostic settings on resources
> - Create a baseline for resources
> - Analyze metrics across subscriptions
> - Create and analyze alerts across subscriptions
> - Create action groups
> - Monitor for unused resources
> - Monitor and report on spend

Configure diagnostic settings on resources

As you know, Microsoft Azure has several different types of logs to generate unique data streams. The Activity log is Azure's control-plane log, and it tracks all resource operations in your subscriptions. You can look at the Activity log as an audit log where you can determine, for example, who shut down a production virtual machine (VM) and when they shut it down.

By contrast, guest operating system-level logs are enabled for individual virtual machines, they require an agent, and they collect machine-specific data from the perspective of the guest operating system.

This exam objective is concerned with Azure resource diagnostic logs, which require no agent and pull their data directly from the Azure Resource Manager backplane.

We can export Azure diagnostic log data to any of these three destinations for storage and further analysis:

- **Azure storage** Depending on the particular diagnostic log stream, Azure may use blog storage and/or table storage.
- **Event hub** The Event hub is capable of high-velocity data aggregation; you can then subscribe to event data funneled into the hub.
- **Azure Monitor logs** Use the Kusto Query Language (KQL) to run interactive queries against Azure diagnostic log data.

Imagine you need to configure diagnostic log collection for a public IP address resource. Follow these steps to enable diagnostic data collection for the resource:

1. Log into the Azure portal and browse to Monitor.
2. Select the Diagnostic settings option in the Settings menu.

3. Optionally, use the filter controls to drill into the target Azure subscription, resource group, resource type, and resource. In Figure 1-1, we've enabled diagnostics on a public IP address resource named vm1-ip.

4. Select the public IP address resource and then click Add Diagnostic Setting; the Diagnostic settings blade appears as shown in Figure 1-1.

5. Provide an informative name for the setting configuration.

6. Select one or more targets for the diagnostic data. As previously mentioned, you can direct diagnostic data to a storage account, an Event hub, and/or to an Azure Log Analytics workspace.

7. Choose the logs and/or metrics for which you need to enable data collection. These options are resource-specific. In the case of public IP address resources, you can collect Distributed Denial-of-Service (DDoS) logs and all available metrics. Typically, Azure writes the logs as blob objects, and metrics as tables.

8. Click Save to complete the configuration.

FIGURE 1-1 Enabling diagnostic settings on an Azure resource

NOTE **UNIVERSAL PROCEDURES**

The procedure given here applies to other Azure resources as well. Please keep in mind that the Azure portal is but one way to configure any Azure resource; other options include Azure PowerShell, Azure CLI, or the Resource Manager APIs directly.

Create a baseline for resources

In Azure a resource baseline is what you develop by studying resource metrics and diagnostics data. The baseline represents the ordinary, expected behavior of your Azure resources.

One truism of Azure architecture and administration is that it's no use enabling diagnostics data collection if you don't spend the time inspecting the data periodically.

To that point, the next section covers how to study Azure resource metrics and then configure alerts to be notified proactively when Azure resource usage goes beyond the bounds of your expected baseline.

Analyze metrics across subscriptions

Metrics in Azure Monitor are measured values and counts that represent a time series and ultimately form your baseline. You can plot multiple metrics on the same chart; the underlying Azure resources can even span multiple subscriptions. Here's how:

1. In Azure Monitor, select the Metrics setting.
2. Change the chart title to something meaningful by clicking the pencil icon, typing the title, and pressing Enter.
3. In the first metric row, click Resource. In the Select A Resource blade, choose a subscription, resource group, resource type, and resource.
4. Choose a metric, namespace metric, and aggregation. These options are resource specific.
5. Note that you can change the chart type, create a new alert rule based on the metric, and pin the resulting chart to the portal dashboard. Figure 1-2 shows the vm1 resource's CPU performance over the past 24 hours.

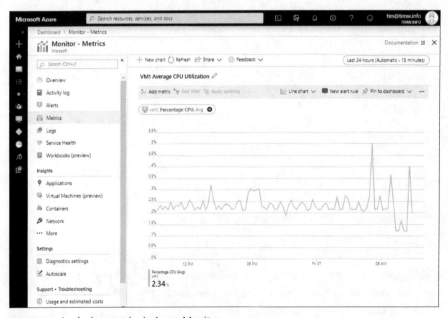

FIGURE 1-2 Analyzing metrics in Azure Monitor

Create and analyze alerts across subscriptions

Alerts are super powerful in Azure because they not only can save you from having to inspect diagnostic logs and metrics manually but you can create action groups that take action automatically when the alert condition is fired.

The following steps demonstrate that you can alert on disparate Azure resources that may span subscriptions. For instance, you may need to be notified when CPU utilization on several VMs exceeds your baseline threshold. Follow these steps to complete the configuration:

1. In Azure Monitor, select the Alerts setting.

2. Click New Alert Rule.

3. Under Resource, click Select. In the Select A Resource blade, choose the Azure resource or resources that will be monitored against your alert condition. Note that you can make selections from more than one Azure subscription.

4. Under Condition, click Add. Your alert can be triggered by two types of signal logic:

    - **Metrics**   Create your alert signal logic by querying Azure resource metric data
    - **Activity Log**   Create your alert signal logic by listening for particular control events in the Activity log

    Depending on the Azure resource and specific metric, you specify the alert logic accordingly. For example, for a VM resource you might select the Percentage CPU metric and fire the alert when average CPU exceeds 80 percent over 5 minutes.

5. Under Actions, click Add. Here you create an action group that determines precisely what happens when an alert is fired. There's more about action groups later in this chapter; for now, understand your action group can take any combination of the following actions:

    - Send an email/SMS/push/voice message
    - Trigger an Azure Function App
    - Trigger an Azure Logic App
    - Send a webhook
    - Integrate with your IT Service Management (ITSM) platform
    - Start an Azure Automation runbook

EXAM TIP

In Azure Monitor, you can have multiple resources targeted by one or more metrics signals, or you can target only one resource at a time with Activity log signals. Keep that in mind in your alert planning.

View alerts in Azure Monitor logs and utilize log search query functions

Of course, you can inspect and manage your Azure alert definitions from the Alerts page in Azure Monitor. However, you can also use KQL from the Logs blade in Azure Monitor to create simple to complex reports on Azure alert behavior.

For example, the following KQL query lists alerts raised during the past 24 hours, grouped by severity:

```
Alert | where SourceSystem == "OpsManager" and TimeRaised > ago(1d) | summarize Count =
count() by AlertSeverity
```

Another cool thing you can do with KQL queries is generate alerts based on them. From the Azure Monitor Logs pane, simply run your KQL query and then click New Alert Rule to generate a new alert that has a condition based on that query.

For instance, here is a sample KQL query that reports on average CPU utilization for all computes associated with your Log Analytics workspace; this query would serve as a nice CPU-related alert definition:

```
Perf | where ObjectName == "Processor" and CounterName == "% Processor Time" and
InstanceName == "_Total" | summarize AVGCPU = avg(CounterValue) by Computer
```

> **NOTE KUSTO QUERY LANGUAGE SYNTAX FOUNDATIONS**
>
> Microsoft developed KQL such that its syntax is immediately familiar to IT operations and development professionals. Its syntax takes as inspiration the Splunk query language, Structured Query Language (SQL), PowerShell, and bash shell scripting.

Create action groups

Action groups represent rich response logic to your Azure alerts. A good general architectural best practice is to create your action groups up front, and then reuse them in subsequent alert definitions. Let's run through the deployment/configuration procedure:

1. In Azure Monitor, navigate to the Alerts blade and click Manage Actions.

2. In the Manage Actions blade, click Add Action Group.

3. Provide a friendly name, short name (no spaces, maximum 12 characters), subscription, and resource group for the action group.

4. Under Actions, choose an action type from the list and configure it accordingly. Figure 1-3 shows configuring multiple email and short message service (SMS) notification.

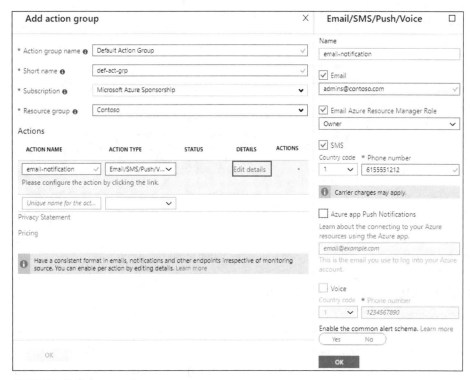

FIGURE 1-3 Defining an action group

Monitor for unused resources

Perhaps the most straightforward way to identify lost, forgotten, or otherwise unused resources is by inspecting the Cost recommendations in Azure Advisor. As an Azure solution architect, I've found that many of my customers rarely if ever think of using Azure Advisor. Given its low cost (free), there's no good reason why you and your customers shouldn't avail yourselves of its benefits.

Not only can Azure Advisor give you a heads-up on unused resources but it can also prompt you to take optimization action on underutilized resources. In Figure 1-4, you see an Azure Advisor recommendation to right-size five underutilized Azure SQL databases.

FIGURE 1-4 Azure Advisor reporting on unused and underutilized resources

Monitor and report on spend

The Usage And Estimated Costs blade in Azure Monitor presents a wonderful summary of your Azure consumption and spend over the past 31 days. If you're in search of more historical data, then browse in the Azure portal to the Cost Management + Billing blade instead.

Here you can perform detailed cost analysis and forecasting for all your Azure subscriptions, and you even can take advantage of Cloudyn optimization advice. Figure 1-5 shows you the Cost analysis blade for a test subscription.

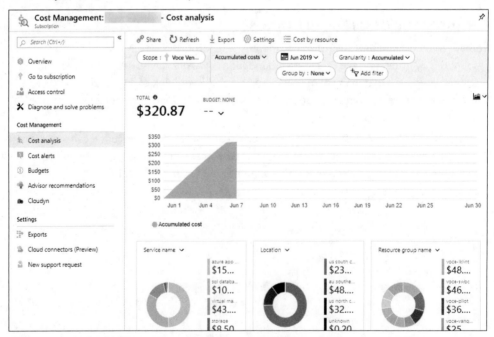

FIGURE 1-5 Using Azure Cost Management to monitor and report on spend

Skill 1.2: Create and configure storage accounts

The Azure storage account is a durable, highly available, scalable, and secure data store for just about any use case.

> **This skill covers how to:**
> - Create and configure a storage account
> - Implement Azure storage replication
> - Install and use Azure Storage Explorer
> - Manage access keys
> - Generate a shared access signature
> - Monitor the Activity Log by using Log Analytics and Azure Monitor

Create and configure a storage account

As stated at the beginning of this chapter, exam AZ-300 presumes that you already have expertise with Azure services. You can use Azure Command-Line Interface (CLI) to create a new storage account.

EXAM TIP

To be successful on all the Microsoft Azure exams, you need to have at least intermediate-level skills with both PowerShell and Azure CLI.

Here's Azure CLI command followed by descriptions of the most important options:

```
az storage account create --name tlwstor170 --resource-group Contoso --kind StorageV2
--access-tier Hot
```

- **--name**   Storage account names must be all lowercase, be 3 to 24 characters in length, contain alphanumeric characters, and be globally unique. (Yes, it's a challenge to satisfy all these requirements.)
- **--kind**   This is the type of storage account. In the Azure CLI, valid options are BlobStorage, BlockBlobStorage, FileStorage, Storage, or StorageV2.
- **--access-tier**   This represents how often you plan to access the data. In the Azure CLI, valid options are Hot or Cool.

Although Azure CLI gives you five options for storage account kind, there really are only three kinds:

- **General purpose v2**   This is the most recommended storage account kind. It gives access to the four storage account services: blob, table, queue, and file.
- **General purpose v1**   This kind is intended for backward compatibility with older deployments; v1 accounts do not support access tiers or zone-level replication.

- **Blob storage** Like General purpose v1, this is a legacy storage account that is used only for businesses that still maintain them. This storage account type can store only VM virtual hard disks, and nowadays it's best practice to place VM disks in managed disk storage instead of in traditional storage accounts.

Microsoft gives customers a price break depending on the access tier; remember that Microsoft charges you not only for the amount of data resident in a storage account but also for outbound (egress) data transfer and every underlying REST API transaction.

Set your blob storage to the Hot tier for frequently accessed data; you get a discount on transaction cost. Set your blob storage to the Cool tier for infrequently accessed data; here, Microsoft grants you a discount on data storage.

Set your blob storage to Archive if you truly don't plan to access the data other than special occasions. Here you must "rehydrate" archived blobs and are charged to do so; make sure you flip the archive bit only if your business requirements mandate it.

The following command sets a new storage account to Cool storage instead of Hot:

```
az storage account update --name tlwstor170 --resource-group Contoso --access-tier Cool
```

> **NEED MORE REVIEW? LEARNING THE AZURE CLI**
>
> If you need some more education concerning the Azure CLI, including installation and configuration instructions, visit the Microsoft Azure docs article "Azure Command-Line Interface (CLI)" at *http://timw.info/azurecli*.

Configure network access to a storage account

Azure general-purpose storage accounts have four internal services:

- **Blob** Binary Large Object data; Intended for text and binary data, including log files, media files, database files, VM disks, and so forth
- **Table** NoSQL data storage that is now part of Azure Cosmos DB product family
- **Queue** Reliable messaging service to support a microservices application architecture
- **File** Managed Server Message Block (SMB) file shares for cloud and on-premises servers

The reason why your storage account name needs to be globally unique is that each of those services is bound by default to a public Azure Resource Manager API endpoint; the well-known URIs are

- **Blob** *http://<account-name>.blob.core.windows.net*
- **Table** *http://<account-name>.table.core.windows.net*
- **Queue** *http://<account-name>.queue.core.windows.net*
- **File** *http://<account-name>.file.core.windows.net*

Of course, unauthenticated access to any Azure storage account is prohibited by default, and you control access by using role-based access control (RBAC) in Azure Resource Manager.

That said, for greater control over access to storage accounts, you can associate them to a virtual network (VNet) in Azure. Because VNets provide an exceptionally strong isolation boundary in Azure, configuring network integration can give your customer more robust control over storage account access.

For example, you might want to ensure that only VMs resident on Contoso-vnet can interact with your storage account. Follow these steps to complete this configuration:

1. In the Azure portal, browse to the target storage account and select the Firewalls And Virtual Networks Settings blade.

2. Under Allow Access From, choose Selected Networks.

3. Click Add Existing Virtual Network and choose the VNet and subnet from which you want to limit access to this storage account.

4. Optionally, under Firewall add IP addresses/address ranges from other clients outside the VNet that need access to the storage account. You can see the Firewalls And Virtual Networks interface in Figure 1-6.

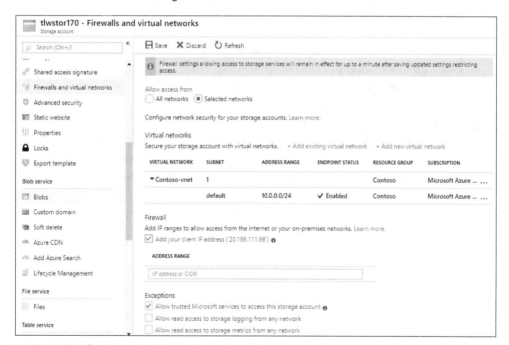

FIGURE 1-6 Configuring network access for an Azure storage account

Implement Azure storage replication

Azure storage replication is what makes your storage accounts highly available. The redundancy option you suggest to your customers depends on their own availability service-level agreements (SLAs) as well as how far-reaching the high availability should be. Here are the storage account redundancy options:

- **Locally redundant storage (LRS)**   Azure makes three copies of the storage account and distributes them throughout a single datacenter in your home region. Here you have protection against the failure of a storage array.

- **Zone-redundant storage (ZRS)**   Azure makes three copies of the storage account and distributes them across multiple datacenters in your home region. Here you have protection against datacenter-level failures. Note that only General Purpose v2 storage accounts can use the ZRS replication option.

- **Geo-redundant storage (GRS)**   Azure makes three copies of the storage account in the home region, and three copies in a second, paired region. Paired regions are geographically close enough to have high-speed connectivity to reduce or eliminate latency. Here you have protection against regional failures.

- **Read-access geo-redundant storage (RA-GRS)**   Same as GRS with the exception that you can access the storage account in the secondary region; the base URL path is *https://<account-name>-secondary.<service>.windows.net.*

To illustrate, the following command for Azure PowerShell sets the stock-keeping unit (SKU) for a storage account to RA-GRS:

```
Set-AzStorageAccount -Name tlwstor170 -ResourceGroupName contoso -SkuName Standard_RAGRS
```

Install and use Azure Storage Explorer

Azure Storage Explorer is a free, cross-platform, closed-source desktop application designed by Microsoft. The tool makes it simple to interact with your Azure storage accounts. Storage Explorer is even built into the Azure portal—simply browse to one of your storage accounts and select the Storage Explorer setting.

You can download Storage Explorer from the Microsoft website; the Windows, macOS, and Linux graphical installers take about 30 seconds to complete. Easy!

At first launch, you're required to authenticate to Azure; connection to Azure public cloud as well as Azure Government is supported. Take a look at Figure 1-7, which demonstrates the Azure Storage Explorer interface. We explain each annotation immediately afterward:

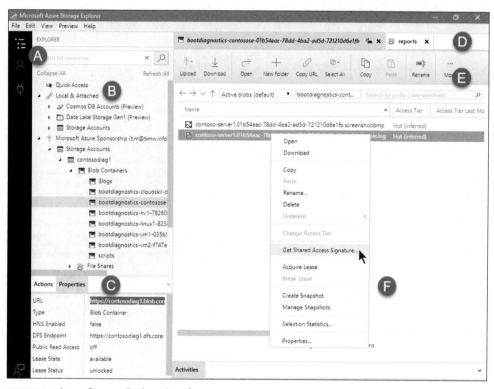

FIGURE 1-7 Azure Storage Explorer interface

- **A**   Switch between the Explorer and Accounts views.
- **B**   Browse your storage accounts and/or other local or remote Azure assets.
- **C**   View properties of selected item; the Actions window displays the same option as right-clicking an object.
- **D**   Multitab interface to view more than one storage object simultaneously.
- **E**   Robust toolbar with upload/download/query controls.
- **F**   Get into the habit of right-clicking objects to see which actions are possible.

You can use the toolbar or drag and drop to upload and download blob objects. The built-in query interface makes it easier to run queries against table storage.

Manage access keys

Each Azure storage account has two interchangeable, 512-bit access keys that you can use to gain programmatic access to your storage account. It's considered best practice to rotate these keys regularly.

The following sample code shows how you can retrieve both keys programmatically by using Azure PowerShell:

```
Get-AzStorageAccountKey -name 'tlwstor170' -ResourceGroupName contoso
KeyName             Value
-------             -----
key1                3oDnt7cci/04/z1ED/uAEwDsU
key2                OMvF4SytaytFJ+U2qh/NGNtC
```

EXAM TIP

You may be asked to remember on the AZ-300 exam that you also can store your storage account access keys in Azure Key Vault to simplify key management. For more information on Key Vault-managed storage accounts, see the docs article "Azure Key Vault managed storage account - PowerShell" at *http://timw.info/keyvault*.

Generate a shared access signature

Azure developers use Azure software development kits (SDKs), Azure PowerShell, or another method to programmatically retrieve access keys to gain authorized access to storage account resources.

But what if you're unwilling to share an access key? A shared access signature (SAS) represents a way to grant limited, time-bound access to individual storage account objects or potentially entire blob service containers.

Specifically, a SAS is a URL that consists of the following components:

- **Protocol**   Will be HTTP or HTTPS; you can optionally require HTTPS only.
- **Address**   Fully qualified path to the storage account object.
- **Permissions**   Standard CRUD (create, read, update, delete) operations.
- **Time interval**   As long as the time interval hasn't expired, anybody on Earth can use the SAS URI. Therefore, you need to be careful in how you create and manage them.

Say you need to provide programmatic access to a JavaScript file named library.js that resides in a container named assets in an Azure storage account named contosostorage704. We can use the following procedure to complete SAS creation by using Storage Explorer:

1. In Storage Explorer, browse to the assets container and locate the target file.
2. Right-click Library.js and select Get Shared Access Signature from the shortcut menu.

3. Complete the Shared Access Signature dialog box as shown in Figure 1-8. Note that you specify start and end times that define the SAS token lifetime; you also add appropriate permissions.

An access policy is essentially a template that defines SAS properties; access policies make it easier to create multiple SAS URIs that share the same settings.

A container-level SAS URI can be dangerous because you open up access to all objects in the current blob container instead of only a single object.

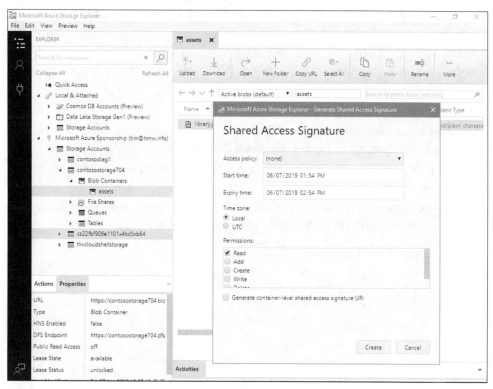

FIGURE 1-8 Creating a Shared Access Signature from Storage Explorer

In our case, the resulting SAS URI looks like this:

```
https://contosostorage704.blob.core.windows.net/assets/library.js?st=2019-06-07T18%3A54%
3A37Z&se=2019-06-07T19%3A54%3A00Z&sp=rl&sv=2018-03-28&sr=b&sig=8B7kWwmysPNuOZDoHslAgBfFv
P5CT9PvCoxfOy5fXBs%3D
```

See that long value after the &sv query string parameter? That's a digital signature. If you change a single character in an SAS URI, it breaks the signature and the SAS URI will no longer work.

Monitor the Activity Log by using Log Analytics and Azure Monitor

Earlier in this chapter, we reminded you that the Activity log is where Azure tracks control-plane actions—essentially, who took what action while in your Azure subscriptions. This exam objective lets you know you can collect and analyze Activity log data from multiple subscriptions by using a Log Analytics workspace in Azure Monitor.

Recall that a Log Analytics workspace is a data warehouse, to which you can link different Azure resources and configure the resources to send their data to the workspace. You then use KQL queries to generate reports on the aggregated data.

Although a single Activity log can be connected only to one workspace at a time, a single workspace can be connected to the Activity log from multiple subscriptions that trust the same Azure Active Directory tenant.

Here's the high-level overview of the configuration:

1. In the Azure portal, browse to your chosen Log Analytics workspace, and select the Azure Activity log setting under Workspace Data Sources.

2. Use the Subscription filter to display an Azure subscription you want to associate with the workspace.

3. In the subscription list, select the subscription and click Connect. Figure 1-9 shows two subscriptions that emit Activity log data into this workspace.

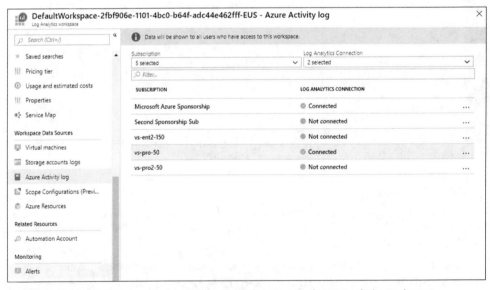

FIGURE 1-9 Linking Activity log from multiple subscriptions to a single Log Analytics workspace

You are then free to write KQL queries in the Azure Monitor log search interface, or install the Activity Log Analytics management solution as your needs dictate. For example, the following KQL query shows the total number of Azure resources that write to the Activity logs and lists the top ten resources with record counts:

```
AzureActivity | summarize AggregatedValue = count() by Resource
```

Skill 1.3: Create and configure a virtual machine for Windows and Linux

Thus far, you've worked with Azure diagnostic data streams and Azure storage. Now it's time to focus on what is likely the first cloud feature most businesses turn to first —infrastructure as a service (IaaS), otherwise known as "virtual machines running in the cloud."

> **This skill covers how to:**
> - Configure high availability
> - Configure monitoring, networking, storage, and VM size
> - Deploy and configure scale sets

Configure high availability

Azure solution architects must remember that availability is a different metric from uptime. Just because a server receives power and is in a started state does not mean that the services offered by the host are functional.

The next sections review ways you can provide various high-availability guarantees to your VM environment in Azure.

Availability sets

If you deploy two or more VM instances into the same availability set, Microsoft provides a 99.95 percent availability SLA. Normally the architectural pattern is to place VM instances of a particular class (for example, web servers) into their own availability set during VM deployment.

> **WARNING AVAILABILITY SET ASSIGNMENT**
> You can add VM instances to an availability set only during VM deployment. If you forget, you'll need to redeploy the VM.

An availability set is a logical container that ensures that your VM instances reside on different hardware hosts on separate racks in your Azure regional datacenter. Availability sets provide protection against

- **Planned maintenance** For instance, if Microsoft needs to restart the hardware host on which your VM resides or take the hardware host offline
- **Unplanned maintenance** Top-of-rack switch failures, power failures

Because the availability set and its members reside in a single datacenter, this architecture can't protect your VMs at the region level.

Availability zones

Availability zones are a newer entry to the Azure high-availability family. Here, you place your VM instances in separate datacenters within the same Azure region. Microsoft connects datacenters within the region with additional, redundant, high-speed network interconnects to ward against latency issues.

> **NOTE   AVAILABILITY SETS AND AVAILABILITY ZONES**
> You can't combine availability sets and availability zones.

Availability zones aren't available for every Azure region, so you need to perform due diligence research with your customers to choose an appropriate region if availability zones are a requirement.

Availability zones protect your VMs against host, switch, rack, and datacenter failures. They don't protect against regional failures.

To provide regional high availability, you should consider deploying additional VM instances to a separate Azure region and using Azure Traffic Manager and Azure public load balancers to direct traffic interregionally. You can see an example of this topology in Figure 1-10.

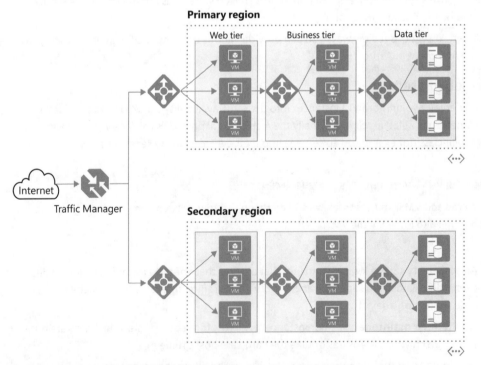

FIGURE 1-10 Providing multi-region high availability for an IaaS deployment.

Single-instance SLA

If you're willing to use high-speed premium storage for your VMs, then you can take advantage of Microsoft's 99.9 percent availability guarantee with single-instance VMs. Here you don't have to use availability sets to attain reasonable high availability.

Configure monitoring, networking, storage, and VM size

Monitoring your Windows and Linux VMs in Azure can take two directions:

- **Azure Diagnostics**   Here you deploy the VMDiagnosticsSettings agent to the VM and collect various guest operating system metrics and log data.

- **Log Analytics**   Here you deploy the Microsoft Log Analytics agent and connect the VM to a Log Analytics workspace.

The advantage of the latter approach is that you can centrally query your VMs from the Azure Monitor log search interface using the previously described KQL. Follow these steps to connect your VM to an existing Log Analytics workspace:

1. In the Azure portal, browse to your Log Analytics workspace.

2. Under Workspace Data Sources, click the Virtual Machines setting.

3. Locate the VM you want to onboard to Log Analytics, and then select the VM. The VM should show a Not Connected status.

4. Click Connect. In Figure 1-11 you can see one VM that is connected to the workspace and one that is not.

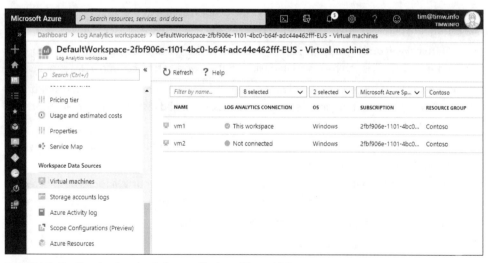

FIGURE 1-11 Configuring Log Analytics monitoring of Azure VMs

With respect to VM networking, you can handle most configuration directly from the Networking blade inside the VM's settings in the Azure portal, shown in Figure 1-12.

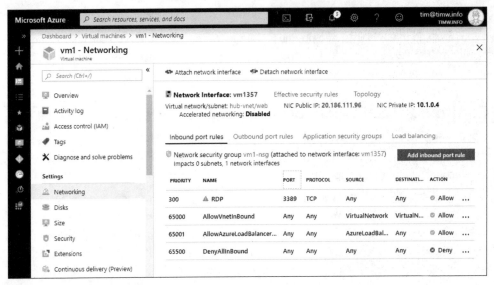

FIGURE 1-12 Virtual machine network configuration

Recall that the networking-related VM elements include the following:

- **Virtual network interface card (vNIC)** A VM can be associated with one or more network interfaces; the interfaces, in turn, can have one or more IP configurations.

- **Private IP address** This IP address originates from the virtual network and subnet on which the VM resides.

- **Public IP address** Optional, but this type of address makes the VM directly reachable from the public Internet.

- **Network security group (NSG)** This software firewall defines inbound and outbound traffic rules. NSGs can be associated with both network interfaces and VNet subnets.

Concerning VM storage, you should recommend your customers use managed disk storage for their VMs and not use traditional storage accounts. Managed disk storage simplifies virtual hard disk management, backup, and security.

Managed disks can be used with standard or premium disk storage. All three VM disk types are also supported: operating system, temporary, and data.

Resizing a VM is a great way to save money and/or "right-size" your VM for its designated workloads. You can resize a VM in all the usual ways; let's use Azure PowerShell in this example.

First, list the VM sizes that are available in the VM's region:

```
Get-AzVMSize -ResourceGroupName 'Contoso' -VMName 'vm1'
```

Second, capture a reference to the target VM in a variable; set the VM's **VmSize** property to the chosen new size; and update the VM's configuration to "set" the change:

```
$vm = Get-AzVm -ResourceGroupName 'Contoso' -VMName 'vm1'
$vm.HardwareProfile.VmSize = 'Standard_D32s_v3'
Update-AzVM -VM $vm -ResourceGroupName 'Contoso'
```

Deploy and configure scale sets

One question to ask Azure architecture clients is, "Are you positive you want to run your workload in VMs?" As you know, IaaS isn't the most horizontally scalable technology.

By contrast, Azure App Service applications can easily autoscale horizontally and potentially vertically; that's one of the greatest benefits of platform as a service (PaaS).

The virtual machine scale set (VMSS) is a way to manually or automatically scale a group of identically configured virtual machines.

Some businesses use scale sets to provide high availability; other companies use scale sets to grind through large batch jobs, taking advantage of both big compute and parallel processing.

Follow these steps for the high-level overview of creating a VM scale set in the Azure portal:

1. In the Azure portal, click Create A Resource and search the Azure Marketplace for the Virtual Machine Scale Set template.

2. In the Create Virtual Machine Scale Set dialog box, provide baseline properties:

   - VM Scale Set Name; each node receives a host name based on the scale set name (for instance, vmss_0, vmss_1, and so forth).

   - OS disk image (Windows Server and Linux are supported).

   - Subscription.

   - Resource group.

   - Location.

   - Availability zone; a single scale set can span availability zones.

   - Administrator username and password.

3. Select a starting instance count and instance size. Remember you will be charged the standard per-minute run time for each running instance in your scale set.

4. Decide whether low-priority VMs are an option. Microsoft gives you a price break by running your workload using unused compute capacity in your Azure region. However, these VMs can be reclaimed by Microsoft at any time, so you need to be sure the workload your scale set processes is truly stateless.

5. Configure autoscale rules. Scale set autoscale has the following configurable properties:

   - Minimum and maximum number of VMs

   - CPU percentage that defines the scale-out and scale-in thresholds

6. Choose a load balancer option. You need either an Azure public load balancer or an Azure application gateway to put in front of your scale set so you have a single entry point into the scale set.

With respect to configuring the scale set to run your workload, there are two factors to keep in mind:

- Your workload should rely upon external storage and be stateless; the idea is that it shouldn't matter which scale set node processes any particular task. You don't want to have workload data permanently resident on your nodes.

- You normally manage the scale set from a jump box VM that you place on the scale set's virtual network.

Take a look at the architectural drawing in Figure 1-13. All the workload components reside in a storage account, and all scale set configuration/management takes place via the jump box VM.

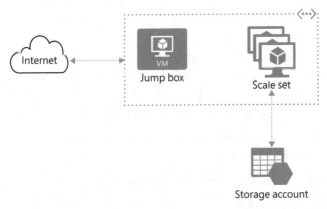

FIGURE 1-13 A representative VM scale set deployment

Skill 1.4: Automate the deployment of virtual machines

Now it's time to review how you can use infrastructure as code to automate VM deployment in Azure. Recall that every Azure Resource Manager (ARM) deployment is recorded in JavaScript Object Notation (JSON). In this section, you use ARM templates to make your VM deployments repeatable, dependable, and fast.

This skill covers how to:

- Deploy Windows and Linux VMs from a template
- Save a deployment as an ARM template
- Modify Azure Resource Manager templates

Deploy Windows and Linux VMs from a template

Visual Studio isn't a tool intended only for developers. As long as you install the Azure workload, Visual Studio is a terrific ARM template editor. Here we use Visual Studio 2019 to create a simple VM by using a brand-new, built-in deployment template.

1. In Visual Studio 2019, click File > New > Project.

2. In the Create A New Project dialog box, search for **resource group**, and select the Azure Resource Group project template.

3. Give the template a meaningful name, choose a project storage location, and click Create.

4. In the Select Azure Template window, set the Show Templates From This Location filter to Visual Studio Templates, select the Windows Virtual Machine template, and click OK to set up the environment.

5. Open the WindowsVirtualMachine.json template file and fill in the parameter values. This template has the following parameters:

   - **adminUsername**   Built-in administrator name
   - **adminPassword**   Built-in administrator password
   - **dnsNameForPublicIP**   Public IP address you use to connect to the new VM after you deploy it
   - **WindowsOSVersion**   Template that includes an allowedValues array that constrains the OS versions the administrator can select

6. To validate the template, right-click the template in Solution Explorer and select Validate from the shortcut menu.

7. Fill in the Validate To Resource Group dialog box. You need to authenticate to Azure and choose a new or existing resource group to house the deployment.

8. Keep an eye on the Output window; if validation completes, you can deploy the VM to Azure by right-clicking the project in Solution Explorer and selecting Deploy from the shortcut menu.

In Figure 1-14 you can see the Validate To Resource Group dialog box as well as partial output from a previous validation in the Visual Studio Output window. I added annotation steps to make the template validation workflow clearer.

Specifically, in (1), you right-click the solution and select Validate from the shortcut menu. You then (2) fill out the deployment metadata, including clicking Edit Parameters to (3) specify deployment-specific input data.

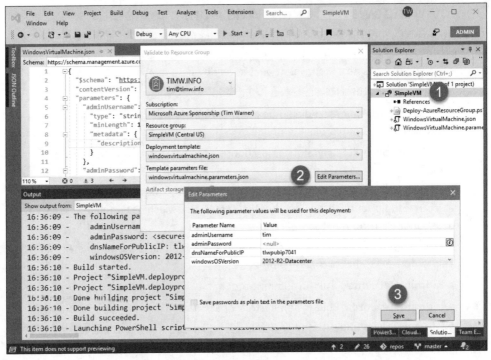

FIGURE 1-14 Using Visual Studio as an ARM template editor

What's so nice about ARM template deployment is that once you have your deployment correct, you can repeat the deployment with no additional debugging effort.

Save a deployment as an ARM template

The Azure portal makes it easy to save the underlying ARM template for any new or existing deployment.

Let's say your customer needs to create 100 storage accounts. As an architect, you can save the customer lots of time by instructing them to create the first storage account, with all requisite properties, in the Azure portal. However, you also need to instruct them to click Download A Template For Automation just prior to clicking Create on the Review + Create screen. This action opens the Template blade as shown in the annotated Figure 1-15.

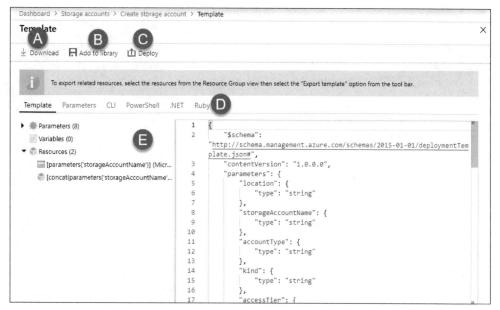

FIGURE 1-15 Save any Azure deployment as an ARM template

The annotations in Figure 1-15 are important:

- **A** Download the JSON template, parameter file, and deployment helper scripts as a single ZIP archive.
- **B** Add this deployment template to an Azure portal-based library stored in your subscription.
- **C** Deploy the template directly from within the Azure portal.
- **D** Edit the underlying JSON.
- **E** JSON outliner, making it easier to navigate the source code.

To save the underlying template for an existing Azure resource, open it in the Azure portal, locate the Export Template settings, and click Download.

Modify Azure Resource Manager templates

The Azure Quickstart Templates gallery (*https://azure.microsoft.com/en-us/resources/templates/*) should be a regular stop for any Azure cloud solution architect. As of this writing, the gallery has 784 prebuilt templates, ranging from simple (deploying a single storage account) to the enormously complex (deploying a three-tier web application with load balancers, gateways, and custom routing).

Follow these steps to edit an Azure Quickstart Template by using nothing other than your web browser and the Azure portal:

1. Make sure you have logged into the Azure portal with appropriate permissions in the current browser session.

2. In another tab, browse to *https://azure.microsoft.com/en-us/resources/templates/*, and in the Search box, type **basic Windows web app**, and press Enter.

3. Select the Deploy A Basic Windows Web App template.

   The template page includes some interesting controls and metadata:

   - **Deploy to Azure**   Launch a custom deployment in the Azure portal in the current browsing session.
   - **Browse on GitHub**   All the templates are housed fundamentally in a GitHub repository.
   - **Parameters**   Inspect the parameters the author included in the template.
   - **Use the template**   Azure PowerShell and Azure CLI sample code show you how to deploy the template.

4. Click Deploy to Azure. This action should spawn another browser tab, log you into the Azure portal under your current credential, and show the Custom Deployment blade.

5. Fill out the Basics and Settings areas. Basics represents the subscription, resource group, and location; Settings lists the parameters defined in the underlying template.

   Alternatively, you can click Edit Template or Edit Parameters to view and modify the template's underlying source code. Be sure to save your changes!

6. Agree to the Microsoft terms and conditions (you may have to scroll the Custom Deployment blade to the very bottom), and then click Purchase to validate and submit the deployment to Azure Resource Manager.

Configure the location of new VMs

Perhaps the most straightforward way to prevent deployment to disallowed Azure regions is by means of an Azure Policy. Let's say you want to bind an Azure Policy to your 'lobapp' resource group that requires deployments to occur only in the East US and East US 2 regions. Let's accomplish this task with Azure PowerShell.

First, you will create a policy definition at the subscription scope. Here it makes sense to use the built-in Allowed Locations policy, which you fetch from its GitHub repository on the web:

```
$definition = New-AzPolicyDefinition -Name "allowed-locations" -DisplayName "Allowed
locations" -Policy 'https://raw.githubusercontent.com/Azure/azure-policy/master/samples/
built-in-policy/allowed-locations/azurepolicy.rules.json' -Parameter
'https://raw.githubusercontent.com/Azure/azure-policy/master/samples/built-in-policy/
allowed-locations/azurepolicy.parameters.json' -Mode Indexed
```

Next, you change your target scope to the lobapp resource group:

```
$scope = Get-AzResourceGroup -Name 'lobapp'
```

Then, you set the policy parameter:

```
$policyparam = '{ "listOfAllowedLocations:: { :value": [ "eastus", "eastus2" ] } }'
```

Finally, you create the policy assignment:

```
$assignment = New-AzPolicyAssignment -Name 'allowed-locations-assignment' -DisplayName
'Allowed locations Assignment' -Scope $scope.ResourceId -PolicyDefinition $definition
-PolicyParameter $policyparam
```

Configure VHD templates

You want to deploy a new virtual machine in Azure by using an ARM template, but instead of using an Azure Marketplace gallery image, you want to use a generalized VHD you have stored in your managed disk library or storage account.

Two ways to get your generalized VHD into Azure are

- Use AzCopy and Azure Storage Explorer to upload your on-premises generalized VHD to the blob service of a storage account

- Use the Azure portal to capture a generalized VM image and store the image in your managed disks library

> **NEED MORE REVIEW?** **UPLOADING ON-PREMISES VHDs TO AZURE**
>
> To learn more about the "hows and whys" of generalizing and uploading on-premises VHDs to Azure, visit the Azure docs article "Prepare a Windows VHD or VHDX to upload to Azure" at *http://timw.info/vhdx*.

In this example, imagine you have a Windows Server 2019 generalized image in your Azure subscription's managed disk library. Your goal is to make an ARM template to simplify deployment of new VMs based on the custom image template. Follow these steps:

1. Create a new Resource Group deployment in Visual Studio 2019.

2. In the Select Azure Template dialog box, set the Show Templates From This Location filter to Azure QuickStart, and load the template 201-vm-specialized-vhd-new-or-existing-vnet.

3. As shown in Figure 1-16, find the parameter osDiskVhdUri. This string value accepts the full URI of the VHD template. You can fetch your image URL from the Images blade in the Azure portal or the blob container as appropriate.

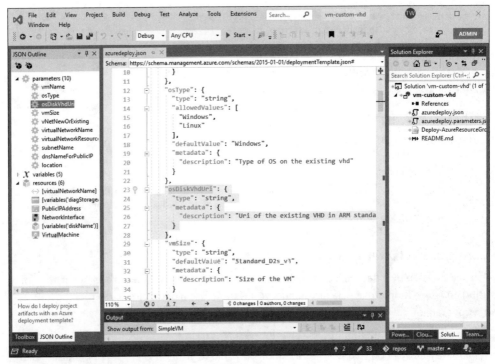

FIGURE 1-16 Deploying a VM by using a VHD template image

4. How you populate the osDiskVhdUri parameter is up to you; you could take any of the following actions:

- Add a DefaultValue key-value pair to the main template file
- Populate the parameter and its value in the template parameter file
- Specify the parameter value at deployment time

Speaking of deployment time, you should quickly review how to use Azure PowerShell to deploy an ARM template. Assuming your template and parameter files exist on your local computer, you can use the following PowerShell command to validate and then deploy the template to Azure by using an existing resource group:

```
New-AzResourceGroupDeployment -Name 'CustomVMDeployment' -TemplateFile '.\azuredeploy.
json' -TemplateParameterFile '.\azuredeploy.parameters.json' -Mode Incremental -Verbose
```

EXAM TIP

Remember that ARM templates can have any name. The file names azuredeploy.json and azuredeploy.parameters.json are simply Microsoft's common convention. On the AZ-300 exam, you will likely see templates with different names.

Skill 1.5: Implement solutions that use virtual machines

This section continues the ARM template discussion and also reviews how to apply whole-disk encryption to your VMs running in Azure.

> **This skill covers how to:**
> - Provision VMs with a new ARM template
> - Configure disk encryption for VMs

Provision VMs with a new ARM template

You can always do Azure deployment work from scratch. Let's finish this section by buzzing through how to get started with an ARM template "from scratch" by using Visual Studio Code.

Visual Studio Code is a free, open-source, cross-platform code editor. Download the software from *https://code.visualstudio.com* and install it on your development workstation; then use VSCode's Extensions tool to add the following extensions:

- **PowerShell** Unlocks PowerShell language and debugging support
- **Azure Resource Manager Tools** Unlocks IntelliSense and debugging support for Resource Manager templates
- **Azure Account** Simplifies VSCode Azure authentication and session management
- **Azure Resource Manager Snippets** Contains a library of handy JSON code segments to make your ARM template development easier

In this example, you use VSCode to create a new ARM template that deploys a storage account.

1. In VSCode, open the Command Palette and type **Azure: Sign in to authenticate to your Azure subscription**.

2. In the Command Palette, type **Azure: Select Subscriptions** and ensure your target subscription is enabled.

3. Click File > New File, and save the file using a meaningful name (for instance, new-storage-account.json).

4. Place your cursor in the first row of the file and type **arm**. You should see a list of ARM snippets. Select the snippet arm! to create a new "skeleton" template.

5. Modify the template to make it more flexible. Edit its source code to match the following:

```
{
  "$schema": "https://schema.management.azure.com/schemas/2015-01-01/
deploymentTemplate.json#",
  "contentVersion": "1.0.0.0",
  "parameters": {
```

```
        "storageAccountType": {
          "type": "string",
          "defaultValue": "Standard_LRS",
          "allowedValues": [
            "Standard_LRS",
            "Standard_GRS",
            "Standard_ZRS",
            "Premium_LRS"
          ],
          "metadata": {
            "description": "Storage Account type"
          }
        },
        "location": {
          "type": "string",
          "defaultValue": "[resourceGroup().location]",
          "metadata": {
            "description": "Location for all resources."
          }
        }
      },
      "variables": {
        "storageAccountName": "[concat('store', uniquestring(resourceGroup().id))]"
      },
      "resources": [
        {
          "type": "Microsoft.Storage/storageAccounts",
          "name": "[variables('storageAccountName')]",
          "location": "[parameters('location')]",
          "apiVersion": "2018-07-01",
          "sku": {
            "name": "[parameters('storageAccountType')]"
          },
          "kind": "StorageV2",
          "properties": {}
        }
      ],
      "outputs": {
        "storageAccountName": {
          "type": "string",
          "value": "[variables('storageAccountName')]"
        }
      }
    }
```

At this point your VSCode environment should match Figure 1-17. Here's an explanation of the preceding code in case you need any additional elucidation:

- **$schema**   Required. Defines the location of the underlying schema against which you validate this template.

- **contentVersion**   Required, but not used by Azure. This is for your own use in versioning the file over its lifecycle.

- **parameters**   Optional, but extremely useful to make the template portable.

- **variables**   Optional, but useful to simplify resource naming.

- **resources**   Required because this is where you deploy the Azure resources to be deployed.
- **outputs**   Optional, but useful at times to display post-deployment metadata to the script runner.

Check the Problems pane in the VSCode terminal to see whether any ARM template validation errors exist. In this particular template, you're likely to see one problem: "String is longer than the maximum length of 24."

You can ignore this error because if you check the source code, the storage account name is derived from a call to the storageAccountName variable, which will be less than the storage account's maximum name length of 24 characters.

6. When you're ready to deploy, run New-AzResourceGroupDeployment in the terminal as shown previously.

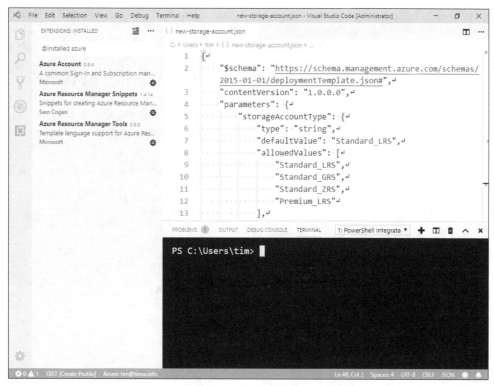

FIGURE 1-17 ARM template development in Visual Studio Code

NEED MORE REVIEW?   **ARM TEMPLATE STRUCTURE HELP**

If you need to brush up on ARM template structure, visit the Azure docs article "Understand the structure and syntax of Azure Resource Manager templates" at *http://timw.info/arms*.

Configure disk encryption for VMs

To satisfy your organizational security policies, you can apply whole-disk encryption, called Azure Disk Encryption (ADE), to your Windows Server or Linux VMs running in Azure. You can encrypt the OS disk as well as any data disks.

The encryption technology depends on the guest operating system: Windows VM disks are encrypted with BitLocker Drive Encryption, whereas Linux VM disks are encrypted with the open-source DM-Crypt library.

You need to provision an Azure Key Vault before using ADE because Azure needs a secure location for the disk encryption keys. The key vault needs to reside in the same region as your target VMs.

Encrypt the operating system and data disks of a running VM by running the following Azure CLI command:

```
az vm encryption enable --resource-group "Contoso" --name "vm1" --disk-encryption-
keyvault "CorpVault" --volume-type All
```

Skill 1.6: Create connectivity between virtual networks

Virtual networks (VNets) in Microsoft Azure represent strong security boundaries for your Azure resources. By default, VMs running in one VNet have no routing path to VMs running in another VNet. This is by design.

So what do you recommend to a customer who has a business need to connect VNets? Well, Microsoft provides two options:

- VNet peering
- VNet-to-VNet virtual private network (VPN)

This section looks at each option in turn.

> **This skill covers how to:**
> - Create and configure virtual network peering
> - Create and configure VNet-to-VNet VPN
> - Verify virtual network connectivity

Create and configure virtual network peering

Azure global VNet peering allows you to connect two virtual networks without the overhead and cost associated with a VPN gateway. Peering is a good choice when a business needs to link VNets and has no requirement for end-to-end encryption.

The "global" part of this feature name signifies that the two VNets to be peered can exist in the same region, different regions, or even across subscriptions. All network traffic occurring over the peer relationship is private and takes place strictly on the Microsoft Azure network backbone.

If VNet Spoke 1 is peered with VNet Hub, and then VNet Hub is peered with VNet Spoke 2, resources in VNet Spoke 1 cannot communicate directly with resources in VNet Spoke 2 because VNet peerings are nontransitive. Transitivity can become an issue with hub-and-spoke VNet architectures, as shown in Figure 1-18. You can force transitivity by linking user-defined routes (UDRs) to each spoke VNet and forcing traffic through a network virtual appliance (NVA) located in the hub VNet.

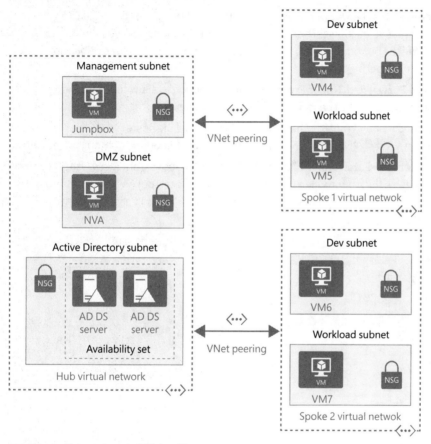

FIGURE 1-18 Hub-and-spoke VNet architecture

Follow this procedure in the Azure portal to create a peering between two VNets in Azure:

1. Locate the first of the two VNets you want to peer. The sequence here doesn't matter; what's important is that you need to configure the peering for both VNets.

2. In the first VNet's Settings blade, click Peerings, and then Add.

3. In the Add Peering blade, shown in Figure 1-19, complete the form:

   ■ **Name** Choose a descriptive name, preferably that defines the peering directionality (for instance, hub-to-spoke1).

- **PeerDetails**   Specify the deployment model, and whether you want to use a resource identifier (ID) to locate the other VNet. This option is necessary if you don't have read access to the destination VNet.
- **Subscription**   Recall that global VNet peering works across Azure subscriptions and regions.
- **Virtual Network**   Choose the VNet that will reside on the other side of the peering.
- **Allow Virtual Network Access From**   The VNet names will be specific to your environment, of course. This option needs to be enabled for VNet peering to work. Disable the option when you need to pause peering, typically for troubleshooting or security response purposes.
- **Allow Forwarded Traffic From**   Enable this option to allow traffic forwarded to your current VNet to be forwarded to the VNet peer.
- **Allow Gateway Transit**   Enable this option to allow the peered VNet to allow the current VNet's VPN gateway. In other words, enable this option only on your hub VNet.
- **Use Remote Gateways**   This option is mutually exclusive from Allow Gateway Transit. You enable this option when you need to allow the local spoke VNet to forward traffic through a hub VNet, typically across a site-to-site VPN to an on-premises network.

FIGURE 1-19 Configuring a VNet peering

4. Click OK to complete the configuration.

Please don't forget that you need to configure the peering on the other VNet as well! Once Azure completes the configuration, you can see it on each VNet's Peerings blade. The Peering Status property should show as Connected.

Create and configure VNet-to-VNet VPN

Before Microsoft announced global VNet peering in Fall 2018, the only option Azure architects and administrators had for cross-region VNet peering was the VNet-to-VNet VPN.

Now, Azure solution architects can recommend the VNet-to-VNet VPN only when it is feasible to do so. The Azure VPN Gateway is a software-defined networking virtual device that forms one side of an Internet Protocol Security (IPSec) VPN tunnel.

As you can see in Figure 1-20, VNet-to-VNet VPN connections fit "hand in glove" with site-to-site VPNs in a hybrid cloud environment. Although VNet-to-VNet VPNs are significantly more expensive than VNet peerings, your organizational security and compliance requirements may require you to configure an environment this way.

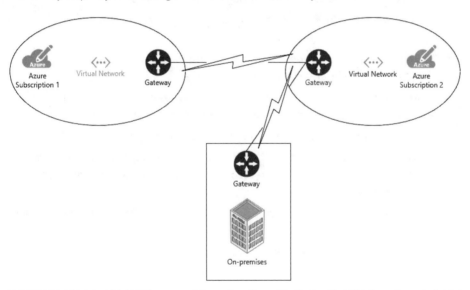

FIGURE 1-20 VNet-to-VNet VPNs can work in conjunction with site-to-site VPNs in an Azure hybrid cloud environment

Follow these steps to configure a VNet-to-VNet VPN in the Azure portal:

1. In the Subnets blade in each VNet's Settings, click Gateway Subnet to define a gateway subnet in each VNet. This empty subnet contains private IP addresses used by the Azure VPN Gateway. Microsoft recommends you use a Common Inter-Domain Routing (CIDR) block of /27 or /28.

2. Open the Virtual Network Gateways blade and click Add.

3. In the Create Virtual Network Gateway blade, complete the form. Some of your key architectural choices include the following:

- **Gateway Type**   An Azure VPN Gateway is used to create either a VPN or an ExpressRoute connection.
- **VPN Type**   You have two routing types to choose from:
  - **Route-Based**   Uses routing tables to make traffic routing and encryption decisions. This VPN type is more widely supported in Azure and with on-premises hardware.
  - **Policy-Based**   Uses static routes. This VPN type is intended for compatibility with older on-premises VPN concentrator hardware. Accordingly, its feature set is much smaller than route-based gateways.
- **SKU**   Higher SKU values denote higher service level (and, accordingly, cost):
  - **Basic**   Intended for proof of concept (POC) or development workloads.
  - **VpnGw1-3**   Supports BGP, up to 30 site-to-site VPN connections and up to 1.25 gigabits per second (Gbps) throughput for the Gw3 SKU.
  - **VpnGw1-3AZ**   These SKUs have the same feature set as VPNGw1-3 but are availability-zone aware.
- **Enable Active-Active mode**   This setting is used when you configure high-availability failover for an Azure VPN Gateway.
- **Virtual Network**   This is the VNet to which the Azure VPN Gateway will reside; Azure will place the gateway in the gateway subnet you created earlier.
- **Public IP Address**   This is the public-facing endpoint for your Azure VPN Gateway.
- **Configure BGP ASN**   You need to assign a Border Gateway Protocol Autonomous System Number (BGP ASN) for advanced configurations; we do not need it for a VNet-to-VNet VPN.

4. Click Create to complete the configuration. Note that Azure VPN Gateway deployment can take quite a while (up to 1 hour on average).

Remember also to repeat these steps to deploy another Azure VPN Gateway on the other VNet.

NEED MORE REVIEW?   **HIGHLY AVAILABLE VPN GATEWAYS**

To learn more about configuring high-availability failover for Azure VPNs, read the Microsoft Docs article "Highly Available Cross-Premises and VNet-to-VNet Connectivity" at *https://docs.microsoft.com/en-us/azure/vpn-gateway/vpn-gateway-highlyavailable*.

Define connections

Simply deploying the Azure VPN Gateways is only step 1 of 2 in our VNet-to-VNet VPN configuration journey. Next, you have to define your connections:

1. Open the first gateway's Settings in the Azure portal, select Connections, and click Add.

2. Fill out the Add Connection form:

- **Connection Type** Choices include VNet-to-VNet, Site-to-site (IPSec), and ExpressRoute.

- **Second Virtual Network Gateway** Select the other VNet's gateway. Note that the First Virtual Network Gateway property points to the local device and is read-only.

- **Shared Key (PSK)** This is a (hopefully) strong passphrase you attach to each gateway to serve as a basic mutual authentication method.

3. Click OK to complete the configuration.

After you've configured the connection, your work is finished. You do *not* need to define a second connection resource for the other VNet. The connection status should appear as Connected in the Connections blade for both Azure virtual network gateways.

Verify virtual network connectivity

A common misconception among newer Azure architects and administrators is that simply defining a peering between two Azure VNets means instant connectivity between them. Not so fast!

Remember that you should have network security groups (NSGs) protecting ingress (incoming) and egress (outbound) traffic through each subnet. Recall, also, that your VMs may have software, host-level firewalls enabled that filter inbound and potentially outbound traffic as well.

> **NOTE BE MINDFUL OF DEFAULT NSG SECURITY RULES**
>
> If you enable default security rules for your NSG, you need to remember that two of these rules (AllowVNetInBound and AllowVnetOutBound) explicitly allow inter-VNet traffic. In the name of least-privilege security, you must work to ensure only required traffic flows are authorized in your Azure design.

Finally, be aware that only VNet-to-VNet VPNs support name resolution for VMs on either side of a connection. If you're doing peering, you need to take additional steps to support name resolution because Azure-provided name resolution can't function across a peering. You can configure the following:

- **A private Azure DNS zone** This is a nonroutable Domain Name system (DNS) zone you can attach to both VNets.

- **DNS servers** Here you deploy a DNS server VM in each VNet, and configure each to forward name resolution requests to the other VNet's name server. If you go this route (so to speak), make sure to update each VNet's DNS server list accordingly.

Network Watcher

Network Watcher is a tremendously useful tool for testing connectivity between virtual networks in Azure. First enable Network Watcher for your target Azure regions by browsing to the Network Watcher Overview blade, right-clicking a region, and selecting Enable Network Watcher from the shortcut menu.

You can then use IP flow verify in Network Watcher to test connectivity between any two IP addresses. As a solution architect you will find Network Watcher in general and IP flow verify in particular to be invaluable in tracking down inter-VM connectivity issues.

Figure 1-21 illustrates a network test we conducted with two VMs in two peered VNets. Here are some of the key IP flow verify options:

- **Virtual Machine**   In the environment, vm1 resides on the local VNet; we want to test connectivity on Transmission Control Protocol (TCP) port 3389 (Remote Desktop Protocol) between vm1 and vm2, which resides on a peered VNet.

- **Network Interface**   Remember that in Azure, IP addresses are associated with virtual network interface cards, not virtual machines.

- **Direction**   Outbound tests connectivity from the local system to the remote; inbound tests the opposite flow.

- **Remote IP Address**   This is the remote node's public or private IP address. In our environment, 10.2.0.4 is the private IPv4 address of vm2, which resides in a peered VNet.

- **Access Allowed**   In Figure 1-21, access is allowed by virtue of the AllowVnetOutBound NSG rule in the routing path.

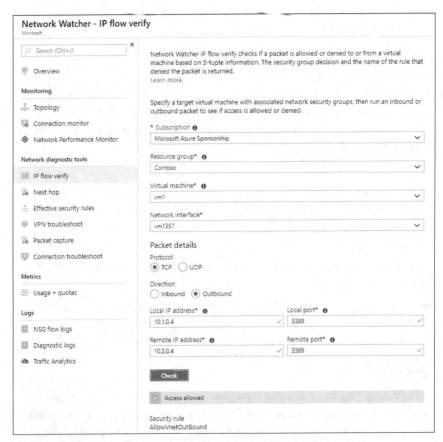

FIGURE 1-21 Using Network Watcher to verify and troubleshoot VNet peering

Skill 1.7: Implement and manage Azure virtual networking

It's time to take a step back from VNet peering and examine virtual networks more generally in Azure. An AZ-300 exam objective is concerned with configuring already created VNets, so that's a good place to begin.

> **This skill covers how to:**
> - Configure virtual networks
> - Configure network interfaces and IP addresses
> - Configure network routes

Configure virtual networks

As an architect, one of your job tasks is to help customers determine how many VNets they require to serve their business, technical, and security requirements. For instance, I have customers who maintain two identically configured VNets: one for production and the other for dev/testing.

Alternatively, a business may want a hub-spoke design pattern to save money and create stronger administrative boundaries among workloads. The following sections describe some of the more common virtual network configuration settings.

Address space and subnets

A customer can have up to 1,000 virtual networks per Azure region, per subscription. A virtual network can have more than one top-level Internet Protocol version 4 (IPv4) address space (useful when transitioning between address spaces, for example). However, once defined, you can't edit an existing address space.

EXAM TIP

The Microsoft Azure certification exams won't require that you recite specific service limit numbers. From what Microsoft Learning has said, their exam writers want to test your knowledge at a higher degree of sophistication.

That said, a worthwhile page for any Azure cloud solution architect's reference is the Microsoft Docs article "Azure subscription and service limits, quotas, and constraints" at *https://docs.microsoft.com/en-us/azure/azure-subscription-service-limits*.

On the other hand, you can have up to 3,000 subnets per virtual network. That seems like an absurdly high number, but at the least, you should consider spreading each workload tier into its own subnet for better organization and traffic routing.

DNS servers

Azure-provided name resolution enables you to resolve DNS hostnames for all resources within a single VNet. However, to facilitate other name resolution scenarios, such as

- Active Directory communications, either within a VNet, between VNets, or between a VNet and on-premises
- Ordinary DNS resolution for VMs spread across different VNets

you need to configure your VNet properties with the IP address(es) of additional DNS servers.

> **NOTE** **DON'T CONFIGURE VM NETWORKING FROM WITHIN THE VM**
>
> An all-too-common rookie mistake with TCP/IP configuration of Azure VMs is attempting to set TCP/IP properties such as IP address, subnet mask, default gateway, and DNS server addresses from within the VM.
>
> If you attempt this, you will almost certainly lock yourself out of the VM. The guiding rule is to configure the networking stack of your VMs from outside the VM session. Use Azure portal, Azure PowerShell, Azure CLI, or the ARM REST APIs instead.

Go to your VNet's Settings list, click DNS servers, and change the DNS Servers property from Default (Azure-provided) to Custom. Next, populate the list with the IP addresses of your custom DNS servers, as shown in Figure 1-22. Please note that Azure-provided DNS will continue to function alongside the custom DNS server addresses you specify here. Specifically, you can configure your custom DNS servers to forward resolution requests to the Azure-provided name servers.

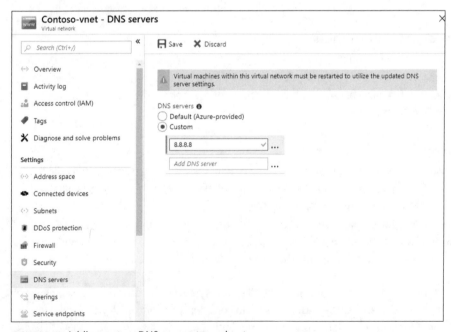

FIGURE 1-22 Adding custom DNS servers to a subnet

Service endpoints

Service endpoints enable you to secure certain Azure resources to particular virtual networks. This is an architectural trend Microsoft has been focusing on for some time. Because the VNet represents such a strong isolation boundary, and its infrastructure remains on the Azure network backbone, why not make use of the VNet in other contexts?

As of this writing, the following Azure products can be integrated into a virtual network via service endpoints:

- Azure Storage
- Azure SQL Database
- Azure SQL Data Warehouse
- Azure Database for PostgreSQL
- Azure Database for MySQL
- Azure Cosmos DB
- Azure Key Vault
- Azure Service Bus
- Azure Event Hub
- Azure Data Lake Store Gen 1

Follow these steps to integrate a general purpose v2 storage account with a virtual network:

1. Find the storage account in question, and click the Firewalls And Virtual Networks setting.

2. In the Configuration blade, change the Allow Access From option from All Networks to Selected Networks.

3. Click Add Existing Virtual Network and select the VNet to which you want to integrate the storage account. Note that you need to specify a subnet on that VNet before you can click Enable and Add.

4. Click Save to save your configuration. Figure 1-23 shows a completed service endpoint.

Enable the exception Allow Trusted Microsoft Services To Access This Storage Account to whitelist all Microsoft-owned IP addresses. Disable this exception and use the Firewall feature to strictly control access to the storage account from (a) VNet resources; and (b) selected additional IP addresses or IP address ranges.

FIGURE 1-23 Configuring a service endpoint for a storage account

Figure 1-24 summarizes the concepts we've been dealing with in this chapter section. Note the following elements in the diagram:

- The application is broken into three subnets along tiered lines. This is probably the most common VNet design pattern.

- In this deployment, Azure-provided name resolution ensures that all VMs within the virtual network can resolve one another's DNS hostnames.

- We created a storage account service endpoint, which limits access to this storage account from VMs on the VNet.

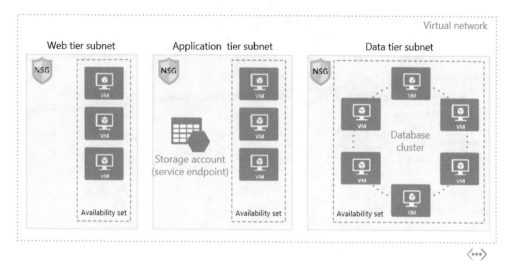

FIGURE 1-24 An n-tier application deployed to an Azure virtual network

Configure network interfaces and IP addresses

We mentioned previously that you should teach your customers to perform all VM TCP/IP configuration from outside the VM session itself. To that point, this section reviews how to assign a virtual machine's network interface public and/or private IP addresses.

1. Locate the network interface that is associated with the VM you want to configure. You can find the interface from the Network interfaces blade, or by navigating to the Networking blade of the VM resource.

2. In the network interface's Settings list, click IP Configurations (step 1 in Figure 1-25).

   By default, every network interface has an initial configuration called ipconfig1. In some cases, you may want to assign a network interface more than one public and/or private IP address; you do this by adding IP configurations.

3. Select the ipconfig1 configuration (step 2 in Figure 1-25); the IP Configurations blade appears.

4. Complete the form (step 3 in Figure 1-25). The options include:

   - **Public IP Address**   The Azure architecture best practice is to assign a public IP address (called a PIP for short) only when the VM has a legitimate use case to do so. The reason for this is that any VM with a public IP address becomes a potential target of a brute-force access attack.

   - **IP Address**   Public IPv4 addresses are tracked as separate resources. These public IP addresses can either be reserved (static) or dynamic. If you choose dynamic, remember you can bind a public DNS name to the network interface to make access easier in the event public IP address changes.

- **Virtual Network/Subnet** Recall that a VM's private IP address comes from its associated VNet address space and subnet ID.

- **Assignment** Dynamic uses Azure-provided Dynamic Host Configuration Protocol (DHCP); Static gives you control over the interface's private IP address.

- **Private IP Address** It's up to you to choose a valid, non-conflicting private IP address.

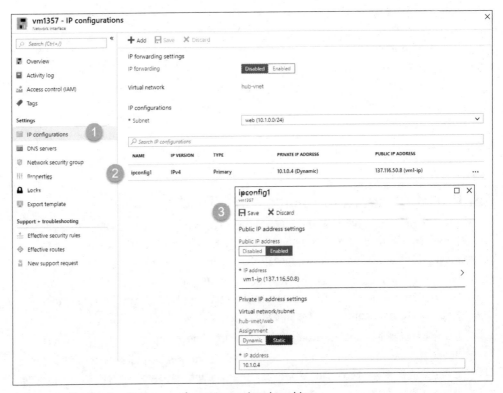

FIGURE 1-25 Configuring IP addresses for an Azure virtual machine

Configure network routes

Earlier in this chapter, we mentioned that VNet peerings are intransitive. This means that, by default, two spoke VNets are unable to communicate through a hub (transit) virtual network.

Remember when we told you that Azure-provided DNS handles name resolution for VMs within a virtual network? Well, Azure system routes are responsible for automatically routing traffic among VMs on different subnets within a VNet.

Azure gives you the ability to create custom route tables that define your own routing paths. Azure route tables are associated at the subnet level.

You can define the following next hop types in an Azure route table:

- **Virtual network gateway**   Use this type when you need to force traffic through an Azure virtual network gateway.

- **Virtual network**   Use this type when you need greater control of traffic between subnets in a VNet.

- **Internet**   Use this type when you need to control Internet-bound traffic.

- **Virtual appliance**   Use this type when you need to route traffic through a central network virtual appliance (NVA), such as an enterprise firewall VM deployed from Azure Marketplace.

Figure 1-26 shows the route table route creation workflow.

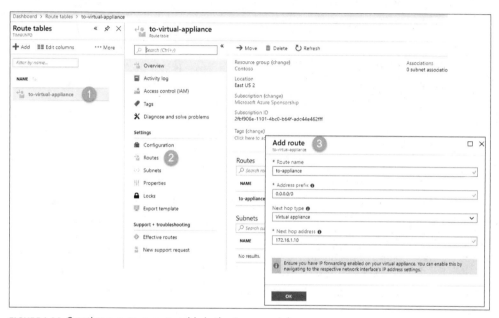

FIGURE 1-26   Creating a custom route table in the Azure portal

---

NEED MORE REVIEW?   **CUSTOM ROUTING IN AZURE**

To learn more about using route tables to customize Azure routing paths, visit the Microsoft Docs article "Virtual network traffic routing" at *https://docs.microsoft.com/en-us/azure/virtual-network/virtual-networks-udr-overview*.

Skill 1.8: Manage Azure Active Directory

Azure Active Directory (Azure AD) is Microsoft Azure's default cloud-based, multitenant identity platform. In this skill, you make sure you understand the "hows and whys" of several key Azure AD architectural and management tasks.

> **This skill covers how to:**
> - Add custom domains
> - Manage multiple directories
> - Configure self-service password reset
> - Implement conditional access policies
> - Perform an access review
> - Configure Azure AD Identity Protection
> - Configure Azure AD Join
> - Configure Enterprise State Roaming

Add custom domains

When you create a new Azure subscription, you receive a default Azure AD instance that has the public DNS name *tenantname*.onmicrosoft.com, where *tenantname* is a globally unique identifier the subscription owner defines.

You can never get rid of the onmicrosoft.com hostname because this is an attribute Azure uses to identify your tenant. However, for ease of use and compatibility with your identity and access use cases, you can and should bind at least one public DNS name you own to your tenant.

> **NOTE ABOUT THE WORD "TENANT"**
>
> By the way, an Azure AD tenant is simply one instance of the Azure AD service. Azure AD is called multitenant because more than one Azure subscription can trust a single Azure AD tenant. By contrast, a single subscription can be associated with only one Azure AD instance at a time.

Follow these steps to associate a public DNS domain with your Azure AD tenant:

1. Browse to your Azure AD tenant, and navigate to the Custom Domain Names setting (step 1 in Figure 1-27).
2. Click Add Custom Domain (step 2 in Figure 1-27).
3. Type your public DNS name. This needs to be a domain that you own, which will become clear in the next step.

4. In your DNS registrar, add a verification mail exchanger (MX) or text (TXT) resource record to your zone file, using the Microsoft-provided values.

   Don't worry about causing a denial of service at your domain registrar; after Microsoft verifies you own the domain, you can delete the verification record.

5. Check that the added domain shows as Verified in the Custom Domain Names blade.

You can use a custom domain with Azure AD at any pricing tier, even the Free tier. Once you verified a custom domain, you can use that domain name as a user account suffix. Specifically, some businesses prefer to identify Azure AD cloud users by a naming format that matches their users' Simple Mail Transfer Protocol (SMTP) email address.

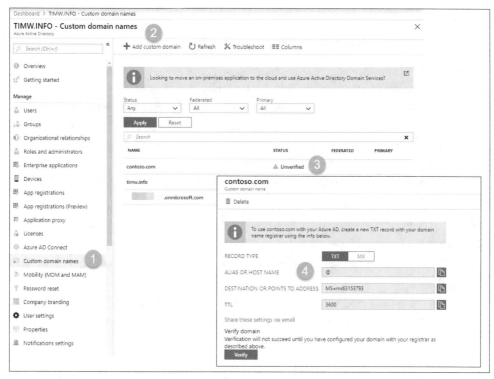

FIGURE 1-27 Associating a custom DNS domain with an Azure AD tenant

Manage multiple directories

As I mentioned a moment ago, a single Azure AD tenant has a one-to-many relationship with Azure subscriptions. In addition, you can deploy additional Azure AD tenants to suit use cases where complete user/service principal isolation is desired.

When you create a new, stand-alone Azure AD instance, the tenant has limited capability unless and until you associate an Azure subscription with it. To do this, open the Subscriptions blade in the Azure portal, select the subscription that is to be associated with the new Azure AD tenant, and click Change Directory.

In the Change The Directory blade, select the target Azure AD directory, and click Change. Note that changing the directory removes access for all role-based access control (RBAC) users.

To switch your administrative user context to a different directory, open the user menu in the Azure portal and select Switch Directory. The Directory + Subscription blade allows you to perform many time-saving tasks, including

- Setting a global subscription filter so that you see data from selected Azure subscriptions
- Setting your default Azure AD directory
- Setting favorite directories to make them easier to find if you manage multiple Azure AD tenants

Configure self-service password reset

Hosting line-of-business web applications that rely on Azure AD authentication can pose challenges for the Azure solutions architect. For example, you may deploy Azure AD Connect to synchronize on-premises Active Directory user identities to an Azure AD tenant.

The benefit here is that your users can log into your cloud apps by using the same credentials they use on-premises. However, what if you need to give the user the ability to change his or her password in the cloud application?

Self-service password reset (SSPR) is supported in all Azure AD editions. To enable SSPR, follow these steps:

1. In the Azure portal, navigate to your Azure AD blade.
2. Select the Password Reset setting.
3. Choose the desired self-service password reset option. Your choices are None, Selected, or All.

   If you choose Selected, you can enable SSPR for individual Azure AD groups. Otherwise, if you choose All, SSPR is enabled for all Azure AD users in your tenant.

EXAM TIP

Keep role-based access control (RBAC) in mind as we work together through this chapter. For instance, to accomplish Azure AD administrative tasks, your Azure AD account should be associated with the Global Administrator Azure AD role.

Give your users the following instructions to reset their Azure AD password:

1. Navigate to the My Apps (*https://myapps.microsoft.com*) and authenticate if necessary.
2. Open the user menu and choose Profile.
3. On the Profile page (shown in Figure 1-28), click Change Password and follow the instructions.

FIGURE 1-28 Self-service password reset in Azure Active Directory

Password writeback

Self-service password reset affects the Azure AD representation of the user account, but what happens to the on-premises version if you're in a hybrid cloud environment? This question falls squarely within the Azure solution architect's wheelhouse.

The solution here is an Azure AD feature called password writeback. Password writeback requires Azure AD Premium P1 or P2 licenses. We cover this subject in more detail later in this chapter.

Implement conditional access policies

Conditional access policy is an Azure AD Premium P1 or P2 feature that allows you to completely shape your Azure AD user's authentication environment. For example, you might create a policy that allows user login to selected Azure cloud apps based on

- **Sign-in risk** Azure AD Identity Protection assigns each enabled user a risk level based on their past and present logon behavior.
- **Network location** You may require authentication only from whitelisted geographic locations.
- **Device management** You may restrict cloud app access from mobile devices or noncompany issued devices.

> *NOTE* **HOW TO UPGRADE YOUR AZURE AD LICENSING**
>
> Somewhat counterintuitively, you cannot purchase Azure AD licenses from the Azure AD tenant settings, or even the Azure portal itself. Instead, log into the Microsoft 365 Admin Center (*https://portal.office.com*) using an Azure AD Global Administrator account, select Billing > Purchase Services, locate the appropriate Azure AD SKU, and then click Buy Now.

Follow these general steps to deploy a conditional access policy in your subscription:

1. In the Azure portal, navigate to the Conditional Access blade, and click New Policy.
2. In the New blade, complete the form.
   - **Users and groups** Scope the policy to particular Azure AD user and/or group accounts.
   - **Cloud apps** Enable or deny authentication to specific Azure AD-backed apps in your subscription.
   - **Conditions** Here you can shape the authentication environment according to sign-in risk, device platforms, locations, client apps (browser, mobile, and/or desktop clients), or device state (whether the client device is Azure AD-joined).
   - **Grant** or block access if all other conditional access policy requirements are true.
   - **Session** For Exchange Online and SharePoint Online, use app-enforced additional restrictions.

In your practice, you doubtless noticed that conditional access policies work on exclusions and inclusions. For example, you may have a conditional access policy that allows authentication to your Cloud App Users Azure AD group but denies access to the Cloud Interns group, as shown in Figure 1-29.

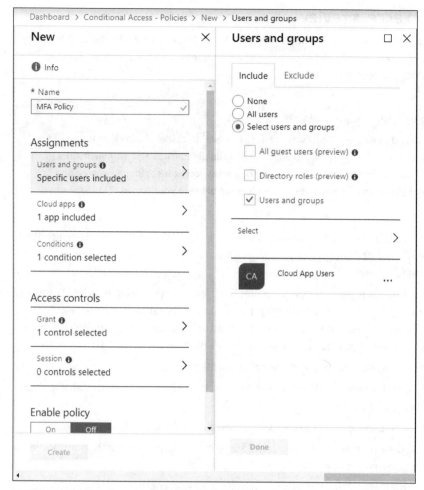

FIGURE 1-29 Configuring a conditional access policy

 EXAM TIP

You're highly likely to be asked on your AZ-300 exam about Microsoft's preferred way to enable Multi-Factor Authentication (MFA) for your Azure AD users. The answer to this is, naturally, via conditional access policy.

Specifically, you need to enable the Require Multi-Factor Authentication property in the Access Controls > Grant Section of your policy.

Perform an access review

Access review is part of Azure AD Privileged Identity Management (PIM). Azure AD PIM requires Azure AD Premium P2, and allows you to enforce least-privilege security for your Azure AD and Azure subscription resources.

> **NOTE** **AZURE AD LICENSE ASSIGNMENT**
>
> Please remember that Azure AD editions are licensed per-user. That means that to use features like Azure AD PIM or password writeback, all involved users and administrators must be assigned the appropriate Azure AD license. You can assign licenses in many ways; one of the most straightforward is to navigate to the Licenses blade in your Azure AD tenant.

For instance, you use PIM to give administrators just-in-time, time-restricted administrative access to Azure AD and/or Azure resource groups. Outside of these elevation windows, Azure admins run as standard users.

Specifically, the access review process simplifies the process of reviewing Azure AD group membership and privileged role assignments for your team. For example, you may want to work with your peers to determine precisely who should be given access to the Global Administrators or Owners roles in your subscription. Here is the high-level configuration workflow:

1. Open the Access Reviews blade in the Azure portal.
2. If this is the first time you've used Access Reviews, then click Onboard to enable access reviews in the current directory.
3. From Settings, choose Access Reviews, and then click New Access Review.
4. Fill out the Create An Access Review form. Some of the major configuration properties of an access review include

   - **Start/End Date** Put a "time fence" around the review period.
   - **Users To Review** These are the Azure AD users or groups whose role membership and resource access we want to scrutinize.
   - **Reviewers** These are the access review participants.
   - **Completion Settings** Whether the access review results should be implemented by Azure.

Azure sends each access review member a notification email, similar to what's shown in Figure 1-30. The reviewers then take action on the review by visiting a special Access Review interface (shown in Figure 1-31). The reviewer can scan who belongs to the given Azure AD group or role and approve or deny their membership.

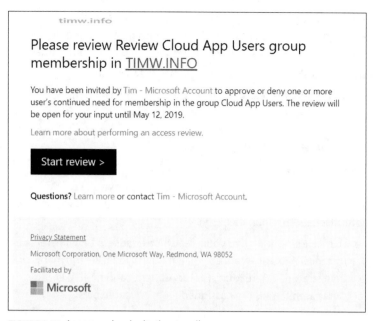

FIGURE 1-30 Access review invitation email message

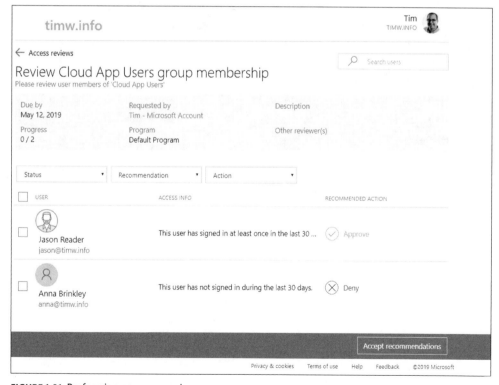

FIGURE 1-31 Performing an access review

In the previous example, we showed you how to perform an access review to audit Azure AD group membership or access to an Azure AD application. It's a bit confusing, but you configure access reviews in two different Azure portal locations, depending on what exactly you're reviewing:

- **For Azure AD groups or applications**   Use the Access Reviews blade.
- **For Azure AD or Azure resource roles**   Use the Azure AD Privileged Identity Management blade.

Configure Azure AD Identity Protection

Azure AD Identity Protection (IdP) is an Azure AD Premium P2 feature that enables you to detect potential vulnerabilities affecting your Azure AD identities and potentially configure automatic remediation for suspicious events (for example, attempted logons for the same user account from two geographical locations simultaneously).

As you can see in Figure 1-32, Azure AD IdP gives you a real-time heads-up on vulnerable Azure AD user accounts. For instance, Azure IdP can tell you if it thinks you have too many Azure AD and/or resource administrators, where Multi-Factor Authentication (MFA) is not required, and which user accounts aren't using their assigned high-privilege roles.

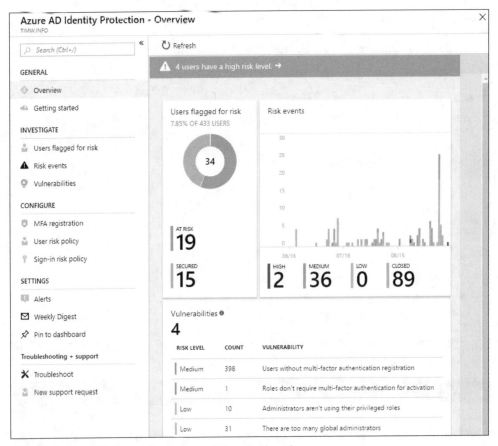

FIGURE 1-32 Azure AD Identity Protection real-time dashboard

With respect to Azure AD IdP configuration, you can configure three policy types:

- **MFA registration policy**   Require your users to specify additional authentication methods to protect their accounts.
- **User risk policy**   Set a minimum user behavior risk threshold that triggers the policy; the policy result either blocks or allows sign-in to your Azure AD-backed apps.
- **Sign-in risk policy**   Set a minimum sign-in risk level to trigger the policy that, in turn, blocks or allows sign-in.

In case you wondered, Azure uses a lot of machine learning and telemetry to calculate risk values for Azure AD users and sign-ins. Microsoft calls this vast artificial intelligence engine the Intelligent Security Graph, or ISG.

Microsoft tells us in their documentation that we should allow Azure an initial learning period of at least 14 days to get a handle on your users' sign-in and application access behaviors.

Configure Azure AD Join

Azure AD Join is what it sounds like to you: the capacity of joining Windows 10 endpoint devices to your Azure AD tenant. You can join Windows 10 devices to Azure AD with any Azure AD SKU; however, advanced features such as mobile device management (MDM) auto-enrollment require Azure AD Premium P1 or P2 licensing.

It's crucial you understand Microsoft's positioning of Azure AD Join and related technologies such as Microsoft Intune. These are mechanisms for endpoint management, not server management.

Azure AD Joined devices may or may not be connected to an on-premises Active Directory Domain Services (AD DS) domain; in any case, Group Policy is not supported in Azure.

Anyway, the high-level Azure AD Join configuration workflow involves the following planning points:

- Whether you will manage the endpoint devices exclusively using cloud products like Intune (this scenario is called MDM-only), or if you plan to split management between Intune and on-premises System Center Configuration Manager (SCCM)
- How you will handle authentication to on-premises and Azure resources
- Which provisioning option makes the most sense for your business (self-service, Windows Autopilot, or bulk enrollment)
- Which MDM provider you'll use to manage Azure AD-joined devices (options include Intune, VMware AirWatch, ManageEngine, and other partners)
- Whether you need conditional access policy for managed devices and users
- What need the business has for enterprise state roaming

Configure Enterprise State Roaming

Speaking of enterprise state roaming, let's consider this feature now. I think of Enterprise State Roaming (an Azure AD Premium P1 or P2 feature) roughly as a public cloud equivalent of roaming user profiles in on-premises Active Directory.

The idea here is your users with their Windows 10 Azure AD–joined devices can synchronize their user and application settings data to the cloud, and have the data be available to all their Windows devices.

Follow these steps to understand the Enterprise State Roaming "big picture":

1. In your Azure AD tenant, browse to Devices, and then click Enterprise State Roaming.

2. Set the Users May Sync Settings And App Data Across Devices property to either All or Selected, depending on whether you want to enable Enterprise State Roaming for all or selected Azure AD users.

3. Click Save to complete the configuration.

Skill 1.9: Implement and manage hybrid identities

For some Azure solution architects, the subject of "hybrid identity" may lead them to think along ExpressRoute or site-to-site VPN lines. Not so fast! With Azure AD Connect, we can link our on-premises Active Directory user accounts with an Azure AD tenant and support single sign-on (SSO) to cloud apps that rely on Azure AD for authentication.

Take a look at Figure 1-33. Your company might have an Office 365 subscription or line-of-business software as a service (SaaS) apps that use Azure AD for authentication.

The last thing you want as an Azure solutions architect is to force your users to have to memorize multiple credential sets. By leveraging Azure AD Connect, you can synchronize on-premises Active Directory identities to your Azure AD tenant, and then instruct your users to use their on-premises credentials to authenticate to the cloud-based apps.

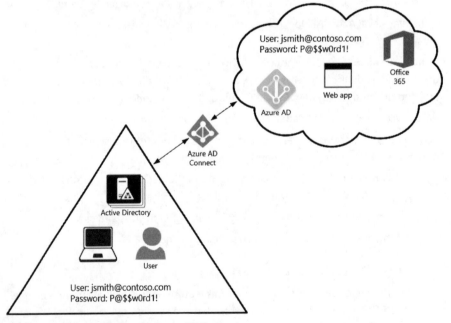

FIGURE 1-33 Hybrid identity with Azure AD Connect

Install and configure Azure AD Connect

Azure AD Connect is a free Microsoft utility that facilitates single sign-on between on-premises Active Directory and Azure AD. You don't need ExpressRoute or a site-to-site VPN to use Azure AD Connect; all communications occur over TCP 443.

Download Azure AD Connect and install on a domain member server. Here are the steps:

1. Start Azure AD Connect, agree to the license terms, and click Continue.

2. Choose the express settings or Customize Installation option. Here's the distinction between the two installation paths:

    ■ **Express settings** Choosing this path synchronizes all identities and attributes in the current Active Directory forest to Azure AD by using password hash synchronization.

    ■ **Customize** Choosing this path gives you complete control over the hybrid identity scenario, including choosing another identity synchronization method.

    In this example, we choose Customize.

3. On the Install required components screen, click Install. You can optionally specify a custom Azure AD Connect installation location, use an existing SQL Server, or use an existing service account.

    The Azure Active Directory Connect Wizard automatically downloads and installs Microsoft SQL Server Express LocalDB for use as a back-end data store. At this point the utility installs the synchronization service; this is the "engine" that powers hybrid identity with Azure AD.

4. On the User sign-in page, choose a sign-on method, as shown in Figure 1-34. This is probably the most important architectural choice you have to make. The sign-on methods are

    ■ **Password Hash Synchronization** This is the simplest option; each on-premises AD identity has an Azure AD representation, and Azure AD Connect keeps the passwords in sync. Specifically, Azure AD Connect maintains user account password hashes both in local AD and Azure AD.

    ■ **Pass-Through Authentication** This method is an alternative to password hash synchronization. With pass-through authentication, no password hashes are kept in Azure AD; this suits businesses whose security requirements prevent cloud-based password hash storage. Note that this sign-on method requires the deployment of agent software on-premises.

- **Federation With AD FS**   Azure AD Connect can largely automate the deployment of an Active Directory Federation Services (AD FS) farm to support token-based SSO.
- **Federation With PingFederate**   is a third-party alternative to AD FS; this option is aimed at businesses that already use PingFederate for token-based SSO.

FIGURE 1-34 Configuring an identity synchronization option in Azure AD Connect

You can optionally combine your preferred sync method with what Microsoft calls Seamless Single Sign-On (it's the Enable Single Sign-On option you see in Figure 1-34). Seamless SSO creates a computer account named AZUREADSSOACC in your on-premises AD domain. This allows Seamless SSO to use local Kerberos for authentication; only Kerberos tickets, never password hashes, travel between your on-premises and Azure AD environments.

In this example, we choose Password Hash Synchronization and then click Next to continue.

5.   In the Connect to Azure AD screen, type your Azure AD Global Administrator credentials, and then click Next.

EXAM TIP

The exam may test your knowledge of the account privileges required to set up Azure AD Connect. Remember that you must have both Azure AD Global Administrator and local AD Enterprise Administrator credentials to complete the configuration.

6.   In the Connect Your Directories screen, verify that Azure AD Connect shows the correct Active Directory forest, and click Add Directory. You're prompted to authenticate as an

Enterprise Administrator. Note that the account must be a member of the Enterprise Administrators universal group; Domain Admins will not be sufficient.

7. In the Azure AD sign-in configuration screen, verify your on-premises Active Directory user principal name (UPN) suffix matches your Azure AD domain name. A couple points to note:

    ■ You must have a custom DNS domain attached to your Azure AD tenant. You're not allowed to configure hybrid identity by using your tenant's default *.onmicrosoft.com domain name.

    ■ You may need to add a UPN suffix to your forest and modify the UPN attributes of your synchronized users if your goal is to simulate their SMTP email address (this is perhaps the most common pattern). For example, your local domain may be called contoso.local, and your email and Azure AD domains may be contoso.com.

8. In the Domain and OU filtering screen, choose Sync Selected Domains And OUs and use the filter controls to manage which identities you want to synchronize to Azure AD. This is an important step for two reasons:

    ■ You don't want to waste expensive Azure AD licenses on non-user accounts.

    ■ You don't want to synchronize high-privilege accounts or service accounts to Azure AD unless absolutely necessary.

In Figure 1-35, you see that we chose to synchronize only the user accounts within our PILOT organizational unit (OU).

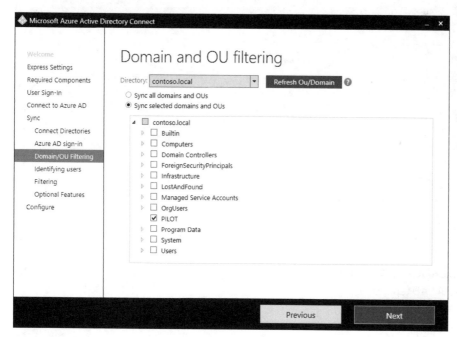

FIGURE 1-35 Customizing synchronized identities with Azure AD Connect

9. On the Uniquely Identifying Your Users screen, click Next to continue. By default, Azure AD Connect uses the UPN attribute to identify your local AD accounts individually. In larger organizations that plan to synchronize users across AD domains and forests, you may need to choose another AD schema attribute to resolve account name conflicts.

10. In the Filter User And Devices screen, click Next. By default, we synchronize all identities within our PILOT OU.

11. In the Optional Features screen, decide whether you need advanced functionality. In this case, we click Next to continue. Later in this section, we show you how to opt-in to any of these features after synchronization has begun.

12. Ensure that the Start The Synchronization Process When Configuration Completes option is enabled, and then click Install to complete the installation.

When account synchronization completes, you can visit the Users blade in your Azure AD tenant to confirm that the on-premises identities show up properly. Take a look at Figure 1-36, which shows a partial user list from my timw.info Azure AD tenant.

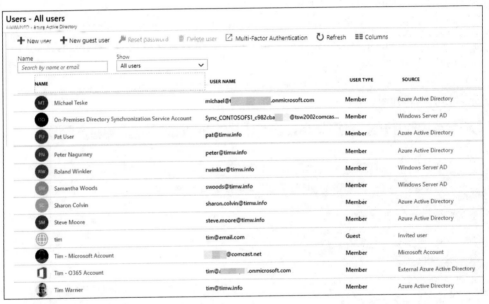

FIGURE 1-36 A multi-sourced Azure AD tenant

In Figure 1-36, pay attention to the Source column. Here's what the different source IDs mean:

- **Azure Active Directory** This is a cloud-native identity that was created directly in the Azure AD tenant.

- **External Azure Active Directory** This is an identity from another Azure AD tenant who was invited to the local directory via Active Directory Business-to-Business collaboration (Azure AD B2B).

- **Invited User** This is an Azure AD B2B guest user who has not yet accepted the invitation to join the local directory.

- **Microsoft Account** External Azure AD B2B guests become Microsoft accounts after they redeem their invitation.

- **Windows Server AD** This is a local Active Directory identity that has been synchronized to the Azure AD tenant.

EXAM TIP

Don't forget to assign your synchronized local AD users appropriate Azure AD licenses! Synchronized identities behave exactly the same as cloud-native identities from Azure AD's perspective.

Manage password sync and writeback

One advantage to Password Hash Synchronization is that it's fast and easy to deploy. One disadvantage is that unless you enable password writeback, your users may change their passwords in the cloud and have their passwords fall out of sync.

First off, understand that password writeback to on-premises AD is supported only in Azure AD Premium P1 and P2. Second, you can enable password writeback after you deploy Azure AD Connect. Here's how:

1. Start Azure AD Connect, and in the Welcome To Azure AD Connect screen, click Configure.

2. In the Additional tasks window, select Customize Synchronization Options and click Next.

3. In the Connect To Azure AD screen, authenticate with a Global Administrator role holder account.

4. In the Connect To Directories screen, confirm your AD forest and directory and then click Next.

5. In the Domain And OU filtering screen, click Next to continue.

6. In the Optional Features screen, shown in Figure 1-37, select Password writeback, and then click Next.

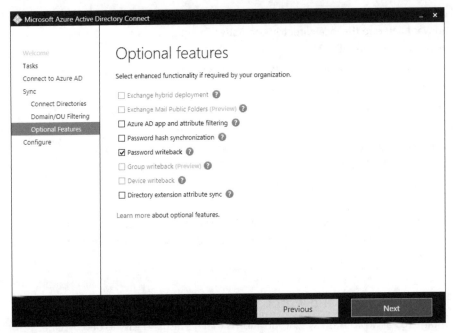

FIGURE 1-37 Enabling password writeback in Azure AD Connect

7. Click Configure to complete the environment change.

> **NOTE CONFIGURE AZURE AD CONNECT HIGH AVAILABILITY**
>
> The Azure AD Connect Additional Tasks screen has an option called Configure Staging Mode. To provide some redundancy to your Azure AD Connect deployment, install Azure AD Connect on at least one other domain member server, but configure it for staging mode. The secondary Azure AD Connect instance remains in "standby"; if the primary Azure AD Connect server goes offline, bring the standby out of staging mode to have it resume identity synchronization as usual.

Manage the scheduler

By default, the Azure AD Sync scheduler runs every 30 minutes. You can find the scheduler service in the Service Control Manager list under Microsoft Azure AD Sync (short name: ADSync). Open an elevated PowerShell session on your Azure AD Connect server and run Get-ADSyncScheduler to view current sync metadata.

To disable the scheduler, run the following PowerShell command:

```
Set-ADSyncScheduler -SyncCycleEnabled $false
```

Configure federation and single sign-on

As an alternative to password hash synchronization or pass-through authentication, you can enable "true" SSO by implementing Active Directory Federation Services (AD FS). What does "true" SSO mean?

Well, honestly, password hash sync is not really "single sign-on" in the true sense of the word. You see, while your on-premises users authenticate to your cloud apps with what they think are their local AD credentials, the app authentication relies strictly on the synchronized Azure AD identities instead.

What I call "true" SSO is an authentication system that uses vendor-neutral tokens (typically in Security Assertion Markup Language (SAML) format) for trusted authentication between two different identity stores.

When you use Azure AD Connect to install or configure a local AD FS farm, a trust relationship is defined between local AD and your Azure AD tenant. Here is a super high-level overview of the authentication flow:

1. A user accesses an Azure AD-based application and types his or her email address (which we know, behind the scenes, represents the user's on-premises AD UPN).

2. Because a federated trust exists, Azure AD redirects the user to the local AD FS farm, where the user may or may not be prompted for their password depending on the environment specifics.

3. User authentication happens strictly locally within AD; the AD FS security token service generates a vendor-neutral token that makes claims about the user's identity, group memberships, and possibly other metadata.

4. The AD FS farm presents the token to Azure AD. Azure AD trusts local AD via the federation, so the user is granted access to the application.

Do you see how that works? At most, all the user needs to provide to the Azure AD application is the username; no password hashes or Kerberos tickets are exchanged over the network connection.

Let's run through the Azure AD Connect federation setup workflow. In keeping with the work we've performed thus far, we will rerun the Azure AD Connect wizard to change from password hash authentication to federated authentication.

1. In the Azure AD Connect Additional tasks screen, choose Change User Sign-In and click Next.

2. In the Connect To Azure AD screen, authenticate as a Global Administrator.

3. In the User Sign-In screen, select Federation With AD FS and click Next.

4. In the Domain Administrator credentials, authenticate to local AD with a domain administrator identity.

5. In the AD FS farm screen, decide whether you want to use an existing AD FS farm or configure a new AD FS farm.

6. Complete the wizard according to your choice in step 5.

NEED MORE REVIEW?   **DEPLOYING AND CONFIGURING AD FS**

Setting up AD FS is beyond the scope of this book. To learn more about AD FS in general, visit the Active Directory Federation Services documentation at *https://docs.microsoft.com/en-us/ windows-server/identity/active-directory-federation-services*.

Manage Azure AD Connect

Besides the ADSync service and the Azure AD Connect wizard itself, Azure AD Connect provides three other graphical utilities to help you manage and customize your hybrid identity environment:

- **Synchronization Service Manager**   View and configure synchronization service properties.
- **Synchronization Service Web Service Configuration Tool**   Control the web services connection between local AD and Azure AD.
- **Synchronization Rules Editor**   Customize the mapping between local AD schema attributes and Azure AD user and group account attributes.

I show you Synchronization Service Manager in Figure 1-38. As you can see, you can force a synchronization run by right-clicking inside the window and choosing Run from the shortcut menu.

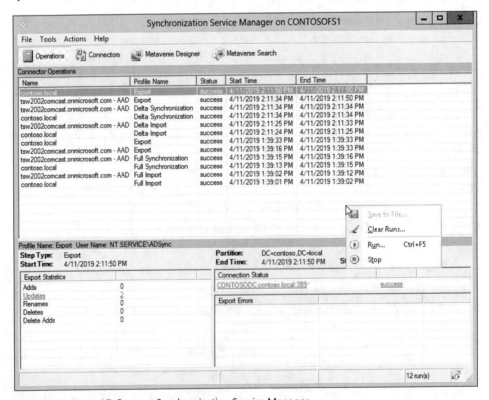

FIGURE 1-38 Azure AD Connect Synchronization Service Manager

Verifying synchronization status in the Azure portal

Lastly, navigate to the Azure AD Connect blade in your Azure AD tenant, as depicted in Figure 1-39. The Azure portal shows you sync status and which user sign-in options you have enabled. In Figure 1-39, the environment uses pass-through authentication and Seamless SSO.

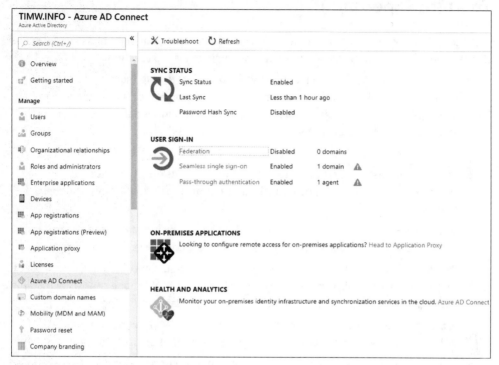

FIGURE 1-39 Verifying sync status in Azure AD

Chapter summary

- Configure diagnostics for Azure resources to create performance baselines and to analyze your consumption.
- Azure Log Analytics provides a centralized analysis engine for all your Azure resources.
- Global VNet peering means the peered VNets can exist in different Azure regions or even different subscriptions.
- Consider a VNet-to-VNet VPN when security needs require the communications.
- You assign public and private IP addresses to VMs through their associated virtual network interface, not the VM resource itself.
- A virtual network (VNet) consists of one or more top-level IPv4 address spaces; the most common design pattern is to create a subnet for each application tier.
- Azure AD Identity Protection is an Azure AD Premium P2 feature that uses Microsoft's Intelligent Security Graph to detect potential vulnerabilities with your user identities.

- Azure AD Join enables you to join Windows 10 devices to your Azure AD tenant and optionally manage them by using Microsoft Intune or another mobile device management (MDM) platform.

Thought experiment

In this thought experiment, demonstrate your skills and knowledge of the topics covered in this chapter. You can find answers to this thought experiment in the next section.

You are an Azure solutions architect hired by Fabrikam, Inc. to help them plan their move to the Microsoft Cloud Platform. Currently, Fabrikam is organized as a single Active Directory domain, with all IT infrastructure located in an on-premises datacenter at corporate headquarters in Sacramento, California.

In your consultation with Fabrikam, you identify the following business requirements:

- Fabrikam leadership wants to make more robust use of its existing Office 365 subscription. Specifically, users should be able to sign into Office 365 by using their fabrikam.com email IDs.

- The Fabrikam compliance department needs to know which IT staff members have administrative privilege in Azure Active AD and in the corporate Azure subscription.

- Fabrikam IT wants to migrate its core infrastructure to Azure and decommission most of their on-premises environment. The on-premises network backbone consists of multiple virtual LANs (VLANs) with no clear management boundary among them.

- Fabrikam IT also needs to be able to manage the cloud VMs from on-premises AD; AD will eventually be migrated to Azure, but that initiative isn't on the near-term roadmap.

With this information in mind, answer the following questions:

1. What solution would you recommend to solve the single-sign on issue to Office 365?

2. How can Fabrikam meet the goal of reporting Azure AD and Azure subscription management access to their compliance department?

3. What kind of network topology would you recommend to Fabrikam IT?

Thought experiment answers

This section contains the solution to the thought experiment. Each answer explains why the answer choice is correct.

1. The reference to Office 365 is a bit of a red herring. It's important for you to understand that many Microsoft cloud products use Azure AD as an identity store, including, of course, Office 365. You should start by teaching Fabrikam how to associate their fabrikam.com DNS domain with the Office 365 Azure AD tenant, after which you can implement Azure AD Connect to facilitate SSO to Office 365. Which account synchronization strategy, or whether AD FS federation is appropriate, will require additional interviews to learn more about Fabrikam's security requirements.

2. We now know that Azure AD PIM has the central use case of reporting on high-privilege access to Azure AD and Azure resources. Thus, you should guide Fabrikam to upgrade their Azure AD licenses as necessary and then show them how to work with Azure AD PIM, particularly access reviews. The reviewers can then send reports to the compliance department to meet their regulatory requirements.

3. The pitfall here that some businesses fall into is the mistaken belief that they must by definition replicate their on-premises network topology to Azure 1:1. Absolutely not! In many cases it's better to consider the Azure environment a "greenfield" deployment, and design the virtual network topology from scratch, keeping in mind security, performance, and availability.

   In this scenario, you might consider either ExpressRoute or a site-to-site VPN to facilitate central management of both on-premises and Azure resources. Depending on business and technical requirements, you might deploy only a single VNet, or you may determine a hub-and-spoke topology makes the most sense.

## CHAPTER 2

Implement workloads and security

Organizations are still working out the details of getting to the cloud. With all of the hardware and servers running in datacenters and in colocation spaces, moving to the cloud still takes a bit of effort.

Architecting solutions in Azure is not just development or infrastructure management in the cloud. It's much more than that, and you need to understand how the Azure resources an organization needs to operate will sometimes be centered in development and sometimes in infrastructure. It's up to you to know enough about these topics.

This chapter helps you understand how you can bring your existing workloads to Azure by allowing the use of some familiar resources (IaaS Virtual Machines) and others that may be new (serverless computing) to your environment. In addition, the use of Multi-Factor Authentication (MFA) is covered here to ensure your cloud environment is as secure as possible. An Azure Solutions Architect may face all these situations in day-to-day work life and needs to be ready for each of them.

Skills covered in this chapter:

- Skill 2.1: Migrate servers to Azure
- Skill 2.2: Configure serverless computing
- Skill 2.3: Implement application load balancing
- Skill 2.4: Integrate an Azure virtual network and an on-premises network
- Skill 2.5: Manage Role-Based Access Control (RBAC)
- Skill 2.6: Implement Multi-Factor Authentication (MFA)

Skill 2.1: Migrate servers to Azure

Because most organizations have been operating on infrastructure running in house, there is a significant opportunity to help them migrate these workloads to Azure, which may save some costs and provide efficiencies for these servers that their datacenters may not. Or they might want to explore getting out of the datacenter business. How can you help your organization or customer move out of a datacenter into the Azure cloud?

The recommended option for this is Azure Site Recovery (ASR), which offers different options depending on the type of workload you're migrating (physical or virtual).

This skill covers how to:

- Configure Azure components of Site Recovery
- Configure on-premises components of Site Recovery
- Replicate data to Azure
- Migrate by using Azure Site Recovery

Configure Azure components of Site Recovery

Azure Site Recovery provides a way to bring your servers into Azure while allowing them to be failed back to your on-premises datacenter should the need arise as part of a business continuity and disaster recovery (BDCR) scenario. An increasingly common practice is to make the failover one-way and use ASR to move servers to Azure. Then you switch off their local counterparts, effectively migrating your environment to Azure.

Follow these steps to configure the Azure resources to migrate existing servers to Azure:

> **NOTE CONSIDER CREATING THE AZURE RESOURCES FIRST**
>
> Creating the Azure resources first prepares the destination and ensures that nothing is missed. Because the process moves files into Azure, this can minimize issues when the transfer begins because the target resources will be identified up front.

1. Log in to your Azure subscription.
2. Create a resource group to hold your Azure Backup Vault.
3. Create a new resource and select Backup and Site Recovery (OMS) from the Storage grouping in the Azure Marketplace as shown in Figure 2-1.

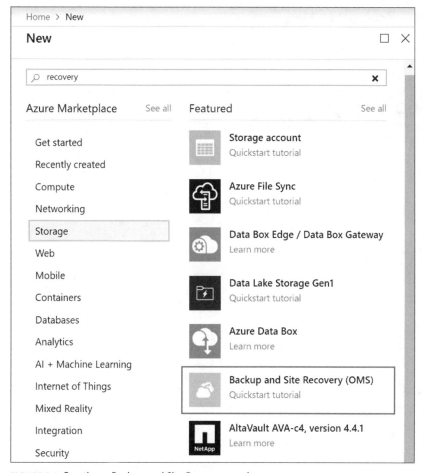

FIGURE 2-1 Creating a Backup and Site Recovery vault

4. In the Recovery Services vault Creation blade, shown in Figure 2-2, complete the form:

- **Name** Choose a unique name for your Recovery Services vault.
- **Subscription** Specify an active Azure subscription.
- **Resource Group** Create a new or select an existing resource group for the Recovery Services vault.
- **Location** Select the region to use for the Recovery Services vault.

> *NOTE* **FEATURE NAME CHANGES HAPPEN AT CLOUD SPEED, TOO**
>
> Backup and Site Recovery (OMS) is the new name for the Recovery Services vault resource. As of this writing, the names have not been updated throughout the portal.

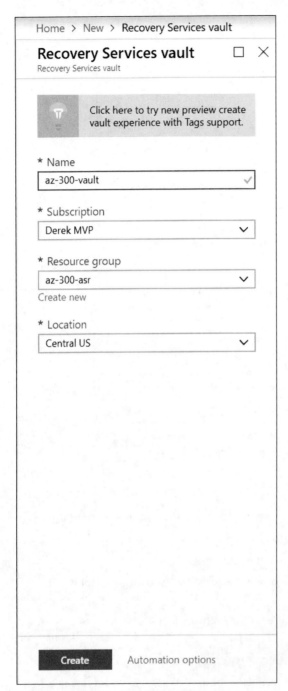

Home > New > Recovery Services vault

Recovery Services vault ☐ ✕
Recovery Services vault

Click here to try new preview create vault experience with Tags support.

* Name

az-300-vault ✓

* Subscription

Derek MVP ⌄

* Resource group

az-300-asr ⌄

Create new

* Location

Central US ⌄

Create   Automation options

FIGURE 2-2 Creating a Recovery Services vault

5. Click the Create button to build the resource, which may take a few moments to complete.

Once the Recovery Services vault is ready, open the overview page by clicking the resource within the resource group. This page provides some high-level information, including any new things related to Recovery Services vault.

Configure on-premises components of Site Recovery

Use the following steps to get started with a site recovery (migration in this case):

1. Click the Site Recovery link under Getting Started in the Settings pane as shown in Figure 2-3.

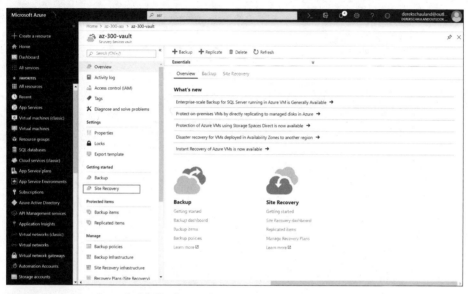

FIGURE 2-3 Getting Started with Site Recovery

2. Select the Prepare Infrastructure link to begin readying on-premises machines.

3. Complete the Prepare Infrastructure steps (shown in Figure 2-4):

   - **Where are your machines located?** On-premises.

   - **Where do you want to replicate your machines to?** To Azure.

   - **Are your machines virtualized?** Select the appropriate response:

     - Yes, with VMware.

     - Yes, with Hyper-V.

     - Other/Not virtualized.

NOTE **ABOUT PHYSICAL SERVERS**

Migrating Physical Servers using P2V, which is covered later in this chapter, uses the Physical/Other option of the Azure Site Recovery configuration mentioned here. Aside from this step, the Azure configuration is the same as discussed here.

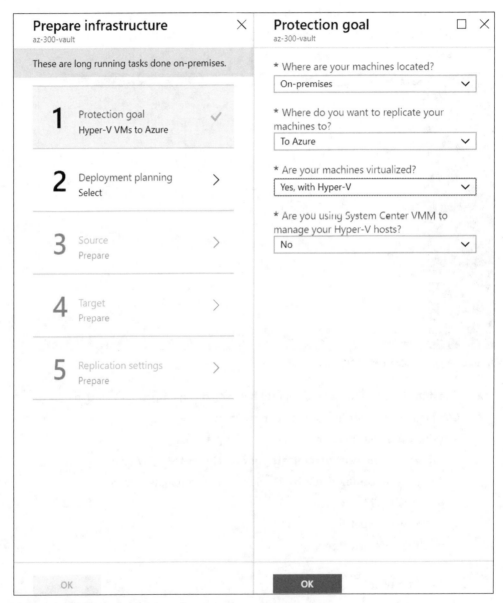

FIGURE 2-4 Configure protection goals

4. Click OK to complete the protection goal form.

Step 2 of infrastructure preparation is deployment planning, which helps to ensure that you have enough bandwidth to complete the transfer of virtualized workloads to Azure. This will take an estimate of the time needed to transfer the workloads to Azure based on machines found in your environment.

Click the Download link for the deployment planner, located in the middle pane of the Deployment planning step, to download a zip file to get started.

This zip file includes a template that will help in collecting information about the virtualized environment as well as a command-line tool to scan the virtualized environment to determine a baseline for the migration. The tool requires network access to the Hyper-V or VMware environment (or direct access to the VM hosts where the VMs are running). The command-line tool provides a report about throughput available to help determine the time it would take to move the scanned resources to Azure.

> **NOTE** **ENSURE RDP IS ENABLED BEFORE MIGRATION**
>
> Ensuring the local system is configured to allow remote desktop connections before migrating it to Azure is worth the prerequisite checks. There will be considerable work to do, including a jump box local to the migrated VMs virtual network if these steps are not done before migration. It's likely that this will be configured already, but it's never a bad idea to double-check.

After the tool has been run, in the Azure portal, specify that the deployment planner has been completed and click OK.

Next the virtualization environment will be provided to Azure by adding the Hyper-V site and server(s).

> **NOTE** **ALL HYPERVISORS WELCOME**
>
> At the time of this writing, the lab used for the examples consists of Hyper-V infrastructure. The examples provided will use Hyper-V as the on-premises source, but ASR is compatible with VMware as well.

To add a Hyper-V server, download the Azure Site Recovery Provider and the vault registration key (see Figure 2-5), and install them on the Hyper-V server. The vault registration info is necessary because ASR needs to know which recovery vault the VMs belong to once they are ready to migrate to Azure.

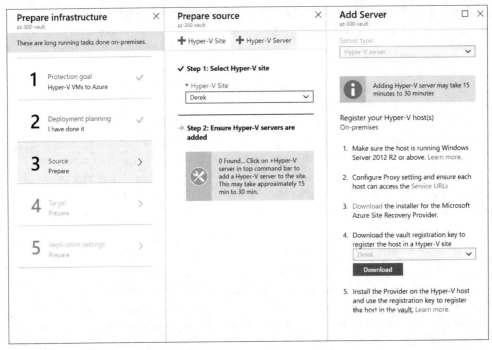

FIGURE 2-5 Preparing the source virtualization environment

Install the Site Recovery Provider on the virtualization host, if you're using Hyper-V as shown in Figure 2-6.

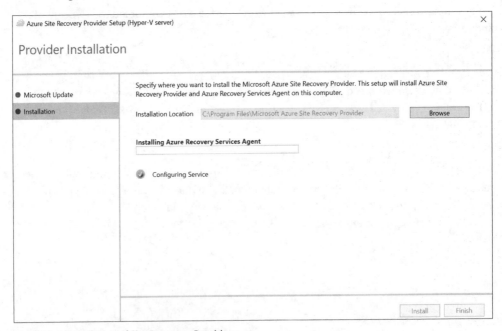

FIGURE 2-6 Installation of Site Recovery Provider

After installation and registration, it may take some time for Azure to find the server that has been registered with Site Recovery vault.

Proceed with infrastructure prep by completing the Target section of the wizard as shown in Figure 2-7.

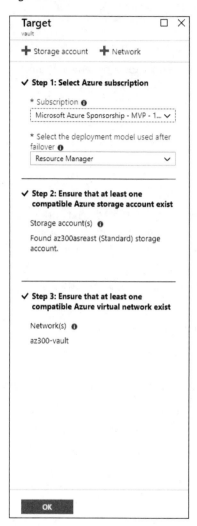

FIGURE 2-7 Preparing the Azure Target

Select the subscription and the deployment model used. (Generally, this will be Resource Manager.)

Click the Storage Account button at the top of the Target blade to add a storage account. Provide the following storage account details:

- Storage account name
- Replication settings
- Storage account type

When this storage account is created, it will be placed in the same region as the replication services vault.

If a network in the same region as the vault isn't found, you can click the Add Network button at the top of the Target blade to create one. Much like storage, the network region will match the vault, other settings, including address range and name, will be available for configuration.

The last requirement for preparing infrastructure is to configure a replication policy. Complete the following steps to create a replication policy:

1. Click Create and Associate at the top of the Replication Policy blade. Enter the following information:

   - **Name** The name of the replication policy.
   - **Source Type** This should be prepopulated based on previous settings.
   - **Target Type** This should be prepopulated based on previous settings.
   - **Copy Frequency** Enter the replication frequency for subsequent copies to be captured.
   - **Recovery Point Retention In Hours** How much retention is needed for this server.
   - **App Consistent Snapshot Frequency In Hours** How often an app-consistent snapshot will be captured.
   - **Initial Replication Start Time** Enter a time for the initial replication to begin.
   - **Associated Hyper-V Site** Filled in based on previous settings.

2. Click OK to create the policy, and Azure builds and associates these settings with the specified on-premises environment.

Replicate data to Azure

After the completion of the on-premises settings, you return to the Site Recovery blade to continue configuration.

To enable replication, complete the following steps:

1. Select the source of the replication—on-premises, in this case.
2. Select the Source location—the Hyper-V server previously configured in these examples, HV001.
3. Click OK to proceed to the target settings.
4. Select the Azure subscription to use with this replication.
5. Provide a post failover resource group, a resource group for the failed over VM.
6. Choose the deployment model for the failed over virtual machine.
7. Select or create the storage account to use for storing disks for the VMs being failed over.
8. Select the option for when the Azure network should be configured: now or later.
9. If you selected now, select or create the network for use post failover.
10. Select the subnet for use by these VMs from the list of subnets available for the chosen network.
11. Click OK.
12. Select the virtual machines to failover as part of Azure Site Recovery.
13. Specify the following default properties and the properties for the selected virtual machines:
    - **OS Type**   Whether the OS is Linux or Windows (available as default and per VM).
    - **OS Disk**   Select the name of the OS Disk for the VM (available per VM).
    - **Disks to replicate**   Select the disks attached to the VM to replicate (available per VM).
14. Click OK.
15. Review the replication policy settings for this replication. They will match the previously specified replication policy settings, but you can select other policies if they exist.
16. Click OK.
17. Click Enable Replication.

With replication options configured, the last part of the configuration to complete is the recovery plan. To configure the recovery plan, use the following steps:

1. On the Site Recovery blade, select Step 2: Manage Recovery Plans and click the Add Recovery Plan button at the top of the screen.
2. Provide a name for the recovery plan and select the deployment model for the items to be recovered.

3. Select the items for a recovery plan. Here you will choose the VMs that will be included in recovery.

4. Click OK to finalize the recovery plan.

5. Once the items are protected and ready to failover to Azure, you can test the failover by selecting the Site Recovery vault resource and choosing Recovery Plans (Site Recovery) from the manage section of the navigation pane.

6. Select the appropriate recovery plan for this failover.

This overview screen shows the number of items in the recovery plan in both the source and target, as shown in Figure 2-8.

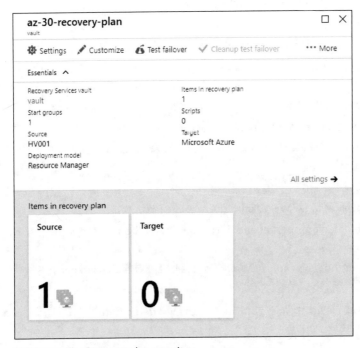

FIGURE 2-8 Site Recovery plan overview

To test the configuration, click the Test Failover button at the top of the Site Recovery Plan blade and complete the following steps:

1. Select the recovery point to use for the test.

2. Select the Azure Virtual Network for the replicated VM.

3. Click OK to start the test failover.

Once the failover completes, the VM should appear in the resource group that was specified for post failover use as shown in Figure 2-9.

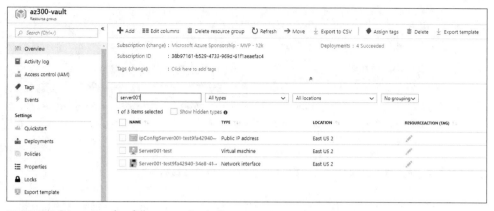

FIGURE 2-9 Resources after failover running in Azure

Migrate by using Azure Site Recovery

Once the test failover has completed, your VM is running in Azure, and you can see that things are as expected. When you're happy with the result of the running VM, you can complete a cleanup of the test, which will delete any resources created as a part of the test failover. Selecting the item(s) in the replicated items list and choosing the option to cleanup test failover. When ready to migrate, use an actual failover by completing the following steps:

1. Select Replicated Items in the ASR Vault Protected Items section.

2. Choose the item to be replicated from the list.

3. Once the item has synchronized, click the Failover button to send the VM to Azure.

Following the failover of the VM to Azure, cleanup of the on-premises environment happens as part of the completion of the migration to Azure. This ensures that the restore points for the migrated VM are cleaned up and that the source machine can be removed because it'll be unprotected after these tasks have been completed.

You may need to tweak settings to optimize performance and ensure that remote management is configured once the system has landed, like switching to managed disks—the disks used in failover are standard disks.

There may also be some networking considerations after migrating the VM. External connectivity may require network security groups to ensure that RDP or SSH is active to allow connections. Remember that any firewall rules that were configured on premises will not necessarily be completely configured post migration in Azure.

After verification that the migrated resource is operating as needed, the last step of the migration is to remove the on-premises resources. In terms of Azure, the resources are still in a failover state because the process was to fail them over with the intention of failing back. An Azure Site Recovery migration is really a one-way failover.

Skill 2.2: Configure Serverless Computing

In the age of the cloud, even using servers is considered legacy technology in some instances because there are platform-based services that will run the code provided rather than deploying applications, functions, or other units of work to a server. The cloud provider—Azure, in this case—takes care of the workings under the hood, and the customer needs to worry only about the code to be executed.

There are more than a few resources in Azure that run without infrastructure—or serverless:

- Azure Storage
- Azure Functions
- Azure Cosmos DB
- Azure Active Directory

These are just a few of the services that are available for serverless compute. Serverless resources are the managed services of Azure. They're not quite platform as a service (PaaS), but they're not all software as a service (SaaS), either. They're somewhere in between.

Serverless objects are the serverless resources to be used in an architecture. These are the building blocks used in a solution, and there will be several types created depending on the solution being presented.

Two of the most popular serverless technologies supported by Azure are logic apps and function apps. The details of configuring these are discussed in turn.

A *logic app* is a serverless component that handles business logic and integrations between components—much like Microsoft Flow, but with full customization and development available.

This skill covers how to:

- Create a simple logic app
- Manage Azure functions
- Manage Azure Event Grid
- Manage Azure Service Bus

Create a simple logic app

To build a simple logic app that watches for files in a OneDrive folder and sends an email when they're found, complete the following steps:

1. Select Create A Resource from the Azure Navigation menu.
2. Type **Logic Apps** in the marketplace search and select the logic app resource.
3. Click Create on the logic app description.
4. Complete the Logic App creation form shown in Figure 2-10 and click Create.
   - **Name** Provide a name for the logic app.
   - **Subscription** Choose the subscription where the resource should be created.
   - **Resource Group** Select Create or Use Existing to choose the resource group where the logic app should be created. If you select Use Existing, choose the appropriate resource group from the drop-down menu.
   - **Location** Select the region where the logic app should be created.
   - **Log Analytics** Specify if log analytics should be enabled or disabled for this resource.

> **NOTE LOG ANALYTICS WORKSPACE IS REQUIRED**
>
> To enable the log analytics feature for a logic app, ensure that the log analytics workspace that will collect the information exists beforehand.

Once a logic app resource exists, you can apply the code to get it to act on resources through predefined templates, custom templates, or using a blank app and adding code to perform actions for the application.

To add code to copy Azure storage blobs from one account to another, complete the following steps:

1. Open the resource group specified when you created the logic app resource.
2. Select the name of the logic app.

   The Logic Apps Designer opens so you can add templates, actions, and custom code to the logic app (see Figure 2-11).

FIGURE 2-10 Creating a logic app resource

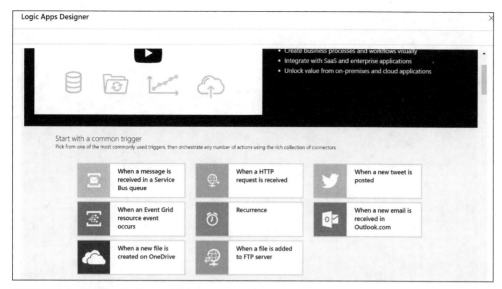

FIGURE 2-11 Logic Apps Designer with common templates

3. From the initial designer page, select the common trigger: When A New File Is Created On OneDrive (refer to Figure 2-11).

   In this example, the logic app watches for new files in OneDrive and sends an email when a new file is landed. It is very simple but is designed to showcase the tools available to work with logic apps.

NOTE **CONNECT TO ONEDRIVE**

A connection to OneDrive will be needed to use this template; clicking to connect a OneDrive account will prompt for login to the account.

---

4. Specify the account credentials for OneDrive to be watched for files, and click Continue.
5. Specify the folder to be watched and the interval for how often the folder should be checked by the logic app as shown in Figure 2-12.
6. Choose a folder to monitor by clicking the folder icon at the end of the folder text box and choosing the root folder.
7. Set an interval. The default is 3 minutes.
8. Click New Step to add an action to the logic app.
9. Select Office 365 Outlook template.
10. Choose the Send An Email option.
11. Sign into Office 365.
12. Specify the To, Subject, and Body of the email as shown in Figure 2-13.

FIGURE 2-12 Specifying the OneDrive folder to be watched for new files

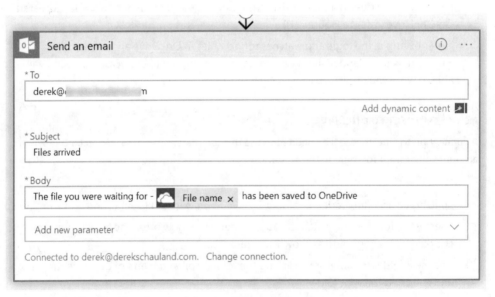

FIGURE 2-13 Configuring an action to send an email from a logic app

13. Click Save at the top of the designer window to ensure the changes made to the logic app are not lost.

14. Click the Run button in Logic Apps Designer to start the app watching for files.

15. Place a new file in the folder being watched by the logic app.

16. The Logic Apps Designer should show the progress of the app and that all steps for finding the file and sending the mail message have completed successfully.

Manage Azure Functions

Azure Functions allows the execution of code on demand, with no infrastructure to provision. Whereas logic apps provide integration between services, function apps run any piece of code on demand. How they're triggered can be as versatile as the functions themselves.

As of this writing, Azure Functions support the following runtime environments:

- .NET
- JavaScript
- Java
- PowerShell (which is currently in preview)

To create a function app, complete the following steps:

1. Select the Create A Resource link in the Azure Portal Navigation bar.

2. Type **function apps** in the marketplace search box and select Function Apps.

3. On the Function Apps overview hub, click the Create button.

4. Complete the Function App creation form shown in Figure 2-14:

- **App Name**   Enter the name of the function app.
- **Subscription**   Enter the subscription that will house the resource.
- **Resource Group**   Create or select the Resource Group that will contain this resource.
- **OS**   Select the operating system that the function will use (Windows or Linux).
- **Hosting Plan**   Select the pricing model used for the app: Consumption (pay as you go) or App Service (specifically sized app service).

> **NOTE   NEW APP SERVICE PLAN IF NEEDED**
>
> If you select the App Service hosting plan, a prompt to select/create it will be added.

- **Location**   Select the Azure region where the resource will be located.
- **Runtime Stack**   Select the runtime environment for the function app.
- **Storage**   Create or select the storage account that the function app will use.
- **Application Insights**   Create or select an Application Insights resource for tracking usage and other statistics about this function app.

5. Click Create to build the function app.

FIGURE 2-14 Creating a function

In the resource group where you created the function app, select the function to view the settings and management options for it.

The Overview blade for the function app provides the URL, app service, and subscription information along with the status of the function (see Figure 2-15).

FIGURE 2-15 The Overview blade for an Azure function

Function apps are built to listen for events that kick off code execution. Some of the events that functions listen for are

- HTTP Trigger
- Timer Trigger
- Azure Queue Storage
- Azure Service Bus Queue trigger
- Azure Service Bus Topic trigger

> **IMPORTANT** **MULTIPLE TYPES OF AUTHENTICATION POSSIBLE**
>
> When configuring a function for the HTTP Trigger, you need to choose the Authorization level to determine whether an API key will be needed to allow execution. If another Azure service trigger is used, you may need an extension to allow the function to communicate with other Azure resources.

In addition to the Overview blade, there is a blade for platform features. These are the configuration items for the App Service plan and other parts of Azure's serverless configuration for this function. Here, you configure things like networking, SSL, scaling, and custom domains, as shown in Figure 2-16.

FIGURE 2-16 The Platform Features blade for an Azure function app

Within the App Settings blade for function apps is the Kudu console, listed as Advanced Tools (Kudu). This console operates much like being logged into the back end of the system or app. Because this is a serverless application, there is no back end to be managed; this tool is used for troubleshooting a function app that isn't performing as needed. Figure 2-17 shows the Kudu back end.

Kudu Environment   Debug console ▾   Process explorer   Tools ▾   Site extensions

Environment

Build	81.10329.3844.0 (14d700a964)
Azure App Service	82.0.7.22 (master-eb6da2b3974)
Site up time	00.00:22:23
Site folder	D:\home
Temp folder	D:\local\Temp\

REST API (works best when using a JSON viewer extension)

- App Settings
- Deployments
- Source control info
- Files
- Log streaming (use curl, not browser!)
- Processes and mini-dumps
- Runtime versions
- Site Extensions: installed | feed
- Web hooks
- WebJobs: all | triggered | continuous
- Functions: list | host config

More information about Kudu can be found on the wiki.

FIGURE 2-17 The Kudu troubleshooting console for a function app

Manage Azure Event Grid

Event Grid is an event-consumption service that relies on publish/subscription to pass information between services. Suppose I have an on-premises application that outputs log data and an Azure function that's waiting to know what log data has been created by the on-premises application. The on-premises application would publish the log data to a topic in Azure Event Grid. The Azure function app would subscribe to the topic to be notified as the information lands in Event Grid.

The goal of Event Grid is to loosely couple services, allowing them to communicate, using an intermediate queue that can be checked for new data as necessary. The consumer app listens for the queue and is not connected to the publishing app directly.

To get started with Event Grid, complete the following steps:

1. Open the Subscriptions blade in the Azure portal.

2. Select Resource Providers under Settings.

3. Filter the list of providers by entering Event Grid in the Filter By Name box.

4. Click the Microsoft.EventGrid resource provider and then click Register at the top of the page.

Once the registration completes, you can begin using Event Grid by navigating to the Event Grid Topics services in the portal, as shown in Figure 2-18.

FIGURE 2-18 Event Grid topics

Once a subscription has topics created, each topic will have specific properties related to the subscription. Click the event grid subscription from the list. From the Topic Overview blade, the URL for the topic endpoint, the status, and the general subscription information is available. You can manage the following items from this point:

- **Access Control** The Azure IAM/Role-Based configuration for which Azure users can read, edit, and update the topic. Access Control is discussed later in this chapter
- **Access Keys** Security keys used to authenticate applications publishing events to this topic.

Ensuring that the applications pushing information to this topic have a key to do so will ensure that the amount of noise sent to the topic is controlled. If the application sends an overly chatty amount of information, the noise may not be reduced.

> ***IMPORTANT*** **SECURITY ITEM**
>
> To ensure the access keys for a topic are secured and kept safe, consider placing them in a Key Vault as secrets. This way, the application that needs them can refer to the secret endpoint and avoid storing the application keys for the topic in any code. This prevents the keys from being visible in plain text and only available to the application at runtime.

With a topic created and collecting information, consuming services that require this information need to subscribe to these events and an endpoint for the subscription. In this case, an endpoint is an app service with a URL that the subscriber services will hit to interact with the topic.

Event subscriptions can collect any and all information sent to a topic, or they can be filtered in the following ways:

- **By Subject** Allows filtering by the subject of messages sent to the topic—for example, only messages with .jpg images in them
- **Advanced filter** A key value pair one level deep

In addition to filtering information to collect for a subscription, when you select the Additional Features tab when you're creating an event subscription shows other configurable features including the following:

- **Max Event Delivery Attempts**   How many retries there will be.
- **Event Time To Live**   The number of days, hours, minutes, and seconds the event will be retried.
- **Dead-Lettering**   Select whether the messages that cannot be delivered should be placed in storage.
- **Event Subscription Expiration Time**   When the subscription will automatically expire.
- **Labels**   Any labels that might help identify the subscription.

Manage Azure Service Bus

Azure Service Bus is a multi-tenant asynchronous messaging service that can operate with first in, first out (FIFO) queuing or publish/subscribe information exchange. Using queues, the message bus service will exchange messages with one partner service. If using the publish/subscribe (pub/sub) model, the sender can push information to any number of subscribed services.

A service bus namespace has several properties and options that can be managed for each instance:

- **Shared Access Policies**   The keys and connection strings available for accessing the resource. The level of permissions, manage, send, and listen are configured here because they're part of the connection string.
- **Scale**   The tier of service the messaging service uses: Basic or Standard.

- **Geo-Recovery**   Disaster recovery settings that are available with a Premium namespace.
- **Export Template**   An ARM automation template for the service bus resource.
- **Queues**   The messaging queues used by the service bus.

Each configured queue displays the queue URL, max size, and current counts about the following message types:

- **Active Messages**   currently in the queue
- **Scheduled Messages**   sent to the queue by scheduled jobs or on a general schedule
- **Dead-Letter Messages**   that are undeliverable to any receiver
- **Transfer Messages**   pending transfer to another queue
- **Transfer Dead-Letter Messages**   Message that failed to transfer to another queue

In addition to viewing the number of messages in the queue, you can create shared access permissions for the queue. This will allow permissions for manage, send, and listen to be assigned. Also, this provides a connection string leveraging the assigned permissions that the listener application will use as the endpoint when collecting information from the queue.

In the properties blade of the selected message queue, the following settings can be updated:

- Message time to live default
- Lock duration
- Duplicate detection history
- Maximum delivery count
- Maximum queue size
- Queue state (is the queue active or disabled)
- Move expired messages to the dead-letter subqueue; keep undeliverable messages in a subqueue to keep this message queue clean

The settings for a message queue are similar to those discussed earlier in the section about Event Grid because they serve a similar purpose for the configured queues.

Skill 2.3: Implement application load balancing

Azure has a couple of different options for load balancing: the Azure load balancer that operates at the transport layer of the networking stack and the Application gateway that adds to the load balancer at layer 4 and adds layer 7 (HTTP) load balancing on top of this configuration using additional rules.

> **This skill covers how to:**
> - Configure Application Gateway and load balancing rules
> - Implement front-end IP configurations
> - Manage application load balancing

Configure Application Gateway and load balancing rules

An Application Gateway has the following settings that you can configure to tune the resource to meet the needs of an organization:

- **Configuration** Settings for updating the tier, SKU, and instance count; indicate whether HTTP/2 is enabled.

- **Web Application Firewall** Allows adjustment of the firewall tier for the device (Standard or WAF) and whether the firewall settings for the gateway are enabled or disabled.

  - Enabling the WAF on a gateway defaults the resource itself to a Medium tier by default.

  - If the Firewall Status is enabled, the gateway evaluates all traffic except the items excluded in a defined list (see Figure 2-19). The firewall/WAF settings allow the gateway to be configured for detection only (logging) or prevention.

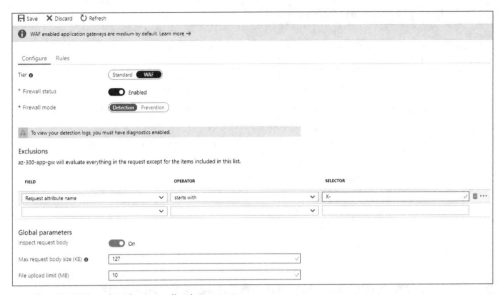

FIGURE 2-19 WAF settings in an application gateway

> *NOTE* **AUDITING AT THE FIREWALL REQUIRES DIAGNOSTICS**
>
> When using the Firewall Settings in WAF mode, enabling detection mode requires diagnostics to be enabled to review the logged settings.

- **Backend Pools** The nodes or applications to which the application gateway will send traffic.

  The pools can be added by FQDN or IP address, Virtual Machine, VMSS, and App Services. For target nodes not hosted in Azure, the FQDN/IP Address method allows external back-end services.

- **HTTP Settings** These are the port settings for the back-end pools. If you configured the gateway with HTTPS and certificates during setup, this defaults to 443; otherwise, it starts with port 80. Other HTTP-related settings managed here are

  - Cookie Based Affinity (sticky sessions)

  - Connection Draining—ensuring sessions in flight at the time a back-end service is removed will be allowed to complete

  - Override paths for backend services—allows specified directories or services to be rerouted as they pass through the gateway

- **Listeners** These determine which IP addresses are used for the front-end services managed by this gateway. Traffic hits the front end of the gateway and is processed by configured rules as it moves through the application gateway. Listeners are configured for IP address and port parings.

- **Rules** The rules for the gateway connect listeners to backend pools, allowing the gateway to route traffic landing on a specific listener to a backend pool using the specified HTTP settings.

Even though each of these items is configured separately in the application gateway, rules bring these items together to ensure traffic is routed as expected for an app service.

Health Probes are used to ensure the services managed by the gateway are online. If there are issues with one of the configured back-end services, the application gateway removes the resource from the back end of the gateway. This ensures that the back-end service being used by the gateway will be less likely to display errored pages for resources that may be down.

> **IMPORTANT   AT LEAST ONE BACK-END SERVICE IS NEEDED**
>
> If all back-end services are unhealthy, the application gateway is unable to route around the issue.

The interval at which health probes are evaluated, the timeout period, and retry threshold can all be configured to suit the needs of the back-end applications as shown in Figure 2-20.

FIGURE 2-20 Configuring a new health probe

Implement front-end IP configurations

An application gateway defaults to a front-end configuration using a public IP address, but you can configure it to use a private IP address for the front end. This might be useful in a multitiered application configuration. Using one application gateway to direct traffic from the Internet to an "internal" gateway that has a private front-end configuration might be a useful configuration in some scenarios.

Configuring virtual IP addresses (VIPs) happens in the settings for the application gateway in the Front-End IP Configuration section shown in Figure 2-21.

FIGURE 2-21 The front-end configuration for an application gateway

When you set the front-end configuration, the default public settings include a configured listener. Each configuration needs a listener to allow it to properly distribute traffic to back-end resources.

Setting up private front-end configurations requires a name and private IP address to be specified if the original header will be modified to a known IP value.

> **NOTE** **UPDATE TIME MAY BE REQUIRED**
>
> When saving settings to some areas of the application gateway resource, the time to update may take longer than expected.

Manage application load balancing

The application gateway handles load balancing at layer 7 (the application layer) of the OSI model. This means it handles load balancing techniques using the following methods:

- **Cookie-Based Affinity** This will always route traffic during a session to the same back-end application where the session began. The cookie-based method works well if there is state-based information that needs to be maintained throughout a session. For client computers to leverage this load balancing type, the browser used needs to allow cookies.

  Cookie-Based Affinity management happens in the HTTP Settings/Backend HTTP Settings blade of the resource (see Figure 2-22).

FIGURE 2-22 Configuring HTTP settings

- **Connection Draining** Enable this setting to ensure that any connections that are being routed to a resource will be completed before the resource is removed from a backend pool. In addition, enter the number of seconds to wait for the connection to timeout.

- **Protocol** Set HTTP or HTTPS here. If you choose HTTPS, you need to upload a certificate to the application gateway.

URL Path-Based Routing

URL Path-Based Routing uses a configuration called a URL Path Map to control which inbound requests reaching the gateway are sent to which back-end resources. There are a few components within the Application Gateway needed to take advantage of URL Path-Based Routing:

- **URL Path Map** The mapping of requests to back-end resources
- **Backend Listener** Specifies the front-end IP configuration and port that the routing rules will be watching
- **Routing Rules** The rules associate the URL Path Map and the listener to ensure that specific requests are routed to the correct backend pool.

PowerShell is necessary to add the configurations to an application gateway for the settings needed for URL Path-Based Routing.

EXAM TIP

Leveraging the examples to help create a PowerShell script that works in your environment is advisable. When reviewing code supplied by others, be sure to look over it in an editor that supports the language—like Visual Studio Code—to help you understand what the code does before you run it in your environment.

A useable example of the following code is at *https://docs.microsoft.com/en-us/ azure/application-gateway/tutorial-url-route-powershell*:

```
#Configure Images and Video backend pools
$gateway = Get-AzApplicationGateway `
  -ResourceGroupName Az-300-RG-Gateway`
  -Name AppGateway
Add-AzApplicationGatewayBackendAddressPool `
  -ApplicationGateway $gateway `
  -Name imagesPool
Add-AzApplicationGatewayBackendAddressPool `
  -ApplicationGateway $gateway `
  -Name videoPool

Add-AzApplicationGatewayFrontendPort `
  -ApplicationGateway $gateway `
  -Name InboundBEPort `
  -Port 8080
$backendPort = Get-AzApplicationGatewayFrontendPort `
  -ApplicationGateway $gateway `
  -Name bport
#configure a backend Listener
$fipconfig = Get-AzApplicationGatewayFrontendIPConfig `
  -ApplicationGateway $gateway
```

```
Add-AzApplicationGatewayHttpListener `
  -ApplicationGateway $gateway `
  -Name backendListener `
  -Protocol Http `
  -FrontendIPConfiguration $fipconfig `
  -FrontendPort $backendPort
#Configure the URL Mapping
$poolSettings = Get-AzApplicationGatewayBackendHttpSettings `
    -ApplicationGateway $gateway `
    -Name myPoolSettings

$imagePool = Get-AzApplicationGatewayBackendAddressPool `
    -ApplicationGateway $gateway `
    -Name imagesBackendPool

$videoPool = Get-AzApplicationGatewayBackendAddressPool `
    -ApplicationGateway $gateway `
    -Name videoBackendPool

$defaultPool = Get-AzApplicationGatewayBackendAddressPool `
    -ApplicationGateway $gateway

    -Name appGatewayBackendPool

$imagePathRule = New-AzApplicationGatewayPathRuleConfig `
    -Name imagePathRule `
    -Paths "/images/*" `
    -BackendAddressPool $imagePool `
    -BackendHttpSettings $poolSettings

$videoPathRule = New-AzApplicationGatewayPathRuleConfig `
    -Name videoPathRule `
    -Paths "/video/*" `
    -BackendAddressPool $videoPool `
    -BackendHttpSettings $poolSettings

Add-AzApplicationGatewayUrlPathMapConfig `
    -ApplicationGateway $gateway `
    -Name urlpathmap `
    -PathRules $imagePathRule, $videoPathRule `
    -DefaultBackendAddressPool $defaultPool `
    -DefaultBackendHttpSettings $poolSettings
#Add the Routing Rule(s)
$backendlistener = Get-AzApplicationGatewayHttpListener `
    -ApplicationGateway $gateway `
    -Name backendListener

$urlPathMap = Get-AzApplicationGatewayUrlPathMapConfig `
    -ApplicationGateway $gateway `
    -Name urlpathmap
```

```
Add-AzApplicationGatewayRequestRoutingRule `
    -ApplicationGateway $gateway `
    -Name rule2 `
    -RuleType PathBasedRouting `
    -HttpListener $backendlistener `
    -UrlPathMap $urlPathMap

#Update the Application gateway
Set-AzApplicationGateway -ApplicationGateway $gateway
```

> **IMPORTANT BE PATIENT WHEN UPDATING APPLICATION GATEWAY**
>
> An update to the application gateway can take up to 20 minutes.

EXAM TIP

Remember to work with the Azure Command-Line Interface (CLI) to understand how the commands work and that they differ from PowerShell. Although PowerShell can handle the command-line work in Azure, there may be some significant Azure CLI items on the exam, and it's good to know your way around.

Once the URL map is configured and applied to the gateway, traffic is routed to the example pools (images and videos) as it arrives. This is not traditional load balancing where traffic would be routed based on load of the device; a certain percentage of traffic goes to pool one and the rest to pool two. In this case the content type is helping to drive the incoming traffic.

> *NEED MORE REVIEW?*   **ADDITIONAL RESOURCES FOR LOAD BALANCING OPTIONS**
>
> Check out the articles at the following URLs for additional information:
>
> - "What is Azure Application Gateway" *https://docs.microsoft.com/en-us/azure/application-gateway/overview*
> - "Custom rules for Web Application Firewall v2" *https://docs.microsoft.com/en-us/azure/application-gateway/custom-waf-rules-overview*
> - "Load balance your web service traffic with Application Gateway" *https://docs.microsoft.com/en-us/learn/modules/load-balance-web-traffic-with-application-gateway*
>
> You also can review the Azure CLI documentation at *https://docs.microsoft.com/en-us/cli/azure/get-started-with-azure-cli?view=azure-cli-latest.*

Skill 2.4: Integrate an Azure virtual network and an on-premises network

Azure supports connectivity to external or on-premises networks via two methods:

- **VPN**   An encrypted connection between two networks via the public Internet
- **ExpressRoute**   A private circuit-based connection between an organization's network and Azure

> **NOTE   SECURITY DETAILS**
>
> The connection made by ExpressRoute runs over private circuits between an organization and Azure. No other traffic traverses these circuits, but the traffic is not encrypted on the wire by default. Some organizations may choose or be required to encrypt this traffic with a VPN.

> **This skill covers how to:**
>
> - Create and configure Azure VPN Gateway
> - Create and configure site-to-site VPN
> - Verify on-premises connectivity
> - Manage on-premises connectivity with Azure
> - Configure ExpressRoute

Create and configure Azure VPN Gateway

The virtual network gateway is a router endpoint specifically designed to manage inbound private connections. The resource requires the existence of a dedicated subnet, called the gateway subnet, for use by the VPN.

To add a gateway subnet to a virtual network, complete the following steps:

1. Select the virtual network that will be used with the virtual network gateway.
2. Open the Subnets blade of the network resource.
3. Click Gateway Subnet at the top of the subnets blade.
4. Specify the address range of the subnet. Because this is dedicated for connecting VPNs, the subnet can be small depending on the number of devices that will be connecting.
5. Edit the route table as necessary (not needed by default).
6. Choose any services that will use this subnet.
7. Select any services this network will be dedicated to supporting.
8. Click OK.

To create a virtual network gateway, complete the following steps:

1. From the Azure portal, select or create the resource group that will contain the virtual network gateway.

2. Click the Add Link at the top of the Resource Group blade.

3. Enter virtual network gateway in the resource search box. Select the virtual network gateway in the search results.

4. Click the Create button to begin creating the resource.

5. Complete the Create Virtual Network Gateway form shown in Figure 2-23:

   - **Subscription**   The Azure subscription that will contain the virtual network gateway resource.

   - **Name**   The name of the virtual network gateway.

   - **Region**   The region for the virtual network gateway. There must be a virtual network in the region where the virtual network gateway is created.

   - **Gateway Type**   ExpressRoute or VPN.

   - **VPN Type**   Route-Based or Policy-Based.

   - **SKU**   The resource size and price point for the gateway.

   - **Virtual Network**   The network to which the gateway will be attached.

   - **Public IP address**   The external IP address for the gateway (new or existing).

   - **Enable Active-Active mode**   Allow active/active connection management.

   - **Enable BGP/ASN**   Allow BGP route broadcasting for this gateway.

6. Click Review and Create to review the configuration.

7. Click create to begin provisioning the gateway.

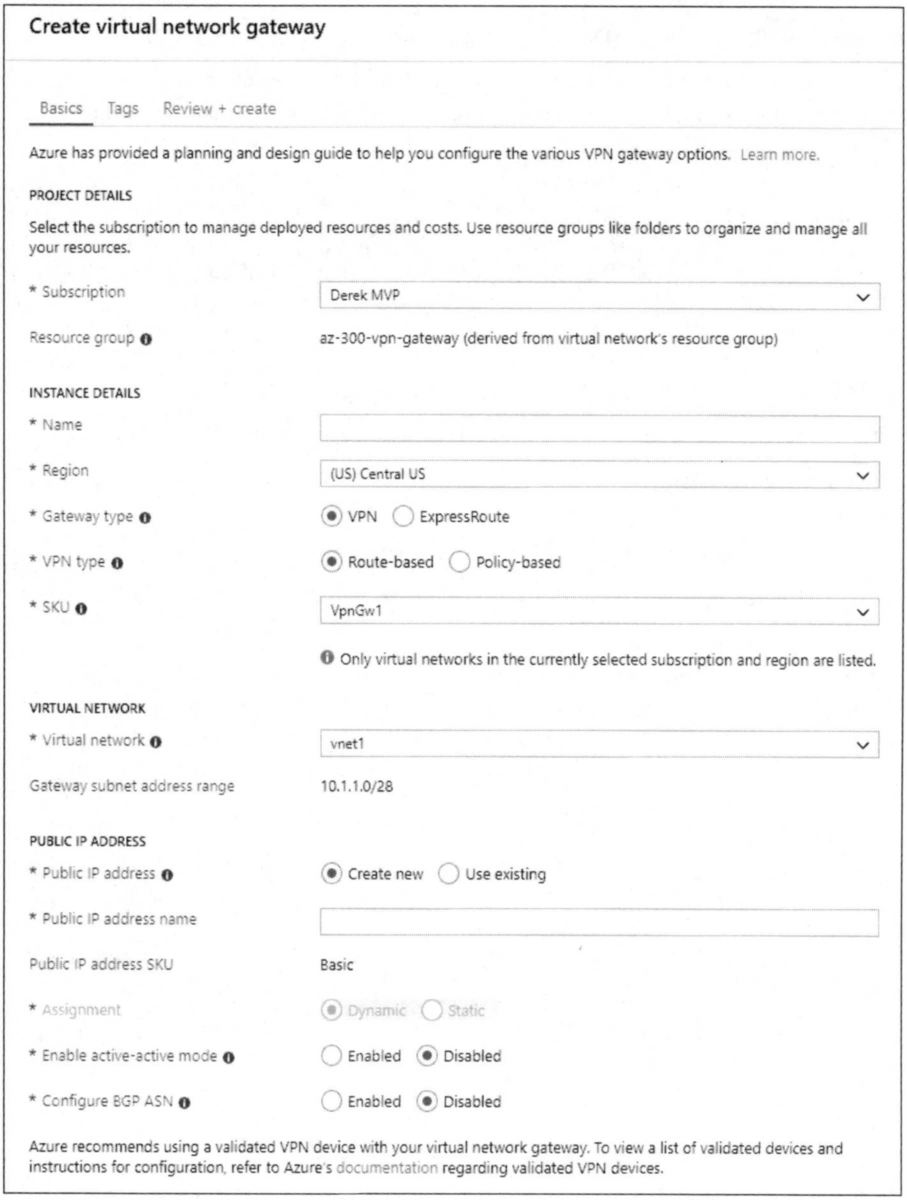

Create virtual network gateway

Basics   Tags   Review + create

Azure has provided a planning and design guide to help you configure the various VPN gateway options. Learn more.

PROJECT DETAILS

Select the subscription to manage deployed resources and costs. Use resource groups like folders to organize and manage all your resources.

* Subscription

Derek MVP   ⌄

Resource group ❶   az-300-vpn-gateway (derived from virtual network's resource group)

INSTANCE DETAILS

* Name

* Region   (US) Central US   ⌄

* Gateway type ❶   ⦿ VPN   ◯ ExpressRoute

* VPN type ❶   ⦿ Route-based   ◯ Policy-based

* SKU ❶   VpnGw1   ⌄

                            ❶ Only virtual networks in the currently selected subscription and region are listed.

VIRTUAL NETWORK

* Virtual network ❶   vnet1   ⌄

Gateway subnet address range   10.1.1.0/28

PUBLIC IP ADDRESS

* Public IP address ❶   ⦿ Create new   ◯ Use existing

* Public IP address name

Public IP address SKU   Basic

* Assignment   ⦿ Dynamic   ◯ Static

* Enable active-active mode ❶   ◯ Enabled   ⦿ Disabled

* Configure BGP ASN ❶   ◯ Enabled   ⦿ Disabled

Azure recommends using a validated VPN device with your virtual network gateway. To view a list of validated devices and instructions for configuration, refer to Azure's documentation regarding validated VPN devices.

FIGURE 2-23 Creating a virtual network gateway

> **NOTE PROVISIONING TIME**
>
> Virtual network gateways can take anywhere from 15 to 45 minutes to be created. In addition, any updates to the gateway also can take between 15 and 45 minutes to complete.

Create and configure site-to-site VPN

Once the virtual network gateway(s) are configured, you can begin configuring the connection between them or between one gateway and a local device.

There are three types of connections available using the connection resource in Azure:

- **Vnet to Vnet** Connecting two virtual networks in Azure—across regions perhaps
- **Site to Site** An IPSec tunnel between two sites: an on-premises datacenter and Azure
- **ExpressRoute** A dedicated circuit-based connection to Azure, which we discuss later in this chapter

For a site-to-site configuration, complete the following steps:

1. In the Azure portal, open the resource group containing the virtual network gateway and Vnet to be used in this configuration.

2. Collect the public IP address and internal address space for the on-premises networks being connected to Azure and the virtual network gateway public IP address and address space.

3. Create a preshared key to use in establishing the connection.

4. Add a connection resource in the same resource group as the virtual network gateway.

5. Choose the connection type for the VPN, site-to-site, the subscription, resource group, and location for the resource.

6. Configure the settings for the VPN as shown in Figure 2-24:
   - **Virtual Network Gateway** Choose the available virtual network gateway based on subscription and resource group settings already selected.
   - **Local Network Gateway** Select or create a local network gateway. This will be the endpoint for any on-premises devices being connected to this VPN.

7. Name the local network gateway.

8. Enter the public (external) IP address of the on-premises device used.

9. Enter the address space for the internal network on-premises. More than one address range is permitted.

10. The Connection name is populated based on the resources involved, but you can change it if you need to make it fit a naming convention.

11. Enter the preshared key for the connection.

12. Enable BGP if needed for the connection. This will require at least a standard SKU for the virtual network gateway.

13. Review the summary information for the resources being created and click OK.

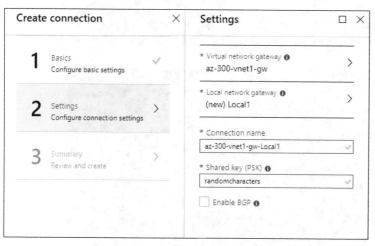

FIGURE 2-24 Configuring the settings for a site-to-site VPN

Verify on-premises connectivity

Once the site-to site-VPN configuration has been completed, verification of the connection will work, or it won't. If you have everything configured correctly, accessing resources in Azure should work like accessing other local resources.

Connecting to the machines connected to the Azure virtual network using local IP addresses should confirm that the VPN is connected, as the ping test shows in Figure 2-25.

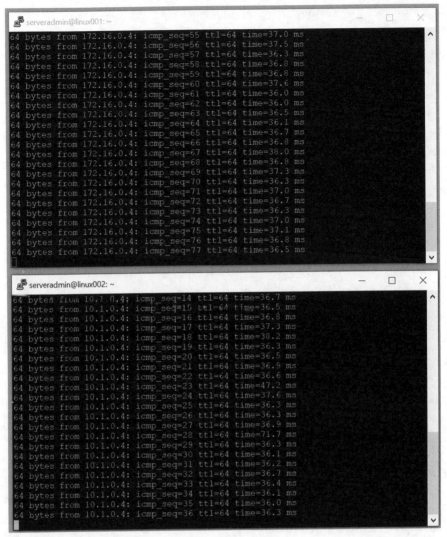

FIGURE 2-25 Traffic between local IP addresses via the VPN

In addition to the ping testing and connections between systems on these networks, the Summary blade for the local connection in Azure shows traffic across the VPN. This is shown in Figure 2-26.

FIGURE 2-26 An active VPN connection in the Azure portal

Manage on-premises connectivity with Azure

In many cases, VPN connections to Azure will be low maintenance once they are connected and in use. There may be times, though, that certain connectivity might need restrictions placed on it—for example, if a server in Azure should be accessed through a load balancer or be accessible only from the local network.

Azure allows these resources to be created without public IP addresses, making them accessible only across the VPN. This is part of the management of these resources; simply removing the public IP takes the machine off of the Internet, but an organization may have additional requirements in that systems in a production environment cannot talk directly to systems in a nonproduction environment. The segregation can be handled via network security groups and routing table entries.

A network security group serves as an ACL list for access (or denial) to resources, so it would help to open or block ports to and from certain machines.

Figure 2-27 shows a simple network security group where port 22 is allowed but only from a source tagged as a virtual network. This allows other resources on Azure virtual networks to reach the device, but nothing from the Internet can connect directly.

Inbound security rules

PRIORITY	NAME	PORT	PROTOCOL	SOURCE	DESTINATION	ACTION	
100	⚠ Port_22	22	Any	VirtualNetwork	10.1.0.4	⊘ Allow	...
65000	AllowVnetInBound	Any	Any	VirtualNetwork	VirtualNetwork	⊘ Allow	...
65001	AllowAzureLoadBalancerInBound	Any	Any	AzureLoadBalancer	Any	⊘ Allow	...
65500	DenyAllInBound	Any	Any	Any	Any	⊘ Deny	...

Outbound security rules

PRIORITY	NAME	PORT	PROTOCOL	SOURCE	DESTINATION	ACTION	
65000	AllowVnetOutBound	Any	Any	VirtualNetwork	VirtualNetwork	⊘ Allow	...
65001	AllowInternetOutBound	Any	Any	Any	Internet	⊘ Allow	...
65500	DenyAllOutBound	Any	Any	Any	Any	⊘ Deny	...

FIGURE 2-27 Network security groups

You can use network security groups at the network interface level for a virtual machine or at the subnet level.

EXAM TIP

Configuring network security groups at the subnet level ensures uniform rule behavior across any devices in the planned subnet and makes management of connectivity much less complicated.

NOTE **SECURITY**

If your organization has requirements for one-to-one access and connectivity, a network security group configured at the interface level for the VM might be necessary to ensure restricted access from one host to another.

Network security groups also allow the collection of flow logs that capture information about the traffic entering and leaving the network via configured network security groups. To enable this, you need two additional resources for all features, as shown in Figure 2-28:

- A storage account to collect the flow log data
- A Log Analytics workspace for traffic analysis

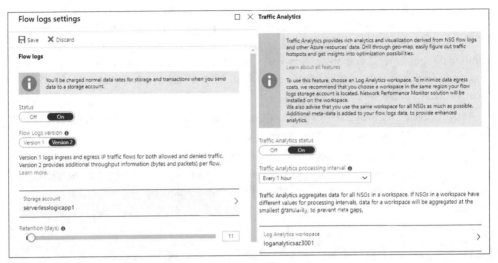

FIGURE 2-28 Flow Log and Traffic Analytics configuration

In addition to network security groups, route table entries can be used to control traffic flow between network resources. With a route table entry, you can force all the traffic between subnets to pass through a specific network or virtual network appliance that handles all the rules and access controls. There are reference architectures for this type of configuration in the Azure documentation that walk through configuring this type of network topology.

Configure ExpressRoute

Before you can use ExpressRoute as a VPN connection type, you need to configure it and prepare it as an Azure resource. Complete the following steps to configure the ExpressRoute Circuit resource in Azure:

1. In the Azure portal, click Create A Resource.
2. Select ExpressRoute from the Networking category.
3. On the Create ExpressRoute Circuit page, select to create a new circuit rather than importing from a classic configuration. To complete ExpressRoute setup, provide the following information:
   - **Circuit Name** The name of the circuit resource.
   - **Provider** Select the name of the provider delivering the circuit.

- **Peering Location**   The location where your circuit is terminated; if you're using a partner like Equinix in their Chicago location, you would use Chicago for the Peering Location.
- **Bandwidth**   The bandwidth provided by the provider for this connection.
- **SKU**   This determines the level of ExpressRoute you are provisioning.
- **Data Metering**   This is for the level of billing and can be updated from metered to unlimited but not from unlimited to metered.
- **Subscription**   The Azure subscription associated with this resource.
- **Resource Group**   The Azure resource group associated with this resource.
- **Location**   The Azure region associated with this resource; this is different from the peering location.

4. Create the resource.

> **NOTE   COSTS AND BILLING**
>
> When you configure ExpressRoute in Azure, you receive a service key. When Azure issues the service key, billing for the circuit begins. Wait to configure this until your service provider is prepared with the circuit that will be paired with ExpressRoute to avoid charges while you're waiting for other components.

Once the service key is issued and your circuit has been provisioned by a provider, you provide the key to the carrier to complete the process. Private peering needs to be configured and BGP allowed for ExpressRoute to work.

ExpressRoute also requires the virtual network gateway to be configured for it. To do this, when creating a virtual network gateway, select ExpressRoute as the gateway type (as shown in Figure 2-29).

Configuring the peering settings for ExpressRoute happens from within the ExpressRoute configuration settings once the circuit has been set up in Azure. From there you see three types of peerings:

- **Azure Public**   This has been deprecated; use Microsoft peering instead.
- **Azure Private**   Peering with virtual networks inside subscriptions managed by your organization.
- **Microsoft**   Peering directly with Microsoft for the use of public services like Dynamics and Office 365.

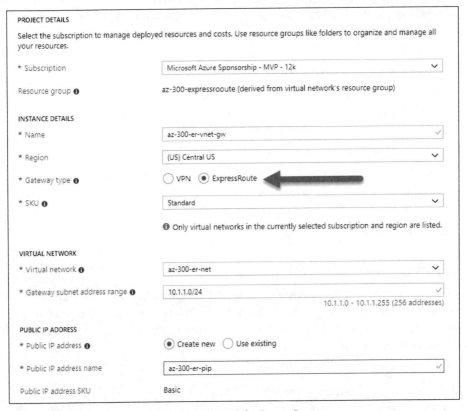

FIGURE 2-29 Configuring a virtual network gateway for ExpressRoute

You need to meet the following requirements for peering:

- A /30 subnet for the primary link.
- A /30 subnet for the secondary link.
- A valid VLAN ID to build peering on; no other circuit-based connections can use this VLAN ID. The primary and secondary links for ExpressRoute must use this VLAN ID.
- An AS number for peering (2 byte and 4 byte are permitted).
- Advertised prefixes, which is a list of all prefixes to be advertised over BGP.
- Optionally, you can provide a customer ASN if prefixes that do not belong to you are used, a routing registry name if the AS number is not registered as owned by you, and an MD5 hash.

Review the peering information and complete the following steps to finish configuring ExpressRoute:

1. Select the type of peering needed and provide the previously mentioned information.
2. Save the connection.

Once you have successfully configured the connection, the details screen shows a status of configured.

Linking (or creating a connection to) ExpressRoute also happens from within the ExpressRoute resource. Choose the Connections option within the settings for ExpressRoute and provide the following:

- **Name**   The name of the connection.
- **Connection Type**   ExpressRoute.
- **Virtual Network Gateway**   Select the gateway with which to link ExpressRoute.
- **ExpressRoute Circuit**   Select the configured circuit with which to connect.
- **Subscription**   Select the subscription containing the resources used in this connection.
- **Resource Group**   Select the resource group containing the resources used in this connection.
- **Location**   Select the Azure region where the resources used in this connection are located.

This is like creating a site-to-site connection, as described earlier, but it uses different resources as part of the connection.

EXAM TIP

ExpressRoute is a private connection to Azure from a given location, and it requires high-end connectivity. Much of the discussion of ExpressRoute presented here relies on Microsoft Documentation because we don't currently have access to an ExpressRoute circuit.

The settings and configurations discussed are high level, but we've provided an overview of the concepts for ExpressRoute for the exam.

Skill 2.5: Manage Role-Based Access Control (RBAC)

Role-Based Access Control (RBAC) provides a manageable way to assign access to resources in Azure by allowing permissions to be assigned across job roles. If you're a server operator, you may be able to start and restart VMs but not power off or delete them. Because every resource in Azure is permissible and requires access, the consolidation of permissions into roles can help keep things organized.

Create a custom role

While Azure provides roles for certain activities—like contributor and reader, which provide edit and read access respectively—there may be job roles within an organization that don't fit nicely into these predefined items. Custom roles can be built to best suit the needs of an organization. To create a custom role, complete the following steps:

1. Log in to the Azure portal and select the resource group containing the items for which access will be customized.

2. In the navigation list for the resource group, select Access Control (IAM).

3. The IAM blade appears as shown in Figure 2-30 with the Check Access tab selected.

FIGURE 2-30 Check access to Azure resources

Before creating a custom role, it's a good idea to check the access for the user or group the custom role will include. In addition to determining the need for a custom role, this check helps ensure existing access is known and can be updated after custom roles are created

4. In the IAM blade, select Roles at the top right to view a list of the access a predefined role already has.

5. Click a role that might have some of the access your custom role will need to review its permissions.

The creation of custom roles happens through the Azure CLI or Azure PowerShell because there's no portal-based method to build roles as of this writing. To create a custom role using PowerShell, complete the following steps:

1. Open a PowerShell console and connect to your Azure Subscription.

2. Use the following PowerShell to collect the role you will start with:

```
$CustomRole = Get-AZRoleDefinition | where {$_.name -eq "Virtual Machine
Contributor"}
```

3. To view the actions this role has already, display the Actions property:

```
$CustomRole.Actions
```

To keep the custom role creation fairly simple, create a role for VM operators that can manage and access virtual machines. The role called out earlier is allowed to manage but not access machines. The Virtual Machine Administrator Login role allows log in but no management of the machine.

```
$AdminRole = get-azroledefinition | where {$_.name -eq "Virtual Machine
Administrator Login"}
```

At this point, the $CustomRole variable should contain an object for the Virtual Machine Contributor role, and $AdminRole should contain an object for the Virtual Machine Administrator Login role.

As you can see from Figure 2-31, the actions allowing access to the VMs are missing from the Virtual Machine Contributor Role.

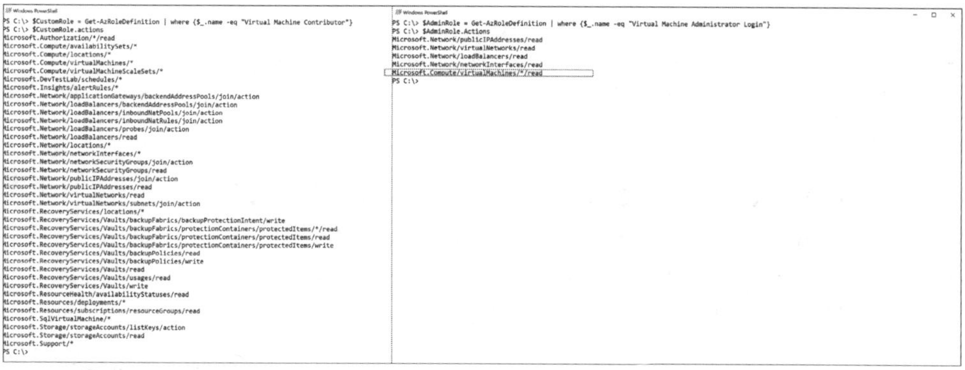

FIGURE 2-31 Missing permissions between built-in roles

4. To complete the custom role, add the missing admin permission to the `$customRole` object:

```
$customRole = get-azroledefinition | where { $_.name -eq "Virtual Machine
Contributor" }
$customRole.id = $null
$customRole.name = "Custom - Virtual Machine Administrator"
$Customrole.Description = "Can manage and access virtual machines"
$customRole.Actions.Add("Microsoft.Compute/VirtualMachines/*/read")
$customRole.AssignableScopes.Clear()
$CustomRole.AssignableScopes = "/subscriptions/<your subscription id>/
resourceGroups/<Resource Group for role>"
New-AzRoleDefinition -role $CustomRole
```

This will create a custom role called Custom - Virtual Machine Administrator and assign all the roles from the Virtual Machine Contributor Role plus the ability to log in to Azure Virtual Machines.

The role will be scoped to the supplied resource ID for the resource group chosen. This way, the added permissions are applicable only to the resource group(s) that need them—perhaps the Servers resource group.

Figure 2-32 shows the output of the command to create this custom role, with sensitive information redacted.

```
PS C:\> $customRole.id = $null
PS C:\> $customRole.name = "Custom - Virtual Machine Administrator"
PS C:\> $Customrole.Description = "Can manage and access virtual machines"
PS C:\> $customRole.Actions.Add("Microsoft.Compute/VirtualMachines/*/read")
PS C:\> $customRole.AssignableScopes.Clear()
PS C:\> #$CustomRole.AssignableScopes = "/subscriptions/<your subscription id>/resoureGroups/<Resource Group for role>"
PS C:\> $CustomRole.AssignableScopes = "/subscriptions/38b97161-b529-4733-969d-61f1aeaefac4/resourceGroups/az300-vault"
PS C:\>
PS C:\> New-AzRoleDefinition -role $CustomRole


Name            : Custom - Virtual Machine Administrator
Id              : 0c41319c-7e7b-4ac9-8c4c-010a691a47b2
IsCustom        : True
Description     : Can manage and access virtual machines
Actions         : {Microsoft.Authorization/*/read, Microsoft.Compute/availabilitySets/*, Microsoft.Compute/locations/*,
                  Microsoft.Compute/virtualMachines/*...}
NotActions      : {}
DataActions     : {}
NotDataActions  : {}
AssignableScopes : {/subscriptions/3                                    4/resourceGroups/a            }


PS C:\>
```

FIGURE 2-32 Newly created custom role

Configure access to resources by assigning roles

Previously, a custom role was created to allow management of and access to virtual machines within an Azure Resource Group. Because the custom role was scoped at the resource group level, it will only be assignable to resource groups.

To make use of the custom role and any built-in roles, the roles need to be assigned to users or groups, which makes them able to leverage these access rights.

To assign the newly created custom role to a group, complete the following steps:

1. In the Azure portal, locate the resource group to which the custom role was scoped.

2. Click the Access Control (IAM) link in the navigation pane.

3. Click Add and select Add Role Assignment.

4. In the Select A Role box, enter the name of the custom role "Custom –" and click the name of the role.

> **NOTE   CUSTOM ROLE NAMING**
>
> Although the type of any custom roles is set to CustomRole when roles are added, we've found prepending the word "Custom –" to the beginning of the name or following a naming standard predefined by your organization may make custom roles easier to find when searching for them at a later time.

5. The Assign Access To drop-down list displays the types of identities that access can be assigned to:
   - Azure AD user, group, or service principal
   - User Assigned Managed Identity
   - System Assigned Managed Identity
     - App Service
     - Container Instance
     - Function App
     - Logic App
     - Virtual Machine
     - Virtual Machine Scale set

   Because virtual machine administrators are generally people, keep the Azure AD user, group, or service principal selected.

6. In the Select box, enter the name of the user or group to which this new role should be assigned.

7. Click the resultant username or group to select them.

> **IMPORTANT   ABOUT GROUPS**
>
> Keep in mind that using a group for role assignments is much lower maintenance than individually assigning users to roles.

8. Click Save to complete the role assignment.

The user (or users if a group was assigned) was assigned new access and may need to log out of the portal or PowerShell and log back in or reconnect to see the new access rights.

Configure Management Access to Azure

Like access to resources running in Azure, access to the platform itself is controlled using RBAC. There are some roles dedicated to the management of Azure resources at a very high level—think management groups and subscriptions.

A management group in Azure is a resource that can cross subscription boundaries and allow a single point of management across subscriptions.

If an organization has multiple subscriptions, they can use management groups to control access to subscriptions that may have similar access needs. For example, if there are three projects going on within an organization that have distinctly different billing needs—each managed by different departments—access to these subscriptions can be handled by management groups, allowing all three subscriptions to be managed together with less effort and administrative overhead.

When you use RBAC roles, the method of assigning access to subscriptions or management groups is the same as other resources, but the roles specific to management and where they're assigned are different. These would be set at the subscription or management group level.

> **IMPORTANT CUMULATIVE BY DEFAULT**
>
> RBAC access is cumulative by default, meaning contributor access at the subscription level is inherited by resource groups and resources housed within a subscription. Inheritance is not required because permission can be granted at lower levels within a subscription all the way down to the specific resource level. In addition, permission can also be denied at any level; doing so prevents access to resources where permission was denied. If denial of permissions happens at a parent resource level, any resources underneath the parent will inherit the denial.

There will always be an entity in Azure that is the overall subscription admin or owner. Usually this is the account that created the subscription but can (and should) be changed to a group to ensure that more than one person has top-level access to the subscription. In addition, this change will account for job changes, staff turnover, and reduce the likelihood that someone forgets about access to Azure during these situations.

To configure access to Azure at the subscription level, complete the following steps:

1. Log in to the Azure portal and select Subscriptions.
2. Click the subscription to be managed.
3. Click the Access Control (IAM) navigation item.
4. On the IAM blade, select Role Assignments.

    The users or groups that have specific roles assigned display. At the subscription level there should be few roles assigned as shown in Figure 2-33. Most access happens at the resource group or resource level.

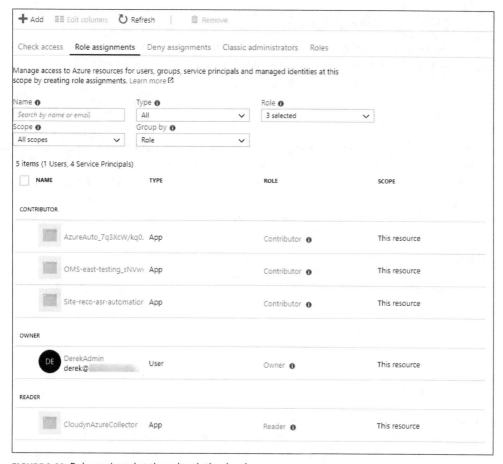

FIGURE 2-33 Roles assigned at the subscription level

5. Click Add at the top of the IAM blade.

6. Select Add Role Assignment.

7. Choose the Owner Role.

8. Leave the Assign Access To drop-down selector set to Azure AD User, Group, or Service Principal.

9. Select a group to assign to the owner role by searching for the group and then clicking it in the results.

10. Click Save.

The group has owner access at the subscription level. This access allows members of the group to create, modify, and remove any resources within the selected subscription.

Management Groups

As mentioned previously, management groups allow RBAC configurations to cross subscription boundaries. Using the scope of a management group for high-level administrative access will consolidate visibility of multiple subscriptions without needing to configure RBAC settings in each of multiple subscriptions. This way, the admins group can be assigned owner access in a management group that contains all the subscriptions for an organization, simplifying the configuration a bit further as shown in Figure 2-34.

FIGURE 2-34 Management groups can be used across subscriptions for access

Top-level access management groups have a top-level root group scoped to the Azure AD tenant. Administrative users can't see this with usual administrative or owner RBAC permissions. To allow this visibility, assign the User Access Administrator role to the group that will be working with management groups.

To add subscriptions or management groups to a management group, complete the following steps:

1. Log in to the Azure portal.
2. Select Management Groups from the All Services list on the navigation pane.
3. If no management group exists, click Add Management Group.
   A. Enter the ID for the new management group (this cannot be changed).
   B. Enter the display name for the management group.
4. Click Save.
5. Click the name of the management group to which items will be added.

   There will likely be very little information visible when viewing a management group. Click the details link next to the name of the group to see more information and take action on the management group, including Adding Management Groups and Subscriptions.

6. For subscriptions, click Add Subscription.

7. Select the subscription to be managed by this group.

8. Click Save.

9. For management groups, click Add Management Group.

10. Select to create a new management group or use an existing group.

    Management groups can be nested to consolidate resource management. This should be used carefully because doing so can complicate management of subscriptions and resources further than necessary.

11. Select a management group to include and click Save.

> **IMPORTANT CHANGING MANAGEMENT GROUPS MAY REQUIRE PERMISSION REVIEW**
>
> When moving items from one management group to another, permissions can be affected negatively. Be sure to understand the impact of any changes before they are made to avoid removing necessary access to Azure resources.

Troubleshoot RBAC

Identifying the cause of problems with RBAC may require some digging to understand why a user is unable to perform an action. When you're assigning access through RBAC, be sure to keep a group of users configured for owner access. In addition to a group, consider enabling an online-only user as an owner as well. This way, if there is an issue with Active Directory, not all user accounts will be unable to access Azure.

Because Role-Based Access Control (RBAC) is central to resource access in Azure, using RBAC carefully is paramount in working with Azure. Like permissions in Windows before it, Azure RBAC brings a fair amount of trial and error to the table when assigning access. Also, because Azure is constantly evolving, there may be times when a permission just doesn't work as stated.

The main panel of the IAM blade has improved considerably in recent time by providing a quick way to check access up front. If someone is questioning their access, an administrator or other team member can easily enter the username or group name where access is being questioned and see which role assignments are currently held. No more sifting through the role assignments list to determine if Fred has contributor or viewer access to the new resource group. This is one of the key tools in troubleshooting—being able to see who has what level of access.

During the times when Fred should have access to a particular resource, but claims to be missing access while Azure shows the correct role assignments, the Roles tab on the IAM blade shown in Figure 2-35 can help determine whether all the needed permissions are available. Sometimes they won't be.

Looking at the list of roles is only somewhat helpful. If Fred claims that he can't read a resource, but he's listed as having the reader role for the resource, there will likely be something going on behind the role. To see the permissions assigned to the listed role, click on the name of the role.

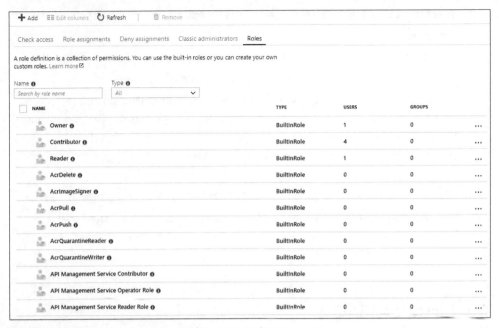

FIGURE 2-35 Reviewing role assignments for groups and users

On the top of the listed assignments page for the role, click Permissions to see the list of permissions that make up the role.

You will see, as shown in Figure 2-36, the list of resource providers that the role meets and whether they have partial access or all access to the provider as well as what data access for a provider the role has.

Permissions (preview)
Reader

RESOURCE PROVIDER	MANAGEMENT	DATA
84codes.CloudAMQP	Partial	--
Azure Data Box	Partial	--
Azure Database Migration Service	Partial	--
Azure IoT Central	Partial	--
Azure Log Analytics	Partial	--
Azure Stack Resource Provider	Partial	--
Bot Service Resource Provider	Partial	--
CloudSimple Private Cloud IAAS	Partial	--
Conexlink MyCloudIT	Partial	--
Crypteron DataSecurity	Partial	--
Domain Services Resource Provider	Partial	--
FriendlyRpNamespace	Partial	--
LiveArena.Broadcast	Partial	--
Machine Learning Services Resource Provider	Partial	None

FIGURE 2-36 Resource provider permissions within a role

Selecting a provider name from this view displays the components used by this role within a given provider and the permissions assigned, as shown for the Azure Data Box provider in Figure 2-37.

FIGURE 2-37 Permissions within the reader role for Azure Data Box

In addition to investigating which permissions get assigned with certain roles, changing roles for certain users or groups to see how access changes is another method that's useful in working through access issues.

There also can be times when changes to RBAC are being cached—when settings changes just aren't appearing once they've been made. In the Azure portal, changes made can take up to 30 minutes to be reflected. In Azure CLI or a PowerShell console, the process of signing out and signing in again will force settings to refresh when making changes to RBAC. Similarly, when using Rest APIs to manage permissions, updating the current access token will refresh permissions.

There are also times when certain resources may require permissions that are higher than the stated need—for example, working in an App Service may require write permission to the underlying storage account to ensure performance monitoring is visible; otherwise, it returns an error. In cases like this, perhaps elevated access (contributor in this case) might be preferable for a time to allow monitoring. This way, the developers get access to the items they need, but maybe the access doesn't remain assigned long term.

Implement Azure Policy

Azure Policy provides a way to enforce and audit standards and governance throughout an Azure environment. Using this configuration involves two top-level steps:

1. Creating or selecting an existing policy definition
2. Assigning this policy definition to a scope of resources

Using policy can streamline auditing and compliance within an Azure environment. However, it can also prevent certain resources from being created depending on the policy definition settings.

> **IMPORTANT REMEMBER TO COMMUNICATE**
>
> Although the intent may be to ensure, for example, that all resources are created in a specified region within Azure, remember to overcommunicate any enforcement changes to those using Azure. The enforcement of policy generally happens when the Create button is clicked, not when the resource is discovered to be in an unsupported region.

Collections of policy definitions, called *initiatives*, are used to group like policy definitions to help achieve a larger goal of governance rather than assigning 10 policy definitions separately. To hit this goal, they can be grouped into one initiative.

To assign a policy, complete the following steps:

1. From the Navigation pane in the Azure portal, select All Services.

2. Search for Policy.

3. Click the star next to the name of the service (will be helpful in the future).

4. Click the name of the policy service to go to the resource.

5. On the Policy Overview blade, compliance information will be displayed (100% compliant if this is not in use yet).

6. Select the Assignments item.

7. On the Policy Assignments blade, shown in Figure 2-38, click Assign Policy.

FIGURE 2-38 Azure policy assignments

8. Complete the following information on the Assign Policy screen:

   - **Scope**   Select the scope at which the chosen policy will be configured.

   - **Exclusions**   Select any resources that will be exempt from the policy assignment.

   - **Policy definition**   Select the policy definition to be assigned.

   - **Assignment Name**   Enter the name for this policy assignment.

   - **Description**   Enter a description for the expected outcome of the policy assignment.

   - **Assigned By**   The name of the Azure logged-in user who is assigning the policy will be listed.

9. Click Assign to save these settings.

When selecting from the list of available definitions, shown in Figure 2-39, pay attention to the name of the policy. Audit policies are used to capture information about what would happen if the policy were enforced. These will not introduce any breaking changes. Policies that aren't labeled audit may introduce breaking changes.

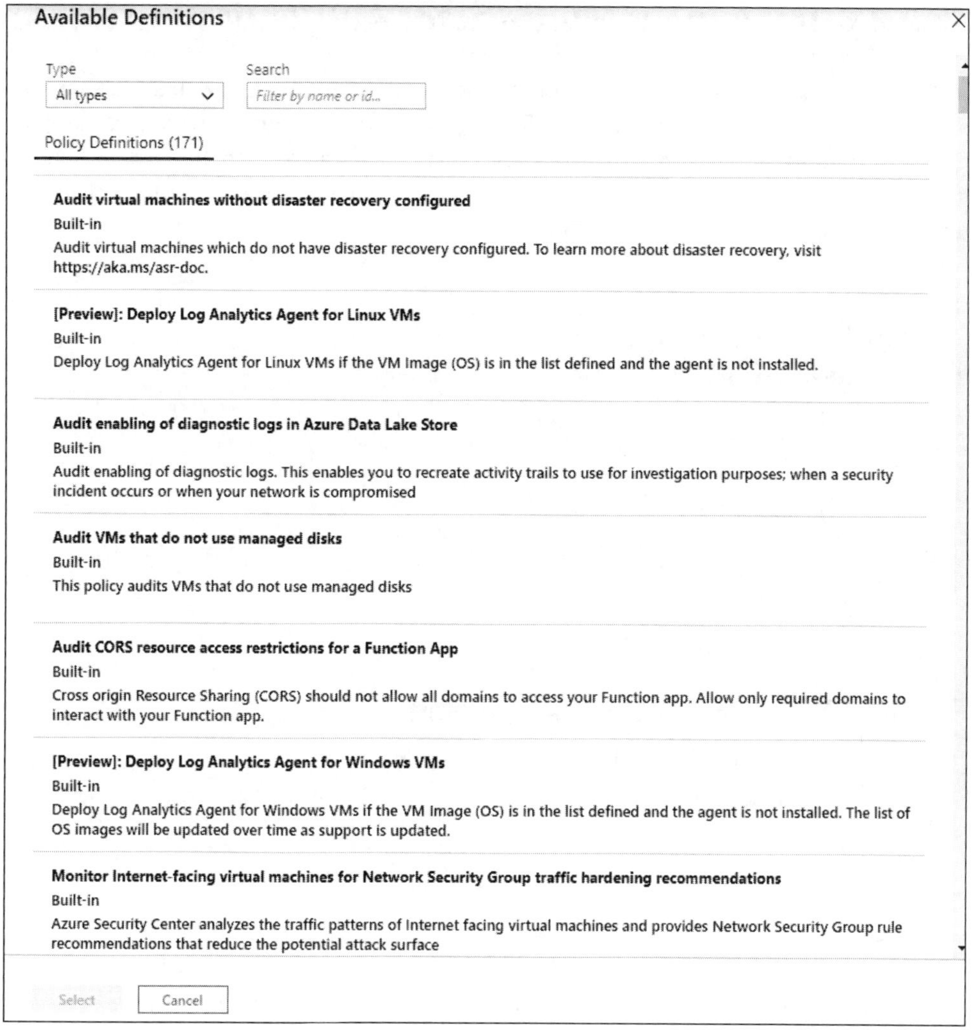

Available Definitions   ×

Type   Search
[All types   ∨]   [Filter by name or id...]

Policy Definitions (171)

Audit virtual machines without disaster recovery configured
Built-in
Audit virtual machines which do not have disaster recovery configured. To learn more about disaster recovery, visit https://aka.ms/asr-doc.

[Preview]: Deploy Log Analytics Agent for Linux VMs
Built-in
Deploy Log Analytics Agent for Linux VMs if the VM Image (OS) is in the list defined and the agent is not installed.

Audit enabling of diagnostic logs in Azure Data Lake Store
Built-in
Audit enabling of diagnostic logs. This enables you to recreate activity trails to use for investigation purposes; when a security incident occurs or when your network is compromised

Audit VMs that do not use managed disks
Built-in
This policy audits VMs that do not use managed disks

Audit CORS resource access restrictions for a Function App
Built-in
Cross origin Resource Sharing (CORS) should not allow all domains to access your Function app. Allow only required domains to interact with your Function app.

[Preview]: Deploy Log Analytics Agent for Windows VMs
Built-in
Deploy Log Analytics Agent for Windows VMs if the VM Image (OS) is in the list defined and the agent is not installed. The list of OS images will be updated over time as support is updated.

Monitor Internet-facing virtual machines for Network Security Group traffic hardening recommendations
Built-in
Azure Security Center analyzes the traffic patterns of Internet facing virtual machines and provides Network Security Group rule recommendations that reduce the potential attack surface

[Select]   [Cancel]

FIGURE 2-39 The policy definitions list available for assignment

Once a policy has been assigned, its compliance state may show Not Started because the policy is new and has not yet been evaluated against resources. Click Refresh to monitor the state of compliance. This may take some time to reflect state change.

If a policy runs against a scope and finds items in noncompliance, it may require remediation tasks to be performed. These tasks are listed under the remediation section in the Policy blade, and they're only applicable to policies that will deploy resources if they are not found.

Skill 2.6: Implement Multi-Factor Authentication (MFA)

Multi-Factor Authentication (MFA) is becoming more and more necessary with the increased number of breaches and security concerns floating around information technology these days. MFA ensures that a log in to a site or application goes a step beyond the username and password by requiring the user to provide something they have (usually in the form of a token received via SMS or an authenticator app).

This skill covers how to:

- Enable MFA for an Azure AD Tenant
- Configure user accounts for use with MFA
- Configure trusted IPs for MFA
- Configure fraud alerts for MFA
- Configure MFA bypass options
- Configure MFA verification methods

Enable MFA for an Azure AD Tenant

To enable MFA for Azure AD, complete the following steps:

1. Log in to the Azure portal.
2. Select Azure Active Directory from the navigation pane.
3. Within Azure Active Directory, select MFA under the security section.

> **IMPORTANT UPGRADED SKU REQUIREMENTS**
> The use of MFA in Azure AD requires the use of a paid SKU for Azure AD.

If your tenant of Azure AD is not at a high enough SKU, you may be able to enable a premium trial to continue configuration.

4. After selecting Azure AD P1 or P2 for the Active Directory SKU, sign out of the Azure Portal and sign back in.

5. Return to Azure Active Directory and select MFA to see available options related to MFA:

- **Account Lockout**   Settings available to ensure incorrect logon attempts will trigger the account to be locked out and options for them to reset on their own.

- **Block/Unblock Users**   Add users to the block list who will be unable to log in. This will set all authentication attempts to be denied and remain in place for 90 days from the first blocked login.

- **Fraud Alert**   Configure fraud reporting for users receiving a second factor request they aren't expecting and configure fraud reporting users be blocked on report of fraud.

- **Notifications**   Enter the recipient email address who will receive alerts generated by MFA. The best practice here would be to use a distribution group for notification.

- **OATH Tokens**   Configure the secret keys (via upload) for associated hardware tokens to allow use of a hardware token as a second factor.

- **Phone Call Settings**   Configure the caller ID number (United States only), whether an operator is required to transfer for extensions, the number of pin attempts allowed per call, and greetings used with the phone calling service.

- **Providers**   The provider settings were disabled as of September 1, 2018.

- **MFA Server Settings**   These settings bring the functionality of Azure AD MFA to an on-premises datacenter.

- **Server Settings**   The number of seconds before the two-factor code times out.

- **One-Time Bypass**   A list of user accounts that will bypass MFA authentication. The default bypass is for 300 seconds.

- **Caching Rules**   Configure MFA so that consecutive authentications don't repeat MFA authentication.

- **Server Status**   Reports the status of an on-premises MFA server.

- **Activity Report**   Shows activity against Azure AD MFA and a connected MFA server.

Configure user accounts for use with MFA

MFA is configured per user account, meaning it can be enabled for one user or all user accounts in an organization. To set up a user account to use MFA, complete the following steps:

1. From the Azure portal, select Azure Active Directory and MFA.
2. Choose Additional Cloud-Based MFA Settings from the Getting Started blade.
3. In the new tab opened for MFA, select Users from the top of the screen, as shown in Figure 2-40.

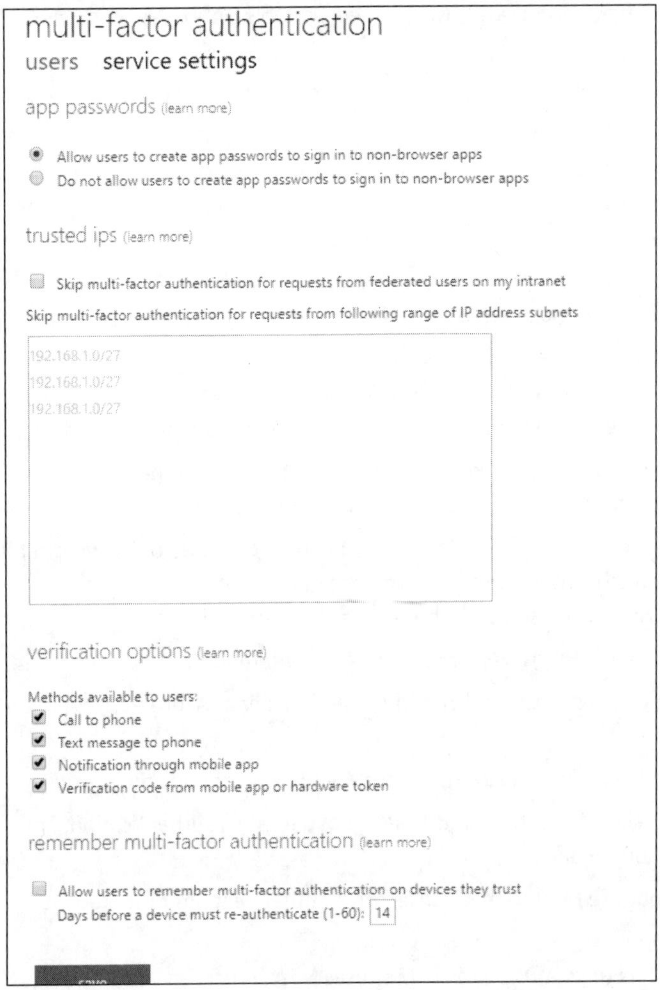

multi-factor authentication

users   service settings

app passwords (learn more)

- ◉ Allow users to create app passwords to sign in to non-browser apps
- ○ Do not allow users to create app passwords to sign in to non-browser apps

trusted ips (learn more)

- ☐ Skip multi-factor authentication for requests from federated users on my intranet

Skip multi-factor authentication for requests from following range of IP address subnets

```
192.168.1.0/27
192.168.1.0/27
192.168.1.0/27
```

verification options (learn more)

Methods available to users:
- ☑ Call to phone
- ☑ Text message to phone
- ☑ Notification through mobile app
- ☑ Verification code from mobile app or hardware token

remember multi-factor authentication (learn more)

- ☐ Allow users to remember multi-factor authentication on devices they trust

Days before a device must re-authenticate (1-60): [14]

FIGURE 2-40 Configuring MFA for users within an Azure AD organization

4. Select the user or users to enable for MFA from the list (see Figure 2-41).

5. With user(s) selected, click the Enable link under the user details on the right of the page.

6. Copy the displayed link if users are not signing in regularly. This way they can be provided an email to establish the needed MFA requirements as soon as they can.

7. Click the Enable Multi-Factor Auth link on the displayed pop-up dialog box.

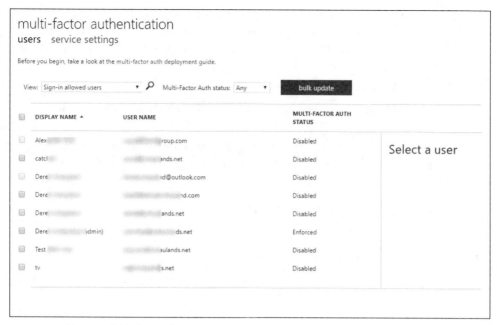

FIGURE 2-41 Users available for configuration with MFA

8. With MFA enabled, additional user settings are available, including

- **Require Selected User(s) To Provide Contact Methods Again** Re-collect additional email addresses and phone numbers used by MFA.

- **Delete All Existing Application Passwords Generated By Selected Users** Any app-level passwords these users have configured as a secure way to authenticate specific applications or devices will be deleted.

- **Restore Multi-Factor Authentication On All Remembered Devices** For devices on which the user(s) have selected options for the device to be remembered. Reset this to require a re-authentication.

The last setting available on this page is Enforce. If this is configured for a user, they will be required to use MFA at sign-in. If the MFA settings are enabled but not enforced, the user will be able to decide if MFA should be used.

Configure trusted IPs for MFA

While MFA provides extra security, many organizations like to reduce the amount of two-factor logins needed by users when they connect from known IP addresses. An example of this might be in the corporate or satellite offices owned and managed by the company. Because the network and systems are managed by a known IT staff, these networks can generally be trusted to not require MFA.

Your mileage may vary because this is configurable. Some organizations may choose to constantly require the use of MFA or only allow the IP of the corporate office to be trusted. This will likely depend on the industry and amount of sensitive information handled by the organization.

To add trusted IPs, complete the following steps:

1. From the MFA Getting Started page, select the Additional Cloud-Based MFA Settings link.

2. On the Multi-Factor Authentication page, check the box labeled Skip Multi-Factor Authentication For Requests From The Following Range Of IP Address Subnets.

3. Enter the IP address ranges to be trusted as shown in Figure 2-42.

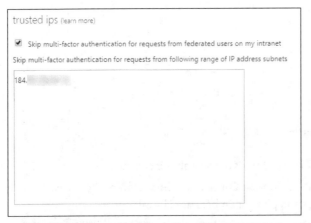

FIGURE 2-42 Trusted Multi-Factor Authentication IP addresses

4. After entering any IP ranges to trust, click Save.

EXAM TIP

Configuring trusted IPs for known locations is great. Pay attention to areas where the location might not have a static IP address (a home office, for example). Configuring an IP that may change, even if it doesn't change often, as trusted could cause issues for users expecting no MFA at their location.

NOTE REMEMBER ME

Another option available on the app settings page for MFA allows users to have their devices remembered by MFA for a set number of days. Check the box at the bottom of the app settings screen and set the number of days (between 1 and 60).

Configure fraud alerts for MFA

Fraud alerts help keep corporate information safe and help employees ensure their access does not fall into the wrong hands. With alerts enabled, anytime a user receives an MFA prompt they did not initiate, it can be reported as fraudulent, which can prompt the account to be locked to prevent further attempts. To configure fraud alerts for MFA, complete the following steps:

1. Log in to the Azure portal.
2. Select Azure Active Directory.
3. Choose MFA in the navigation pane.
4. Select Fraud Alert to open the Configuration blade (see Figure 2-43).

FIGURE 2-43 The MFA Fraud Alert Configuration blade

5. Enable the setting by selecting to turn on the Allow Users To Submit Fraud Alerts option.
6. The Automatically Block Users Who Report Fraud option is enabled by default; toggle the option to Off to disable this feature.
7. The Code To Report Fraud setting, set to 0 by default, allows users who choose to get called by the MFA service to enter a code before pressing # to report the contact as fraudulent.

> **NOTE UPDATE THE DEFAULT**
>
> Consider the option to change the default fraud code—0#. If it is modified, a custom greeting is necessary to ensure the call recipients know that they can enter a different code before pressing # to report fraud.

8. Once the settings for fraud reporting have been configured, click the Save button at the top of the blade to update the option.

Configure MFA bypass options

When using MFA, there may be a use case to allow some employees to bypass MFA in certain situations. This is outside of the configuration of trusted IPs because it bypasses all MFA for the configured accounts for the preset time limit, which has a default of five minutes.

From the MFA blade of Azure Active Directory, select One-Time Bypass to display the bypass list shown in Figure 2-44. Then complete the following steps:

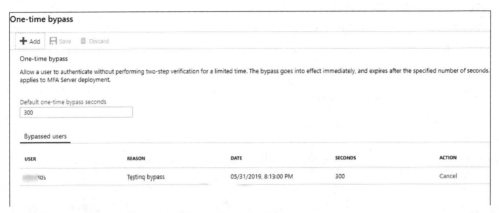

FIGURE 2-44 Configuring the one-time bypass list for MFA

1. Click the Add button.
2. Enter the user account the bypass will impact.
3. Enter the number of seconds the bypass will last, if you're using something different than the default.
4. Enter a reason for configuring the MFA bypass.
5. Click OK.
6. Once the user(s) have been added to the bypass list, click Save at the top of the blade to immediately enable the MFA bypass.

Configure MFA verification methods

There are several ways that users can verify their identity when MFA is configured. These include:

- **Microsoft Authenticator App**   A phone app that delivers a one-time use token to provide the second factor of authentication.
- **SMS**   Users can opt to receive a text message with a code to prove their identity.
- **Voice Call**   Users can opt to be called by the MFA service to prove their identity.

Other options are available for use with self-service password reset only:

- **Email Address**   A link for password reset is delivered via email.

- **Security Questions** A series of questions are configured and answered during onboarding. They are stored with the Azure Active Directory user object and not visible to any other users.

Each of these options' configuration steps will be discussed in turn.

To configure the Microsoft Authenticator App, complete the following steps:

1. Click Next on the More Information Required screen.

2. Select the method of contact as mobile app on the Additional Security Validation page shown in Figure 2-45.

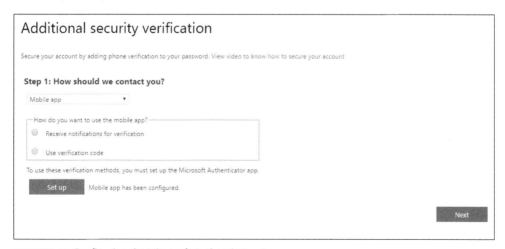

FIGURE 2-45 Configuring the Microsoft Authenticator App

3. Select how the app should alert for authentication requests:
   - Receive notifications
   - Use verification code

4. Click Set Up to configure the mobile app.

5. From the installed Microsoft Authenticator App on a mobile device, scan the QR code displayed on the configure mobile app dialog box (see Figure 2-46).

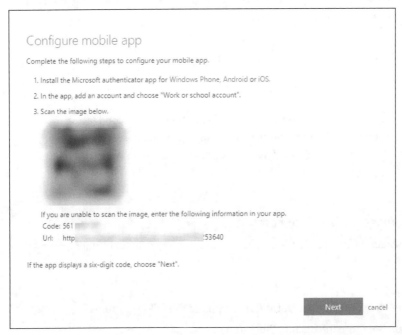

Configure mobile app

Complete the following steps to configure your mobile app.

1. Install the Microsoft authenticator app for Windows Phone, Android or iOS.

2. In the app, add an account and choose "Work or school account".

3. Scan the image below.

If you are unable to scan the image, enter the following information in your app.
Code: 561
Url: http   53640

If the app displays a six-digit code, choose "Next".

Next   cancel

FIGURE 2-46 Displays the connection QR code for configuring the Authenticator app

6. If scanning from the app is not possible, you can enter the displayed code into the app by browsing to the displayed URL.

7. Click Next after completing this step.

8. Following the activation confirmation, click Next.

9. Wait for the test code to be sent to the configured device and approve it to verify receipt.

10. Click Done.

Advanced MFA settings are managed through the user account page. To change or add verification methods once MFA is enabled and the initial sign-in has completed, complete the following steps:

1. Log in to the account where MFA is enabled and select the account from the top of the page.

2. On the menu, select View Account (see Figure 2-47).

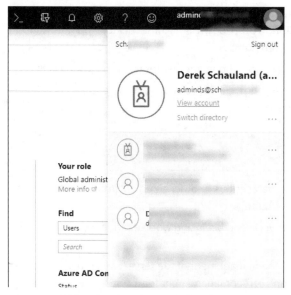

FIGURE 2-47 Accessing the account settings for a user account

3. On the account screen, select Additional Security Verification to see the MFA settings for the account, as shown in Figure 2-48.

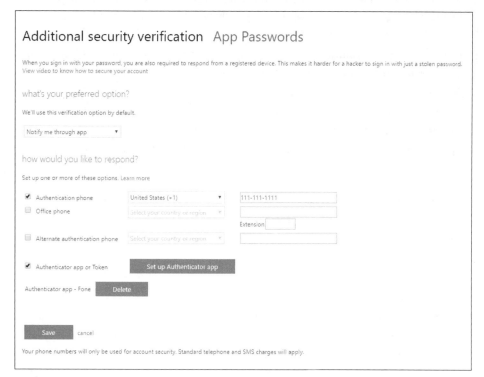

FIGURE 2-48 Advanced security settings for a user account with MFA configured

On the Additional Security Verification screen, select the default method of contact from the What's Your Preferred Option drop-down list : Authenticator App notification, SMS message, or phone call to desired number.

Also, on this screen, set the authentication phone number for texts and phone calls.

4. After configuring the SMS and call settings, click Save at the bottom of the page to enable these settings for this user account.

Chapter summary

- Virtual machines from on-premises datacenters or other cloud environments as well as Physical servers can be migrated to Azure.

- Application load balancing and network load balancing work in tandem to ensure an all-around solution.

- Serverless compute resources take the management of the servers and move it into the platform, reducing the organization's server management footprint.

- Logic Apps perform custom integrations between applications and services both inside and outside of Azure.

- Virtual network peering allows communication between networks in Azure without need for a VPN, whereas Site-to-Site VPNs connect Azure to existing on-premises networks and ExpressRoute provides completely private connections to Microsoft services from an on-premises environment.

- Role-Based Access Control aligns user access to Azure resources more closely with job roles. Keep in mind that this alignment is not always perfect and multiple roles may be necessary to provide the correct access.

- Policies in Azure help to ensure that resources can be audited for compliance and deployment controlled as required by the organization.

- Multi-Factor Authentication should be used wherever possible, especially for sensitive (think administrative) access. Configurations like trusted IP and One-Time bypass will help reduce the amount of MFA requirements from known networks and simplify troubleshooting of MFA. While SMS-based authentication is better than not using MFA, be aware that it can be spoofed more easily than an app configured for use with a specific account.

Thought experiment

In this thought experiment, demonstrate your skills and knowledge of the topics covered in this chapter. You can find the answers to thought experiment questions in the next section.

You're an Azure solutions architect hired by Tailspin Toys to help them with security configuration and Multi-Factor Authentication setup for their planned migration to the Azure cloud platform.

When discussing the configuration plan with Tailspin, you discovered the following items as requirements:

- Some virtualized workloads running Linux or Windows will be migrated to Azure.
- Access to the migrated servers is limited to the help desk being able to reboot servers as needed and the server admins team getting full control of the machines.
- Admin-level users in Azure need to use strong passwords and another level of authentication. All the admins are smartphone users.

Considering the discovered requirements, answer the following questions:

1. What solution would you recommend to ensure the server workload(s) get moved to Azure with minimal downtime?

2. What technology can help Tailspin Toys meet the requirement allowing different access based on group membership?

3. How can accounts have security increased for the IT admins without causing disruption to other users within the organization?

Thought experiment answers

This section contains the solution to the thought experiment for this chapter. Please keep in mind there may be other ways to achieve the desired result. Each answer explains why the answer is correct.

1. Azure Site Recovery can be used to migrate physical servers, VMWare virtual machines, and Hyper-V virtual machines. Using this method will also allow Tailspin Toys IT to test the configuration and try a failover before migrating the machines to Azure.

2. Using multiple RBAC roles, or a custom role created to specialize the access of the Tailspin Toys help desk users will ensure that the IT admins group maintains full control over the Azure migrated machines. Using groups in this situation as the entities to which the roles are assigned further simplifies management and maintenance because it allows users to be moved from one level of access to another with little administrative effort.

3. Because the users of the privileged accounts are carrying smartphones, the Microsoft Authenticator app can be used as a second factor for authentication with MFA. The ability to configure MFA settings at the user level reduces the worry that this will affect existing organizational employees.

## CHAPTER 3

Create and deploy apps

Azure App Service is a managed platform used to quickly build, deploy, and scale web apps in the cloud. App Service supports applications built using common frameworks such as .NET, .NET Core, Node.js, Java, PHP, Ruby, or Python. One of the biggest advantages to using App Service is the ability to instantly achieve enterprise-grade performance, security, and compliance without having to worry about routine maintenance and operational tasks.

In this chapter, you learn how to create and deploy web applications that run in the Azure App Service environment, and you'll gain an understanding of modern patterns and practices used to build and deploy containerized applications.

Skills covered in this chapter:

- Skill 3.1: Create web apps by using PaaS
- Skill 3.2: Design and develop apps that run in containers

Skill 3.1: Create web apps by using PaaS

Azure App Service gives you the ability to build and host web apps, mobile back ends, and RESTful APIs without getting bogged down in the depths of managing traditional infrastructure. Offloading the heavy lifting of server maintenance, patching, and backups gives you the freedom to concentrate on your application. App Service includes Microsoft's best practices for high availability and load balancing as part of this managed service offering. You can easily enable and configure autoscaling and deploy Windows or Linux-based applications from common deployment sources such as GitHub, Azure DevOps, or any local Git repo.

This skill covers how to:

- Create an Azure App Service web app
- Create an App Service web app for containers
- Create documentation for an API
- Create an App Service background task by using WebJobs
- Enable diagnostics logging for web apps

Create an Azure App Service web app

Microsoft offers a variety of methods for deploying web apps in Azure App Service. The term *web app* simply refers to a managed application running in App Service. You can use the Azure portal to create a web app, and you also can use the Azure CLI, PowerShell, and other IDE-based tools such as Visual Studio that provide integration with the Azure platform.

To create an Azure App Service web app, start by signing in to the Azure portal and use the following procedure:

1. Navigate to the App Services bookmark on the left side of the Azure portal.

2. Click on Add to create a new web app.

3. On the Web App screen (see Figure 3-1), configure the following options and then click Review and Create:

   - **Subscription** Select the appropriate subscription for the web app resource. You may have different subscriptions in your enterprise that are dedicated to development or production environments or are dedicated to use by specific teams in your organization.

   - **Resource Group** Select an existing or new resource group where the web app will reside. Remember that you can deploy multiple resources into a group and delegate access control at the resource group level if needed.

   - **Name** Enter a globally unique host name for your web app under azurewebsites.net. This may take several attempts as many host names are already in use. Enter the name for your web app in all lowercase letters. It should have between 3 and 24 characters.

   - **Publish** Select Code as the publish option unless you're deploying a web app that has been packaged into a Docker container image.

   - **Runtime stack** Select the appropriate runtime stack for your application. Multiple runtimes are supported in App Service, including .NET Core, ASP.NET, Java, Node, and Python.

   - **Region** Choose the appropriate region to host your web app. Keep in mind that proximity between users and application infrastructure may be very sensitive depending on the type of web application you're deploying. It's a common practice to host cloud resources in regions closest to end users.

   - **App Service Plan** Select a new or existing App Service Plan, which is the managed infrastructure hosting your web apps. Various pricing tiers are available that provide everything from basic capability all the way to very advanced capabilities. The Standard S1 plan is the recommended minimum pricing tier for production web apps.

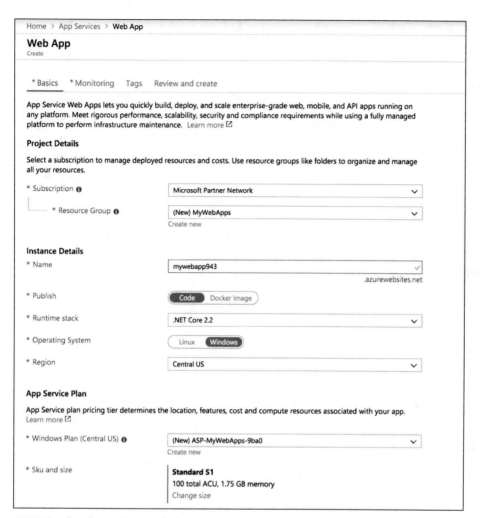

FIGURE 3-1 Creating an App Service web app

EXAM TIP

You can also use the command line to deploy your web apps. For example, use the *az webapp create* command with the Azure CLI to perform this task from your local terminal or Azure Cloud Shell instance.

Create an App Service web app for containers

The ease of Azure App Service makes deploying Windows or Linux container-based web apps a simple process. You can pull Docker container images hosted in the Docker Hub or use your own private Azure Container Registry. One of the greatest benefits to this approach is that you can include all the dependencies you need for your application inside your container images. Microsoft will take care of the patching, high availability, and load balancing that powers the underlying infrastructure.

Creating a web app for containers is a similar process to building a standard web app. Use the following procedure in the Azure portal to create a containerized web app in App Service:

EXAM TIP

Azure PowerShell is a common command-line alternative used to deploy web apps. You can use the *New-AzWebApp* cmdlet to script the deployment of standard or containerized web apps in App Service.

1. Navigate to the App Services bookmark on the left side of the Azure Portal.
2. Click Add to create a new web app.
3. Provide all of the required details for your web app and make sure to set the Publish option to Docker Image; then click Next.
4. Enter the details for your Docker container image, as shown in Figure 3-2, and then click Review and Create:
   - **Options** Selecting a Single Container is the most common option. Multicontainer support using Docker Compose is currently planned for future release.
   - **Image Source** The Docker Hub is the default container registry for public images. You also can select your own private registry or an Azure Container Registry resource.
   - **Access Type** Public images are the default access type for Docker Hub; however, private images are also supported with App Service web apps. If you select private for your access type, you're prompted to enter your registry credentials.
   - **Image and Tag** Enter the name of your container image and corresponding tag (optional).
   - **Startup Command** Optional startup scripts or commands are supported. This is often unnecessary because container images can be built to use a specific startup command by default.

Web App
Create

* Basics   * Docker   Tags   Review and create

Pull container images from Azure Container Registry, Docker Hub or a private Docker repository. App Service will deploy the containerized app with your preferred dependencies to production in seconds.

Options	Single Container ⌄
Image Source	Docker Hub ⌄

Docker hub options

* Access Type	Public ⌄
* Image and tag	nginx ✓
Startup Command ❶	

FIGURE 3-2 Configuring the Docker image settings

NEED MORE REVIEW? APP SERVICE OVERVIEW

To review further details about Azure App Service, refer to the Microsoft Azure documentation at *https://docs.microsoft.com/en-us/azure/app-service/overview*.

Create documentation for an API

It's quite common for development teams to host RESTful APIs as web apps in Azure, and the App Service environment provides support for documenting those APIs through metadata. The OpenAPI Specification (formerly Swagger Specification) is an API description format for REST APIs. An OpenAPI file allows you to describe your entire API, and this file can be used to generate documentation automatically.

Self-documenting APIs open up some interesting capabilities for your web apps running in Azure. In addition to helping with documentation, RESTful APIs that offer a Swagger definition file also can be used by Azure Logic Apps and the built-in HTTP + Swagger connector. This provides a seamless experience when you use the Logic Apps Designer with your custom-built APIs.

The process for creating documentation for an API requires the following procedure:

1. Application developers need to add support for generating Swagger documents into the codebase for the API. For example, .NET developers can use the Swashbuckle or NSwag open source packages to add Swagger support to the project.

2. You need to add a Swagger definition file to the project. This definition file is simply a JSON document that describes the API methods that are available when consuming the API. This file is typically generated by the Swagger tool chain or through third-party implementations.

3. After development of the API is complete, it should be deployed to an existing Azure web app resource. This can be done in a variety of deployment sources such as GitHub, Azure DevOps, or any local Git repo.

4. Once the application is up and running in App Service, navigate to the properties of the web app resource in the Azure portal.

5. Navigate to the API Definition screen and configure the API definition location, as shown in Figure 3-3.

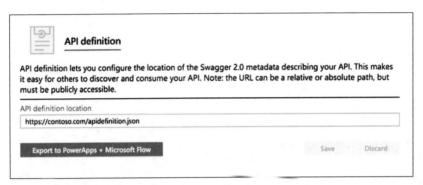

FIGURE 3-3 Setting the API definition location

EXAM TIP

The terms "web app" and "API app" can be used interchangeably when it comes to working with Azure App Service applications. An API app is the same resource as a web app in App Service. The only difference is it has an API definition configured.

6. After the API definition location has been set, teams can use tools like the open source Swagger UI to generate documentation for their API.

NOTE CROSS-ORIGIN REQUESTS (CORS)

You may need to enable support for CORS depending on how the API and tools are used with your API definition. For more details, see *http://docs.microsoft.com/en-us/azure/app-service/ app-service-web-tutorial-rest-api in the Azure documentation.*

Create an App Service background task by using WebJobs

App Service Plans host the infrastructure that runs your web app resources. Although App Service is a managed offering, there are still virtual machines handling all of the work behind the scenes. This means that if you have an App Service Plan, you likely have idle compute infrastructure and resources available for running background tasks.

This is where WebJobs come into play. If you want to run a program or script on your Windows-based App Service infrastructure, you can do so on-demand, or on a schedule.

Use the following procedure to create a WebJob that can run as a background task:

1. Navigate to the properties of an existing web app in the Azure portal.

2. Scroll down on the left-hand side and select WebJobs.

3. Click the Add button to create a new WebJob, as shown in Figure 3-4, and then click OK. The form fields you'll need to provide values for are described here:

   - **Name**   Provide a meaningful name for your WebJob.

   - **File Upload**   Upload your code. Note that the supported file types are Windows (.cmd, .bat, .exe), PowerShell (.ps1), Bash (.sh), PHP (.php), Python (.py), Node.js (.js), Java (.jar).

   - **Type**   Continuous WebJobs are always running, which is useful for background jobs executing on an endless loop. WebJobs also can be configured with *Triggered* as the type, meaning it can be invoked manually or through a schedule that you define.

   - **Scale**   App Service supports the concept of autoscaling, so it's possible that your web app might be powered by multiple virtual machines. If so, you can leave the Scale setting configured as Multi Instance, meaning your background jobs will run on every virtual machine hosting your web app.

FIGURE 3-4 Creating a WebJob in the Azure portal

EXAM TIP

Make sure you remember the supported file types that can be used as scripts for your WebJobs in App Service.

Enable diagnostics logging for web apps

One of the biggest challenges with supporting managed services is the trade-off of convenience versus control. When another company is managing your infrastructure, you gain a lot of efficiency but lose the ability to see everything that is happening under the hood. Fortunately, Microsoft understands how important debugging is for developers and operations staff. App Service provides built-in diagnostics to assist with debugging your web apps, and you can retrieve both web server and application diagnostic logs to aid in your troubleshooting processes.

Complete the following steps to enable diagnostic logging for web apps running in App Service:

1. Navigate to the properties of your web app in the Azure portal.

2. Scroll down and select App Service Logs in the left-hand pane.

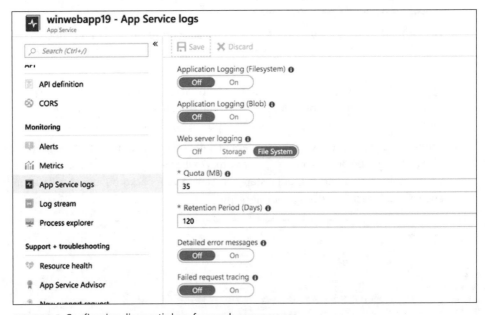

FIGURE 3-5 Configuring diagnostic logs for a web app resource

3. Click the On button for each desired logging feature, as shown in Figure 3-5, and then click Save. The settings on this screen are described here:

   - **Application logging (Filesystem)** Enable this setting to collect diagnostic traces from your web application code. Keep in mind this setting is used for interactive troubleshooting and when using real-time log streaming. This setting turns itself off after 12 hours.

   - **Application logging (Blob)** To persist diagnostic log data for long periods of time, you can configure logging to Blob storage. Enabling this setting requires that you associate the configuration with your Azure Blog storage account.

   - **Web Server logging** You can enable web server logging to gather diagnostic information specific to the web server hosting your application. These logs can be stored on the file system or in Azure Blob storage.

- **Detailed error messages** Enable this setting when you need more detailed error messages from the platform.
- **Failed request tracing** Enable this setting when you need in-depth diagnostic information about failed requests and other errors being thrown by your web applications.

> **NOTE STREAMING LOGS**
>
> It's often useful to get near real-time logging information during the development process of an application. See the Azure docs for more details at *http://docs.microsoft.com/en-us/azure/app-service/troubleshoot-diagnostic-logs.*

Skill 3.2: Design and develop apps that run in containers

Containerization has completely disrupted the IT industry over the past several years, and there's no sign of the trend slowing down. The Azure team understands this and has gone to great lengths to make it incredibly simple to deploy containerized applications in App Service.

This skill covers how to:

- Create a container image by using a Dockerfile
- Publish an image to the Azure Container Registry
- Implement an application that runs on an Azure Container Instance
- Manage container settings by using code
- Create an Azure Container Service (ACS/AKS)

Create a container image by using a Dockerfile

Container images are the artifacts that make it possible to deploy modern applications at speeds never seen before. Applications run inside containers, which are launched from container images. Think of container images as templates that can be used to start up containers. We use container images to package up our code and application dependencies, and then we can invoke running instances of these images to create containers. The Docker toolset has become the gold standard for managing this entire process.

You need to be familiar with the following procedure for creating Docker container images:

1. Create a new text file called Dockerfile (make sure you do not add a file extension).

```
1  FROM node:alpine
2
3  WORKDIR /usr/app
4
5  COPY . .
6  RUN npm install
7
8  CMD ["npm", "start"]
```

FIGURE 3-6 Writing a Dockerfile

2. Add commands, like those shown in Figure 3-6, to automate the build process for a Node.js application packaged into a container image. Each instruction in the Dockerfile adds a read-only layer to the container image.

   - **FROM** Create a layer uslng the official Node.js container image based on Alpine Linux.
   - **WORKDIR** Set the working directory for the application.
   - **COPY** Add files from the developer machine into the Docker image.
   - **RUN** Install all of the required npm packages that the application will need.
   - **CMD** Use to specify the command to run when the container is started.

3. The final step is to use the Docker client to build your container image. Docker Desktop, which runs on Mac and Windows, is used by millions of developers to develop apps locally with Docker. You can use the *Docker Build* command after you've installed Docker Desktop to create a container image using your Dockerfile, as shown in Figure 3-7.

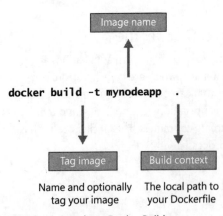

FIGURE 3-7 Running a Docker Build

> **NOTE** DOCKERFILE REFERENCE
>
> The Docker image build process is incredibly versatile. To learn more about writing your own Dockerfile, visit the official Docker reference at *http://docs.docker.com/engine/reference/builder.*

Publish an image to the Azure Container Registry

Container registry services are used as a central location for storing container images. The Azure Container Registry (ACR) is a fully managed Docker registry service based on the open-source Docker Registry. You can build an ACR resource and integrate a variety of Azure services with your container registry. This is useful for keep images in close proximity to application infrastructure, and you can use native security controls in Azure to permit or deny access to ACR.

After you've built your own container images, you can push them to an ACR instance. Complete the steps in the following procedure to build an ACR resource to store your container images:

1. Log into the Azure portal and click Create A New Resource.

2. Select Containers from the Azure Marketplace and click Container Registry.

FIGURE 3-8 Creating an ACR resource

3. Enter the registry details, as shown in Figure 3-8, and click Create.

- **Registry Name**   Enter a globally unique hostname under azurecr.io. Follow standard DNS naming rules and use alphanumeric characters only.

- **Admin User**   Enable to use an ACR-specific username and password to log into the registry using tools like the Docker CLI.

- **SKU**   Select the pricing tier. The tier you select dictates the performance and scalability of your ACR resource.

4. Navigate to the properties of your ACR resource after provisioning has completed. Click Access Keys under Settings to retrieve the login server details and password for your ACR admin user account.

5. Log in to your ACR instance using the Docker client (for example, `docker login <your ACR name>.azurecr.io`).

```
$ docker tag mynodeapp contoso.azurecr.io/mynodeapp
$
$
$ docker push contoso.azurecr.io/mynodeapp
The push refers to repository [contoso.azurecr.io/mynodeapp]
27036f822fba: Pushed
9adffa35f891: Pushed
2edfc06ca0f7: Pushed
662f8f5a2b7a: Pushed
00210cd15c5c: Pushed
ffa1cdbe8bf7: Pushed
f1b5933fe4b5: Pushed
```

FIGURE 3-9 Tagging and pushing a container image to ACR

6. After logging into ACR, you can publish images using the Docker CLI, as shown in Figure 3-9.

- `docker tag`   Use the `docker tag` command to tag your image with the ACR name in the format of *<ACR hostname>/<your image name>*. Note that this can also be done during build time when creating the image with docker build.

- `docker push`   Publish the image to ACR using the registry hostname included as part of the image name.

EXAM TIP

You can use an Azure AD service principal to delegate access to your ACR resource in addition to an admin user.

Implement an application that runs on an Azure Container Instance

The ability to quickly spin up applications inside containers opens numerous possibilities. In addition to running containers in App Service, you also can take advantage of a model that provides containers as a service. Azure Container Instances (ACI) are a service offering that allows you to spin up containers on demand, without any existing infrastructure such as virtual machines or even App Service Plans. ACI enables you to design and deploy your applications instead of managing the infrastructure that runs them.

Use the following procedure to create an Azure Container Instance:

1. Log into the Azure portal and click Create A New Resource.

2. Select Containers from the Azure Marketplace and click Container Instances.

FIGURE 3-10 Creating an Azure Container Instance

3. Enter the ACI details, as shown in Figure 3-10, and click Create.

- **Container name**   Enter a meaningful name for your container.

- **Image type**   Select Public if your image is hosted in a public registry. Otherwise, choose private to enable the options to include your registry login details.

- **Image name**   Enter the exact name of your container image.

- **Image registry login server**   Provide your login server fully qualified domain name. If you're using ACR, this will be your ACR login server name.

- **Image registry user name**   Enter the username for your registry.

- **Image registry password**   Provide your registry password.

- **OS type**   ACI supports both Linux and Windows-based containers. Select the appropriate OS type from the list.

- **Size**   ACI requires that you set resource limits for each instance of your application. This also controls the pricing for the ACI resource, and you can change the size at any time after the ACI resource has been provisioned.

EXAM TIP

ACI is a great solution for basic applications and task automation. For production scenarios that require full orchestration, Microsoft recommends running containers on Azure Kubernetes Service (AKS).

Manage container settings by using code

The Azure platform provides access to numerous language-specific SDKs and tools that you can use to programmatically manage your infrastructure. Developers can use .NET, Java, Node.js, PHP, Python, and Go to build applications that interact with your Azure resources.

In addition to the SDKs, Microsoft offers support for PowerShell and the Azure CLI for authoring operational scripts and for running ad-hoc administration commands locally or in the interactive Cloud Shell.

Azure solution architects are expected to understand how to tap into these automation capabilities to manage container settings using code. This is true whether the code is part of a robust application built by developers or used in provisioning scripts created by the DevOps team. Since the SDKs and command-line tools are all leveraging the Azure RESTful APIs behind the scenes, Azure solution architects can leverage any tool of their choice to get the job done.

Use the following procedure with Azure CLI to discover the commands you can use to manage container settings using code:

1. Navigate to shell.azure.com in your web browser and start a new Cloud Shell instance.

2. Run the following command to review all of the subcommands available to manage your Azure Container Registry (ACR) instances:

```
az acr --help
```

3. Run the following command to review all of the subcommands available to manage your Azure Container Instances (ACIs):

```
az container --help
```

4. To create a resource, such as an Azure Container Instance (ACI), use the `az container create` command:

```
az container create \
--resource-group Core-Infrastructure \
--name mynodeapp \
--image mynodeapp:latest \
--cpu 1 \
--memory 1
```

5. Once you have an ACI instance running, you can manage the settings and life cycle of the instance using code, as shown in the following command that restarts the instance:

```
az container restart --name mynodeapp
```

EXAM TIP

Microsoft may test your knowledge using performance-based hands-on tasks that need to be completed in the Azure portal. Be prepared to use the Cloud Shell to gain access to Azure CLI or PowerShell, and make sure you understand how to use the help system to discover commands and the appropriate syntax to complete the task.

Create an Azure Container Service (ACS/AKS)

For production-grade applications, Microsoft recommends running containers using the fully managed Azure Kubernetes Service (AKS), making it quick and easy to deploy and manage containerized applications. AKS eliminates the burden of ongoing operations and maintenance required by managing your own Kubernetes deployment. As a hosted service, Azure handles critical Kubernetes tasks like health monitoring and maintenance, and the AKS is free to use. You pay only for the agent nodes within your clusters, not for master nodes controlling your clusters.

Use the following procedure to create an Azure Kubernetes Service (AKS) cluster using the Azure CLI:

1. Navigate to shell.azure.com in your web browser and start a new Cloud Shell instance.

2. Create a new resource group using the following Azure CLI command:

```
az group create \
--name AKS \
--location eastus
```

3. Create a new AKS cluster using the following Azure CLI command:

```
az aks create \
    --resource-group AKS \
    --name AKSCluster01 \
    --node-count 1 \
    --enable-addons monitoring \
    --generate-ssh-keys
```

4. After the AKS cluster has been created, you can connect and manage the cluster from the command line. First, install the AKS CLI inside your cloud shell instance using the following command:

```
az aks install-cli
```

5. Download your AKS credentials and configure the AKS CLI to use them within your shell session:

```
az aks get-credentials \
--resource-group AKS \
--name AKSCluster01
```

6. Verify that your connection to the AKS cluster is working properly by using the kubectl command to retrieve a list of cluster nodes.

```
kubectl get nodes
```

> **NOTE AZURE CONTAINER SERVICE (ACS)**
>
> Prior to releasing the Azure Kubernetes Service (AKS), Microsoft offered the Azure Container Service (ACS) as a managed solution that provided multiple orchestration systems as a service, including Kubernetes, Docker Swarm, and DC/OS. ACS has been deprecated, and existing ACS customers will need to migrate to AKS.

Chapter summary

- Azure App Service gives you the ability to build and host web apps, mobile back ends, and RESTful APIs without having to manage server, network, and storage infrastructure.
- App Service supports applications built using common frameworks such as .NET, .NET Core, Node.js, Java, PHP, Ruby, or Python.
- You can deploy web apps using the Azure portal, CLI, PowerShell, or any of the available SDKs provided by Microsoft.
- App Service supports both Windows and Linux applications, including Docker containers.
- Azure web apps are instances of an App Service that run within an App Service Plan.
- Azure Container Instances have no dependencies on an App Service Plan.
- Azure provides rich support for Docker containers and images can be built and stored in the Azure Container Registry (ACR).

- The Azure Kubernetes Service (AKS) is a fully managed container orchestration system that makes it easier for teams to run containers in production.

Thought experiment

In this thought experiment, demonstrate your skills and knowledge of the topics covered in this chapter. You can find answers to this thought experiment in the next section.

You're an Azure architect for Contoso Ltd. You've been asked to design and implement a solution to run a collection of line-of-business applications in the Azure cloud. Answer the following questions about leveraging Azure App Service to deploy your solution for Contoso.

1. You need to move a web application to Azure that the Human Resources department uses to train corporate employees in the Los Angeles branch office. The web app implements an embedded video player that serves video training content to each user. All videos are produced in the highest possible quality. How should you architect the solution to reduce the latency between the end-users and the application infrastructure?

2. You've been tasked with refactoring an on-premises web application to run inside a Docker container in Azure App Service. You need to ensure that container images can be accessed only by certain members of the IT staff. How can you accomplish this with the least amount of administrative effort?

3. You currently have a nightly task that runs a PowerShell script on an on-premises Windows server. The process generates a report and sends the output to the IT support staff at Contoso headquarters. You need to move this process as part of Contoso's migration to Azure, but you need to do so using the least amount of administrative effort. You already have plans to deploy several websites in Azure App Service. What should you do to run the nightly process in Azure?

Thought experiment answers

This section contains the solution to the thought experiment. Each answer explains why the answer choice is correct.

1. Deploy the App Service infrastructure in a west coast-based Azure region. This will put the infrastructure in close proximity to the users in the Los Angeles branch office. For global applications, consider using the Azure CDN service to distribute static content to edge locations available across the Azure global infrastructure.

2. Deploy an Azure Container Registry (ACR) resource inside your Azure subscription. Disable admin access and delegate control to the ACR resource using Role-Based Access Control (RBAC).

3. Create an Azure WebJob within one of the existing web app resources running in your Azure subscription. Upload the PowerShell script and configure a triggered WebJob that runs on a daily schedule.

## CHAPTER 4

Implement Authentication and Secure Data

You've deployed infrastructure and configured platform as a service (PaaS) applications in many forms, web apps, containers, functions, or logic apps. Running through all of this is your customers' data, which is the most valuable piece of any organizations' digital estate.

Access to this data needs to be controlled using one of the four pillars of great Azure Architecture: Security. As an architect, you need to be keeping security at the heart of any design. It extends through implementation and deployment and is at every stage in the life cycle of the application. In the mindset of a good architect, *security* is not a dirty word!

For the AZ-300 certification exam, you need to understand how to secure access to your applications and how to protect the integrity of the data with security tools like encryption.

> **NEED MORE REVIEW?**   **SECURITY**
>
> You can find the full "Azure security documentation" at *https://docs.microsoft.com/en-us/azure/security*. This documentation includes best practices, which are a must read for any architect.

Skills covered in this chapter:

- Skill 4.1: Implement authentication
- Skill 4.2: Implement secure data solutions

Skill 4.1: Implement authentication

You've deployed applications, but how do you control who or what is accessing those applications? What can you recommend to your customers so that they can ensure their applications are accessed only by users and applications that have been granted access? The answer is that you use the authentication implementations available to you through Azure services. As an architect, you need to be aware of the available choices when you make recommendations, and you need to know how to implement the options.

- Implement authentication by using certificates, forms-based authentication, tokens or Windows-integrated authentication
- Implement Multi-Factor Authentication by using Azure AD
- Implement OAuth2
- Implement Managed Identities for Azure Resources Service Principle authentication

Implement authentication by using certificates, forms-based authentication, tokens or Windows-integrated authentication

Authentication is the process where a user, application, or service trying to gain access is verified as the entity it claims to be, therefore allowing "entry" to the app and its services. Authentication is not the services a user or application can access once access is granted into the application; that is *authorization*.

Azure gives your customers multiple ways of authenticating depending on use case. When you're recommending authentication mechanisms, you need to be aware of how they work and how to configure them.

> **NEED MORE REVIEW?**   **AUTHENTICATING WEB APPS**
>
> To learn about the options available for authentication, visit the Microsoft Docs article "Authentication and authorization in Azure App Service" at *https://docs.microsoft.com/en-us/azure/app-service/overview-authentication-authorization*.

Authentication by certificate—TLS mutual authentication

You can configure an Azure web app or API to require client certificate authentication to enable TLS mutual authentication on an Azure web app or API. When this is enabled, the web app or API requests a certificate from the client application during the SSL handshake. The web app or API then uses the certificate to authenticate the client. This is a form of machine-to-machine authentication that you often see in business-to-business applications; it's a way for a front-end application to securely interact with a back-end service.

Azure App Service doesn't have a direct connection to the internet. It's proxied through other services, so to forward the certificate after SSL termination, the terminating Azure service injects the client certificate as a Base64 encoded value into the HTTP request header. It's this value that is read by the application. So, to use this form of authentication, your customers' web application must contain custom code to read the header and perform the authentication.

To look at configuring TLS mutual authentication for a web application, first follow the SSL Termination walkthrough in Skill 4.2. TLS mutual authentication requires that HTTPS Only is set on the web app; otherwise, the SSL certificate won't be received. Therefore, as in the SSL Termination walkthrough, you need a B1 App Service Plan Tier or higher for SSL support. Once SSL Termination has been set up, complete the following steps to enable authentication by certificate:

1. Navigate to the SSL Settings section on the App Service blade, and set Incoming Client Certificates to On. The change is automatically saved. You can also enable this by using the following command in the Azure command-line interface (CLI):

    ```
    az webapp update --set clientCertEnabled=true --name <app_name> --resource-group
    <group_name>
    ```

2. Open a new browser and enter the app service URL. The browser asks for a client certificate because it's the client interpreting the request from the app server. If you deny the app server a certificate, you receive a 403 Error "Forbidden: Client Certificate Required." If you send a certificate, you're granted access because no further authentication is required.

The same process is used to secure function apps through Networking -> SSL from the Platform Features section of the function app. Other applications, including logic apps, that can present the correct certificate may now access the web app or function app.

> **NEED MORE REVIEW?** **CLIENT CERTIFICATES**
>
> To learn more about enabling client certificates, visit the Microsoft Docs article "Configure TLS mutual authentication for Azure App Service" at *https://docs.microsoft.com/en-us/azure/app-service/app-service-web-configure-tls-mutual-auth#enable-client-certificates*.

Forms-based authentication

A legacy form of authentication is forms-based authentication. You may have come across this when you've been looking to rearchitect legacy on-premises applications to the cloud. This method of authentication has an HTML-based web form, which means it must be viewed and filled in on a browser. Therefore, the use case for this authentication is purely user intervention login; the user fills in information on the form, normally a username and password to authenticate against. One of the advantages to using this method was that the user didn't have to be part of the domain to authenticate because the authentication process could be performed against a username and password stored within a database. Figure 4-1 shows the general flow of forms-based authentication, which works like so:

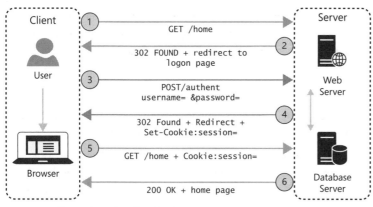

FIGURE 4-1 Forms-based authentication process

1. The user opens a website, and the browser requests a page that requires authentication.

2. The web server receives the request and serves a page with the login form.

3. The user enters credentials and submits them to the form. The form posts the credentials to the web server (in plaintext).

4. The web server authenticates the customer against the data stored in the database. If the information is correct, the user is redirected back to the application entry page with a session cookie.

5. The browser sends the session cookie to receive the original resource requested in step 1.

6. The server grants the request because it includes the authentication cookie. The server serves the page and resources.

There are security issues with this implementation that you need to be aware of when you're determining whether to rearchitect or lift directly into the cloud:

- The credentials are sent as plaintext. You must be securing any traffic to this site with HTTPS, although this is always best practice.

- The credentials are stored in a database. If the database uses poor encryption or no encryption of the passwords, the data is susceptible to attack. Encrypt the passwords with strong, salted encryption.

- Forms use cookies that are vulnerable to cross-site request forgery (CSRF). In CSRF, a rogue site uses a cookie stored on a machine to influence the site that created the cookie to perform an action of which the user is not aware. If the user is an administrator of the site, this could allow the attacker to gain control of the site. This is mitigated using antiforgery techniques that must be coded into the application to create further security tokens to verify the source of requests.

The Azure Web Application Gateway, previously covered in Chapter 2, Skill 2.3 "Implement application load balancing" has a web application firewall. This firewall contains cross-site scripting protection, so it also provides protection against CSRF if you placed it in front of the web application.

EXAM TIP

Knowing how to set up forms-based authentication using .NET or any other language is beyond the scope of the exam. However, understanding the concepts of how it works, why it is used, and how to mitigate the security concerns around it is important.

Application authentication with Azure AD

As mentioned earlier, forms-based authentication is a legacy mechanism. Where possible, you need to recommend that your customers move to modern, secure authentication.

You can see such a mechanism when you log into the portal. To the user, this login looks like the same functionality as web forms; however, the login uses Azure AD as the back end. This method, where Azure AD authenticates the user and grants access to the portal, can be extended to your customers' applications.

To set this up, you need to register an application with Azure AD and then use this registration on the web app to perform the authentication for you. To explore how this works, follow these steps:

1. Using knowledge from previous chapters in this book, create a web app service. Select to publish a Docker Image of Quickstart and Sample of Python Hello World on the app service. Note that on the lower tiers, the container can take a while to pull down. Enter **Container Settings** on the app blade to check the log for progress.

> **NOTE   APP SERVICE TIER**
>
> If you're planning to use authentication via Azure AD for your app, you have to be using HTTPS. Therefore, if you're using a custom domain, you need your SSL bindings set (see Skill 4.2 "SSL/TLS") and at least a B1 App Service Plan.

2. Copy the web app URL from the Overview section of the Web App blade. Save the URL for later.

3. Navigate to Azure Active Directory, select App Registration, and select New Registration. Fill in the following information:

   A. **Name**   Enter a name that will make the app easily identifiable to you and any users.

   B. **Account Types**   If you're developing an internal-use app, choose this organizational directory only. Use Any Organizational Directory for internal use and guests within any Azure AD. The final choice, Accounts In Any Organizational Directory and Personal Microsoft accounts, allows you to also include any Microsoft personal accounts (Skype and so on).

   C. Ignore the Redirect URI for now.

   Click Register to save the application definition into Azure AD. You now need to define how the service will use it.

4. The application is listed in the app registrations page. Click the one you just created. You need to set up the link to the web app by doing the following:

   A. Click Branding on the app registration blade, and paste the URL you copied in step 2 into the Home Page URL field. Click Save. Here you're setting up the URL for the home page of your web app.

   B. Click Authentication. Under Redirect URIs, make sure Web is selected as the Type, and paste the URL from step 2 into the Redirect URL but add `/.auth/login/aad/callback` to the end. It should look like this:
      `https://<webappname>.<domainname> /.auth/login/aad/callback`

   Click Save. Here you're establishing that you want to send the authentication information back to the page your user logged in from.

   C. Select the box for ID Tokens. This is only required in this example because we're using a single-page application with no back end to accept the authorization information. Otherwise the authentication of the application will return an error message. Click Save.

5. You need to copy some values so that you can point your web app to authenticate using this application registration.

   A. In the App Registrations blade, choose Quickstarts. Copy the Application (client) Id from App properties on the right. Keep this for later use; it uniquely identifies your application.

   B. In the App Registrations blade, choose Overview and then Endpoints, copy the WS-Federation Sign-on Endpoint and save this for later use. This endpoint allows the authentication information to be stored in the session.

6. You're ready to configure your web app. Navigate to it in the portal and choose Authentication/Authorization to enable it, but you need to configure it to use Azure AD:

   A. In the Action To Take When Request Is Not Authenticated drop-down menu, choose Log In With Azure Active Directory.

   B. Select Azure Active Directory under Authentication Providers, and in Management mode choose Advanced.

   C. Paste the Application client ID you saved in step 5a into the Client ID.

   D. Paste the WS-Federation Endpoint URL from step 5b into the Issuer URL field, but remove /wsfed from the end. This is pointing the web app at the Single Sign-On URL for your Azure AD.

   E. Click OK to save the Active Directory Authentication settings, and then click Save on the Authentication/Authorization settings.

7. Open a new private browsing window to ensure you're not logged in and navigate to your web app URL. You can authenticate with any user from the Azure AD you registered the app to and be authenticated to the Hello World page.

> *NEED MORE REVIEW?* **APP REGISTRATION AND AUTHENTICATION**
>
> To learn more about enabling web app authentication through Azure AD, visit the Microsoft Docs article "Register an application with the Microsoft identity platform" at *https://docs.microsoft.com/en-us/azure/active-directory/develop/quickstart-register-app*. Then check out "Configure a client application to access web APIs" in the "Next steps" section on the same page.

Tokens

In the walkthrough of the previous section for web application authorization with Azure AD, you registered an application for authentication. This process registers the app with the Microsoft identity platform. Microsoft identity platform is an identity provider that verifies the identity of users and applications against an organization's directory. Once the identity platform has successfully authenticated a user or application, it issues security tokens back to the calling application. The calling application must then validate the tokens to ensure authentication was successful. These tokens are the refresh token from Azure AD, which is returned on authentication, and the access token from the application, which verifies the user's access to the application.

Once tokens are returned to the web app, the App Service Token Store automatically collects and stores the tokens to make it easy for the application to access them by making them available in the request header for back-end code or by sending a GET request to the authentication endpoint. If your customer doesn't need to do anything with the tokens once the user is authenticated, you can turn off the token store. Continuing with the earlier example, use the following steps to turn off the store:

1. Navigate to the app in the portal and choose Authentication/Authorization, and then scroll to the bottom of the page.

2. On Advanced Settings, set Token Store to Off.

3. Execute the authentication URL once more, and the token is no longer on the address bar.

Integrated Windows Authentication (IWA)

On-premises web applications often leverage Windows Active Directory (AD) as a user store, authenticating a user's login using Active Directory. The web servers can be configured to use Single Sign-On, which is when the user signs into the client once, and the credentials are sent silently to the web application to use for authentication so that the user does not need to sign in again. This is Integrated Windows Authentication (IWA), and it can be achieved with Window AD configured to use NTLM or Kerberos.

One of the issues with this authentication implementation is the client must be able to complete part of the authentication process by communicating with the IdentityServer, in this case Windows AD. Therefore, the client needs to be on the domain. However, with applications moving to the cloud and remote work becoming more common, this isn't always possible. In this scenario, as new applications are written or migrated, you should recommend hybrid identity management so that authentication and authorization of users is available wherever they are located.

You explored configuring Azure AD Connect in Chapter 1, Skill 1.9 "Implement and manage hybrid identities," including the User Sign-In screen shown in Figure 4-2. (Note this is from the edit screen of AD Connect configuration rather than the setup screen.)

FIGURE 4-2 Hybrid identities and sign-on options

Note now the Enable Single Sign-On check box at the bottom of the page. If this is selected and Password Synchronization or Pass Through Authentication is also selected, with some more configuration steps, single sign-on capabilities of IWA can be available to your customers' applications in the cloud.

Implement Multi-Factor Authentication by using Azure AD

The previous section explains using Azure AD to provide the authentication mechanism for a web app. When you set up an account type in step 3 of the section "Application authentication with Azure AD", you selected the value Any Organizational Directory. Selecting this setting means any user in the entire directory can be authenticated. Even for a line-of-business application, granting access to every user in the directory is unlikely. Therefore, you need to be able to educate your customers on how to grant access to their applications only to the users that require it. You can achieve this by looking at the Enterprise Applications settings in Azure AD using the following steps:

1. Follow the web app and app registration configured for "Application authentication with Azure AD" in the previous section, or use the web app created from the same section.

2. Navigate to Azure AD and select Enterprise Applications in the AD blade. Click the application you registered in step 1.

3. Choose properties on the Web Apps Enterprise Application blade, change the value on User Assignment Required to Yes, and click Save.

4. In a private browsing window, open the URL to the web app you created in step 1 and sign in as any user from the directory. You see a 401 access denied error; this confirms that the user assignment required setting is functioning correctly.

5. Go back to the Web Applications Enterprise Application blade, and select Users and groups. This is where you can assign users and groups access to the application. Click Add User at the top to open the Add Assignment wizard. Select Users on the left, and then select the user(s) you'd like to grant access to. Click Select at the bottom when all users have been chosen. Click Assign, and the selected users are assigned access to the application.

6. In a private browsing window, navigate back to the web app you created in step 1. Log in with one of the users you selected in step 5 to be authenticated.

Your customers may want to enable users who are outside their organization or users with specific rights on the web application to authenticate by using extra security measures. When architecting such a solution, Microsoft recommends you use conditional access policies and authenticate with Multi-Factor Authentication. Conditional access gives your customers the ability to enforce access requirements when a specific set of conditions occurs. The remaining steps in this section go through how this works for a web application.

EXAM TIP

Don't forget you need an Azure AD premium subscription P2 or P1 to take advantage of conditional access.

For this part of the walkthrough, you need two users in Azure AD: one in a group and one in a different group.

1. If you don't have a group set up, navigate to Azure AD in the portal, select Groups in the blade, and then select New Group. The group type is a Security Group because you're using it to set up a security-related feature. Enter an appropriate Group Name and Group Description; the Membership Type must be Assigned. Click Members, select the members to assign to your group, click Select, and then click Create.

2. Navigate back to Azure AD and Enterprise Applications on the Azure AD blade; select the web app you registered in step 1. In the Web App Enterprise Application blade, select Conditional Access. Following are the requirements to enforce MFA for a Group:

   A. Select Add New Policy at the top.

   B. In Name, use something relevant to the Access Policy being defined.

   C. Click Users and Groups, select to Include Select users and groups, and select the Users and Groups check box. Click Select; then select the Group created in step 1 of this section. Click Select, and then click Done.

   D. You entered Conditional Access through the web app in Enterprise Applications, so the app is already selected in Cloud Apps or Actions. If it was not, select Apps, and then click Select; select the app, click Select, and then click Done.

   E. For this use case, you want every user in the admin group to use MFA, regardless of how they log in, so skip over Conditions.

   F. Select Access Controls, click Grant Access, and then select Require Multi-Factor Authentication. Click Select.

   G. Click Enable Policy and click Save.

3. Configuration for MFA is complete. Now you can test MFA on the created group. Open a private browsing window and enter the URL of your web app to log in as a user who was not placed in the group. You'll be logged in to the web app and see the Hello World page.

4. Open another private browsing window. This time, log in to the web app as the user in the group assigned in step 2c of this section. You're asked to fill in the additional security verification shown in Figure 4-3.

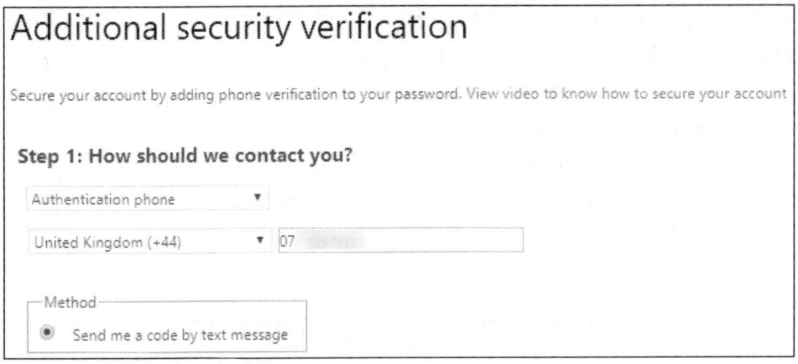

Additional security verification

Secure your account by adding phone verification to your password. View video to know how to secure your account

Step 1: How should we contact you?

Authentication phone ▼

United Kingdom (+44) ▼ | 07

┌─ Method ─────────────────────
│ ⦿ Send me a code by text message

FIGURE 4-3 Multi-Factor Authentication additional security

5. Select the country you're in and enter your mobile number. Once this is completed, you receive a text on your mobile phone to verify the phone is accessible to you. Future logins for this user will always require a code be sent to this phone number (see Figure 4-4).

■■ Microsoft

for   @   .onmicrosoft.com

Enter code

💬 We texted your phone +XX XXXXXXXXX .
    Please enter the code to sign in.

Code

FIGURE 4-4 Entering a security code to verify the mobile phone is accessible

You can check that MFA is being enforced only for the application by logging the same user into the Azure Portal. The MFA code is not requested.

6. If the user switches phone numbers, the number needs to be reset. To enforce this, enter Azure AD in the portal, select Users, select the user you added to the group. In the User blade, select Authentication Methods. Here you can change the user's phone number, or select Require Re-Register MFA. Re-registering sends the user back through the security validation process, and the person can change his or her own phone number. Also note the Revoke MFA Sessions option, which expires the user's refresh tokens so he or she is required to complete an MFA log on the next attempt to log in.

Now the Admin group is secured, it's time to require MFA for your application for anyone outside the organization's network. To do this, you need to set up a named location in Conditional Access. First, you need to set up a named location by following these steps:

1. In the portal, enter Azure AD and click Security in the Azure AD blade. In the Security blade, click Conditional Access and Named Locations. Complete the following fields:

    A. **Name**   Enter a name for your organization.

    B. **Location**   Here you could set up a named location for countries or region, which you could use to deny access to that region.

    C. **IP Ranges**   Add your static IP address ranges. Note that this uses CIDR notation.

2. Click Create.

Now you're ready to configure a location-based conditional access policy. Follow these steps to create the configuration:

1. Select Add New Policy.

2. In Name, enter something relevant to the Access Policy you're defining.

3. Click Users And Groups. Select Include Select Users And Groups and then select the Users And Groups check box. Click Select, and then select the user not in the group earlier in this example. Click Select, and then click Done.

4. You entered Conditional Access through the web app in Enterprise Applications, so the app is already selected in Cloud Apps or actions. If it wasn't, select Apps, and then click Select and select the app. Click Select, and then click Done.

5. For this use case, you want every user outside of the corporate network to log in using MFA, so select Conditions and then click Locations. Click Yes to enable this feature, and then click Exclude because you want to exclude the corporate network. Select the locations, click Select, and select the named location you created earlier. In this example, it's named "My Office." Click Select, and then click Done.

You also see trusted IPs listed in the named location. You could add your IP range to the trusted IPs (by selecting Azure AD > Security > MFA); however, this has further implications to security beyond just this application.

The other conditions available to select are:

- **Sign In Risk**   Azure calculates the likelihood that a sign in isn't coming from the owner of the account.

- **Device Platforms**   You can select mobile platforms here to force MFA from a mobile device.

- **Device State**   You can use this to enforce MFA on unmanaged devices.

EXAM TIP

Know the conditions that can be applied to a Conditional Access Policy. Check out the Need More Review documentation for a deeper dive into these.

---

6. Select Access Controls. Click Grant Access and select Require Multi-Factor Authentication. Click Select.

7. Click Enable Policy and click Save.

8. The configuration of a location-based conditional access policy is now complete. You can see an example of this configuration in Figure 4-5. You need to test to make sure it's functioning correctly. Using the user that was not placed in the group earlier in this example, log in to your application using a browser that is accessing from the IP you added to the address range. You're logged in without MFA because you're accessing from the excluded IP. Now try the same thing on your phone on a cellular network, and you're asked for your MFA code. Finally, log in as the user you added to the web app admins group earlier in the example from your excluded IP range. MFA is still triggered because of the group conditional access policy.

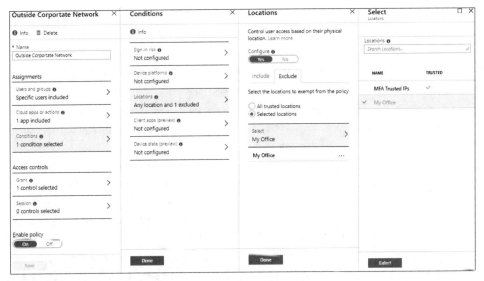

FIGURE 4-5 Location-based conditional access configuration

> **NOTE CONDITIONAL ACCESS**
>
> Here we've covered conditional access of a web app hosted in Azure. The process is identical for on-premise applications published through Application Proxy.

> **NEED MORE REVIEW? IMPLEMENT MFA WITH AZURE AD**
>
> To learn more about enabling MFA for a web application through Azure AD, visit the Microsoft Docs article "Require MFA for specific apps with Azure Active Directory conditional access" at *https://docs.microsoft.com/en-us/azure/active-directory/conditional-access/app-based-mfa*. Also see the generic conditional access documentation at *https://docs.microsoft.com/en-us /azure/active-directory/conditional-access/*.

Implement OAuth 2.0

You may have heard OAuth being discussed in the same breath as authentication. However, OAuth 2.0 is not an authentication protocol, although it's a common misconception that it is. OAuth is an authorization protocol that's used in tandem with authentication protocols. Here's an example of the differences using a real-world example of checking in to take a flight:

- **Authentication** You go to the check-in desk, you hand over your passport, and the check-in officer verifies your identity against the passport because it's a trusted document. It doesn't say whether you can fly or not, but it proves you are who you say you are.

- **Authorization**   You also hand over your flight ticket or proof of booking. At this point, the combination of the passport and ticket enables the check-in officer to authorize you have the correct permissions to go on the flight. The check-in officer hands you a boarding pass, which is your proof of authorization for the flight.

If we map the flight example to a solution, we could have authentication by an authentication protocol such as OpenId. OpenId is an extension of OAuth, and it provides identity information as part of an ID token (id_token). It's this identity information that is the extension; OAuth has no method for this in its definition. In the walkthrough for the section "Application authentication for Azure AD," the authentication endpoint selected was WS-Federation. However, you could have chosen the OpenId endpoint. The additional identity information is sent in the form of claims. Key value pairs present in the ID Token such as email or name.

Going back to the flight example, OAuth would check whether you can have access to the flight (resource), by validating the id_token and checking against the booking (permissions, dependent on resource type). It would verify authorization when you hand over a boarding pass (access token), so that you may board your flight (access your resource). There is also the scope of the access. In other words, what does the token grant you access to in the resource? In the context of the example, this could be first-class or economy seating.

It's important that solution architects understand the differences between these protocols and how they are implemented. Microsoft identity platform enables the implementation of OpenId and OAuth to allow your customer's developers to authenticate using many identities, including Azure AD work and school accounts, personal Microsoft accounts (Xbox, Outlook, and so on) and social accounts such as Facebook or GitHub. The identity platform returns access tokens in the form of JSON Web Tokens (JWTs), these are also known as "bearer tokens" because the bearer of the token is granted access.

OAuth authorization is implemented using "flows." There are different flows depending on the client type and what the application they are accessing needs to achieve:

- **Implicit Grant Flow**   Browser-based client accessing a single-page application, such as a JavaScript application.
- **Authorization Code Flow**   Application installed on a device—either mobile or desktop—that requires access to resources such as Web APIs.
- **Client Credentials Grant**   Server-to-server communications happening in the background and utilizing service accounts or daemons.
- **On-Behalf-Of (OBO) Flow**   An application calls a web service that invokes another web service. The first web service gets consent to use the second web service on behalf of the user.

Figure 4-6 shows the flow of access requests and tokens between the client, APIs, and the Microsoft identity platform.

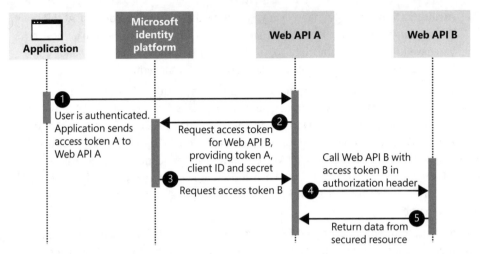

FIGURE 4-6 On-Behalf-Of flow

Instead of talking through this, we're showing you how to set it up using a function app and Microsoft graph. We note where each part of the flow occurs based on the numbered circles in Figure 4-6:

1. Create an Azure Function using the instructions from Chapter 2, Skill 2.2 "Configure Serverless Computing." Select a windows function running PowerShell. Create a new quickstart function, select In-Portal Editing, and then select Webhook+API. Test that the function app is functioning correctly from a browser before you continue.

2. Follow steps 2 through 7 from the section "Application Authentication with Azure AD" earlier in this skill and secure the function app against a directory. For steps 5 and 6 of this same section, use the OpenId endpoint, rather than WS-Federation. While in the App Registration Endpoint, copy the OAuth 2.0 token endpoint (v2) for use later. Note that Authentication/Authorization for a function app is under Platform Features. Test that the function app is functioning correctly with authentication from a browser before continuing.

   This is Circle 1 in Figure 4-6. The user is authenticated, and you have an id_token to send, but you can't see it yet.

3. In the app registration blade, select Certificates & Secrets, click New Client Secret, enter an appropriate description and an expiry of 2 years, and click OK. You have created this for the flow; it requires an application to prove its identity using a Client ID and Client Secret. Copy the Client Secret and paste it into the AD Authentication configuration in the Function App Authentication/Authorization Client Secret (Optional) field. Click OK to save the change.

4. Go to Azure AD in the portal and navigate to the App Registration for the function app created in step 1 of this walkthrough. Click View API Permissions from the Overview in the App Registration blade:

   A. Select to Add a permission.

   B. Select Microsoft Graph at the top.

C. Select Delegated Permissions and then select On Behalf Of, Access API As Signed In User. Note here the Application Permissions option would be used in the Client Credentials Grant Flow.

D. Scroll to the bottom, select User Permission and User.Read. This is the scope. The API requires read access to the user record.

E. Select Add Permissions. Permissions are added and you are returned to the API permissions.

5. Run the function app from a browser once more, and you see a second page after the authentication login as in Figure 4-7.

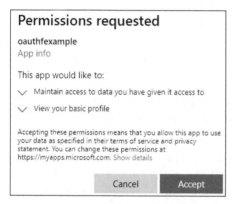

FIGURE 4-7 Consenting for an application to use a secured resource

Click Accept to grant the function app consent to use the permissions listed on your behalf. This consent stays in place until either the user or admin revokes it. The function app should still work correctly once consent is given.

6. Go back to the function app and edit the function code to call the Microsoft Graph API by doing the following:

A. Delete everything from between

```
Write-Host "PowerShell HTTP trigger function processed a request."
```

to

```
# Associate values to output bindings by calling 'Push-OutputBinding'.
```

B. Paste in this code under the Write-Host:

```
$status = [HttpStatusCode]::OK
$aadToken = $Request.headers['x-ms-token-aad-id-token']
```

The first line sets up a 200 OK parameter to return at the end. The second line is part of Circle 1 from Figure 4-6. The Token Store of the function app (refer to the "Tokens" section from this skill) contains your id_token. It's been injected into the header so you can pick it up for use here.

C. Paste in the next bit of code. You need the tenantId taken from the OAuth 2.0 token endpoint from step 2:

```
$uri = "https://login.microsoftonline.com/<tenantid>/oauth2/v2.0/token"
# Body required for on behalf of flow
$body = @{
    client_id            = "$env:WEBSITE_AUTH_CLIENT_ID"
    assertion            = $aadToken
    scope                = "https://graph.microsoft.com/user.read"
    requested_token_use  = "on_behalf_of"
    client_secret        = "$env:WEBSITE_AUTH_CLIENT_SECRET"
    grant_type           =
"urn:ietf:params:oauth:grant-type:jwt-bearer"
}
# Get OAuth 2.0 access and refresh tokens with user.read scope for microsoft graph
$tokenRequest = Invoke-WebRequest -Method Post -Uri $uri -ContentType
"application/x-www-form-urlencoded" -Body $body
$token = ($tokenRequest.Content | ConvertFrom-Json).access_token
```

Following this code through, you're setting up a web POST using the Client ID, Client Secret, and id_token from the authorization, stating that the request is for the On-Behalf-Of flow and the token being sent is of type JWT Bearer. The POST is invoked and the access token for the scope Microsoft Graph user.read is stored. See Circle 2 and Circle 3 from Figure 4-6.

D. Paste the final section of code:

```
# Pass the authorization token to graph
$graphResp = Invoke-RestMethod -ContentType "application/json" -Headers
@{Authorization = "Bearer $token"} `
                -Uri  https://graph.microsoft.com/v1.0/me `
                -Method Get
```

This invokes a RESTful call to the Microsoft Graph API to send the Bearer token on the Header. The /me returns user information for the logged in user. This is Circle 4 and Circle 5 from Figure 4-6.

E. Change the OutputBinding Body to the Graph API response:

```
Body = $graphResp
```

7. Run the function app in a browser once more, you'll see the JSON for the user record of the logged in user as shown in Figure 4-8. This is the full On-Behalf-Of flow in action.

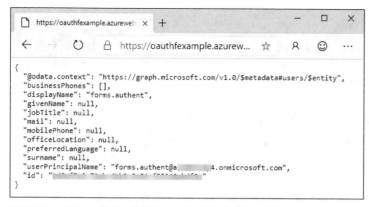

FIGURE 4-8 Microsoft Graph API metadata for the logged in user

8. Now you can revoke the permission for access. Here you are revoking the token. The user must grant their consent once more before the function app can access Microsoft Graph on behalf of the user. Login to *https://myapps.microsoft.com* as the user who was running the function app and had consented to the permission request. Right click on the ellipses next to the app's name, and select Remove as shown in Figure 4-9.

FIGURE 4-9 Revoking consent for an application

This will expire the access token and revoke the consent given by the user.

> **NOTE VALIDATING THE TOKENS**
>
> The example given here doesn't validate the JWT tokens after they're returned. You should be ensuring your customer's developers are validating tokens against the signature on return to make sure they were issued by the correct identity provider. This is best practice, along with validating some claims within the token—in particular the audience's claim to ensure that the ID token was meant to be used by your customer's application.

Protecting an API with Azure API Management and OAuth 2.0

You have explored the methods to secure calls between APIs, web apps, and devices using OAuth 2.0. However, these have been predominantly geared to interactions between your customer's products. What if you need to architect a solution that requires APIs to be accessed externally? For this, you could recommend Azure API Management rather than exposing the APIs directly.

Azure API Management is a service that sits between back-end services (APIs) and the applications that call them. The Azure API Management service at its basic level is a proxy. It enables organizations to securely publish APIs internally and to partners or other third parties that want to leverage their data through the API gateway. The combination of the API gateway and developer and admin portals delivers the following features:

- Onboard developers with a portal that can be branded
- Response caching for performance
- Protects APIs from misuse with security verifying tokens, certificates, and other credentials
- Protects APIs from abuse by throttling using rate limits and quotas
- Gives usage metrics for each API to the owners of the managed APIs and the developers subscribed to them
- Allows on-premise use of the APIs, custom APIs in Azure, or third-party APIs

Open, standardized data exchange is a key component to enabling digital business, and solution architects need to know the services available to deliver this and how to configure them. API management is crossing the blurred line between architecting a solution and developing one. However, as mentioned previously, a good architect will have some development skills as part of their armory.

To explore using API management to secure an API using Azure AD and OAuth 2.0, you need to create an API and an API management instance, and then you configure the app to be protected by the instance. The following example looks at this using an Azure logic app because logic apps have integration built in to API Management:

1. Create a logic app in the portal using the guidance from Chapter 2, Skill 2.2 "Configure Serverless Computing." In this case, it doesn't matter what your logic app does, but it needs to be triggered from an HTTP POST and return a response, so you can test it.

2. Create an API Management Instance. Search for API Management in the portal and click OK. You should see API management services.

   A. Click Add; add a name for the Management Service.

   B. Select your Subscription, Resource Group, and Location.

C. Enter your Organization Name. This is used on the developer portal and in email notifications—for example, notification to a developer that their quota is nearly exhausted.

D. Enter the Administrator Email. This is the email address that will receive any system notifications.

E. Select a Pricing Tier. Note you can't use Basic or Consumption because they have no Azure AD integration, which is required in this walkthrough.

F. Click Create. When the service is ready to go, the admin email designated in step 2d receives an email.

3. Let's have a quick look at products in the API Management service. Products contain APIs with quota definitions and terms of use. You aren't going to edit any of these; you're just getting a grasp of what API Management has to offer:

A. In the API Management Service blade of the API Management service created in step 2, click Products, and then click Starter. In Settings, look at the Requires Subscription check box. When checked, this forces a developer to subscribe before the product and its APIs can be used. The state must be published before APIs in a product can be called.

B. It lists the APIs in the Starter product.

C. In Policies you see a limit of 5 calls every 60 seconds and 100 calls total in a week. This is for the product Starter.

D. Access control is where you can add groups that are created in the Users And Groups section of the API Management blade.

E. Subscriptions are required if a subscription key is needed to access an API.

4. Now publish an API using the API Management service:

A. Select the API Management service created and then select APIs in the Management Service blade.

B. Here you select what type of API to add. There's obviously tight integration to Azure services, so you can select logic app, API app, or function app directly. For other external services, you can pick one of the others as appropriate. Note the Echo API on the left. This is used to create an API which echoes back the response headers and body, which is useful if your back-end API isn't quite ready, and you need to test. Select Logic App.

C. Click Browse to find the logic app you created in step 1 and select it. The first three lines of the form are auto populated. Set the URL Suffix to a relevant suffix and in the Product select Starter, the product you explored in step 3a. Click Create. The logic app is ingested.

5. Your API is listed under APIs on the API Management Service blade. You now need to check that the response is returned correctly:

A. Click Test, select POST manual-invoke, and scroll down. Take a copy of the Request URL.

B. Open PowerShell and execute the following command to call the API, ensuring you are not logged into the Azure AD account that owns the API Management service (or use Postman/equivalent):

```
invoke-webrequest -method Post -uri "<Request URL from Step 5a>"
```

C. An error is returned because there is no subscription key because this is an anonymous request:

```
invoke-webrequest : { "statusCode": 401, "message": "Access denied due to
missing subscription key. Make sure to include subscription key when making
requests to an API." }
```

D. You're not going to secure this API using subscriptions because you're going to secure with Azure AD and OAuth 2.0. Go back to the Test tab, but this time select Settings to the left of it, scroll down and unmark Subscription Required. Click Save and try the call once more. You see a 200 OK response with the logic app response in Content.

6. You now have the building blocks in place to protect the logic app API with Azure AD. To protect any app or API with secure AD, the app or API needs to be registered. Navigate to Azure Active Directory and select App Registration, and then select New Registration:

   A. Enter a Name that will make the app easily identifiable to yourself and any users for the back-end API.

   B. Select Account Types – Any Organizational Directory because it's a good fit for internal use and guests within any Azure AD.

   C. Ignore the Redirect URI for now. Click Register.

   D. Copy the Application ID from the newly registered app's Overview and save for later use.

7. Now you need to expose this application as an API. This will allow you to grant delegated permissions to it:

   A. Select the app registration you created earlier and select Expose An API in the blade.

   B. Select Add A Scope.

   C. In Scope name, enter App.Read. This is the scope of the permission.

   D. In Who Can Consent, select Admins And Users. Admins can consent for the tenant; users can consent for themselves.

   E. In Admin Consent Display Name And Description, put Application Read And Return Response.

   F. The Status should be Enabled. Click Add Scope.

8. All client applications that use your API are registered against Azure AD. Rather than building another application, you can test this using the API Developer portal.

   A. Register another application. This time, put the URL to your APIs development portal as the Redirect URL: *https://<apiname>.developer.azure-api.net/signin*.

   B. Click Register and copy the Application ID for the client application registration from its Overview page.

C. Staying in the new App Registrations blade, select Certificates And Secrets and generate a New Client Secret. Keep a copy of this for later use.

D. Again staying in the App Registrations blade select API permissions. Select Add a permission, then My APIs. Select the back-end API registration created in steps 6 and 7 of this walkthrough. Select Delegated Permissions and select App.Read. Click Add Permission.

9. While in the app registrations section of the Azure AD blade, select Endpoints and note the authorization and token endpoint for OAuth 2.0 v1. Also note the OpenId Endpoint. You'll need these to set up OAuth Authorization and Authentication validation.

10. Your app registrations are now in place, so you need to join the dots with an OAuth Server in the API Management Service:

A. Navigate to the API Management Service you created in Step 2. Click OAuth 2.0 in the Management blade. Click Add.

B. In the Display name, select a relevant name for the OAuth2 service. Note that this auto populates ID.

C. For the client registration page URL, you can use any URL because no users will be registering their own accounts for OAuth2 for this example. Enter **http://localhost**.

D. Select Authorization Code Grant Type. This corresponds to the grant types listed in how OAuth2 works at the beginning of the OAuth 2.0 section of this Skill.

E. In the Authorization Endpoint URL, paste in the OAuth 2.0 authorization endpoint you copied in step 9 of this walkthrough.

F. The API is stateless, so you don't require a state parameter. Leave the authorization request method as Get.

G. In the Token Endpoint URL, paste in the OAuth 2.0 token endpoint copied in step 9 of this walkthrough.

H. Scroll down to Client Credentials, paste the Application ID from the back-end app registration in step 8b to Client ID and the Secret from step 8c of this walkthrough to Client Secret.

I. Copy the redirect_uri (it's grayed out) by selecting the box and pressing Ctrl + C. Save this for later.

J. Click Create.

11. Navigate back to the app registration created in step 8 of this walkthrough, select Authentication on the App Registration blade, and overwrite the Redirect URI with the URL copied in step 10i. Click Save.

12. Navigate back to the API Management Service you created in step 2 of this walkthrough. Select APIs in the blade and pick the logic app API created in step 4 of this walkthrough. Click Settings at the top then scroll down to Security. In User Authorization, select OAuth 2.0 and then the server created in step 10 of this walkthrough. Click Save.

13. Now call the API once more as in step 5b of this walkthrough. The API returns 200 OK and the Content is the response. Why is this when you haven't obtained an id_token or logged in to an app? The OAuth 2.0 configuration is performing correctly, but at the moment the token (or lack of token) is not being checked; therefore, the call proceeds successfully. To preauthorize a request in API management, you need to add a policy named validate-jwt to the inbound policy section of the API:

   A. Navigate back to the API Management Service you created in step 2 of this walkthrough. Select APIs in the blade, and pick the logic app API created in step 4 of this walkthrough.

   B. Click Design, and then select Add Policy in the Inbound Processing section.

   C. Select Other Policies. Paste this into the inbound policy directly under <inbound> and above <base/>; do not overwrite any other text that may be present between these two tags. Note that you need to replace the back-end App ID and OpenID endpoints into this code block:

   ```
   <inbound>
           <validate-jwt header-name="Authorization" failed-validation-
   httpcode="401" failed-validation-error-message="Unauthorized. Access token is
   missing or invalid.">
               <openid-config url="<OpenID Endpoint>" />
               <issuers>
                   <issuer>https://sts.windows.net/<TenantId from OpenId
   Endpoint>/</issuer>
               </issuers>
               <required-claims>
                   <claim name="appid">
                       <value><Client Application Id - Step 8 ></value>
                   </claim>
               </required-claims>
           </validate-jwt>
   ```

   D. Staying in the inbound policy configuration section, logic apps cannot handle the Authorization header and error with "The request must be authenticated only by Shared Access Scheme." To mitigate this, you need to strip it from the header, and add a line above </inbound>:

   ```
   <set-header name="Authorization" exists-action="delete" />
   ```

14. Retest the API call using PowerShell. You'll receive a 401 Unauthorized message; the protection is now working correctly. To test this further, click Developer Portal at the top of the APIs part of the API Management service. The developer portal opens, and you're already logged in as your user (authentication complete with token in the header). Now call the API:

   A. Select APIs at the top.

   B. Select the name of the API you published in step 4 of this walkthrough.

   C. Before clicking Try It, note that the portal has picked up the Authorization request header with the OAuth 2.0 access token.

D. Scroll to the bottom of the page, and click Send. The response is still Unauthorized. Scroll up and look at the Authorization section. You see the name of your OAuth 2.0 server from step 10 of this walkthrough and next to it the choice of No Auth. Change this to Authorization Code; a permissions request will display because this application requires you use the permission to access your API with App.Read and Graph API. If you recall, this was the scope created in step 7 of this walkthrough. Click Accept. The 200 OK Message and content and other metadata displays.

> **NEED MORE REVIEW?** **PROTECTING AN API WITH OAUTH**
>
> For more on protecting APIs using OAuth 2.0 and API Management, read "Protect an API by using OAuth 2.0 with Azure Active Directory and API Management" at *https://docs.microsoft. com/en-us/azure/api-management/api-management-howto-protect-backend-with-aad.*

EXAM TIP

Understanding that Azure AD Authentication is available only in certain API Management pricing tiers and having a general grasp of the core features of API Management is good to know. The best practice of validating the JWT token, whether in API Management or a custom application, may also prove useful.

Implement managed identities for Azure resources service principle authentication

One of the issues we face when architecting solutions is managing the credentials that are required when integrating Azure resources. Ideally, the solutions being architected should not have credentials out in the open, and developers should not have access to them. Managed identities for Azure resources (formerly Managed Service Identity or MSI) provides this feature, authenticating Azure services through Azure AD using an automatically managed identity. This managed identity can be used to authenticate any service that supports Azure AD, and once the identity is assigned, authorized actions can be performed against this service without having to store credentials in the code. Architects need to understand how this works and how it's configured.

There are two types of managed identity: system and user. Let's look at system-assigned managed identity first.

When you enable a system-assigned identity on an Azure service, Azure AD creates an AD identity and then creates a service principal that can be used to represent the service for Access Control, Access Policies, and Role-Based Access Control (RBAC)—whichever is supported by the Azure service. If you delete the Azure resource, the identity is automatically deleted; it's required only for the lifetime of the resource. To see this in action, set up a blob to be read and output by an Azure function by completing the following steps:

1. Create a storage account with a publicly accessible blob container following the guidance from Chapter 1, Skill 1.2 "Create and configure storage accounts." Upload a text file with a simple sentence in it to the container and copy the blob URL to this file for later use. Check that the URL returns the file by opening it in a browser.

2. Create an Azure Function following the instructions from Chapter 2, Skill 2.2 "Configure serverless computing." On creation, select a windows function running PowerShell. Create a new quickstart function and select In-Portal Editing and then Webhook+API.

3. Edit the function to the following by pasting your blob URL from step 1 of this walkthrough into $blobURL=:

```
using namespace System.Net
# Input bindings are passed in via param block.
param($Request, $TriggerMetadata)
# Write to the Azure Functions log stream.
Write-Host "PowerShell HTTP trigger function processed a request."
$status = [HttpStatusCode]::OK
$blobURL = "<Place Blob URL here>"
# Grab the text from the Blob
$blobText=invoke-webrequest -URI $blobURL
# Associate values to output bindings by calling 'Push-OutputBinding'.
Push-OutputBinding -Name Response -Value ([HttpResponseContext]@{
    StatusCode = $status
    Body = $blobText.Content
})
```

Save and run the function. You see the sentence from the blob in the Output pane on the bottom right. This is due to the blob being publicly accessible.

4. Return to the blob container in the portal and click the ellipsis to the right of the storage container. On the container blade, select Overview, and then Change access level and select Private.

5. Rerun the function URL in the browser. The blob is inaccessible, so only the 200 OK is returned; the webpage is empty.

6. Go back to the function and set up a managed identity:

   A. Select Platform Features at the top of the function app.

   B. Click Identity.

   C. In the System Assigned section set Status to On.

   D. Click Save.

7. Once the assignment is complete, go back to the storage account to assign access to the identity:

   A. Return to the blob container in the portal and click the ellipsis to the right of the storage container. Select Container Properties. On the Container blade, select Access Control (IAM).

   B. Click Add at the top, and then Add Role Assignment. Add Role Assignment opens.

   C. Select Storage Blob Data Reader for Role.

   D. In Assign Access To – Function App, select the function app created in step 2 of this section. The role assignment selection is shown in Figure 4-10. Click Save.

FIGURE 4-10 Add role assignment for managed identity

8. Now go back to the function app and edit the PowerShell snippet. You made the blob container private in step 4 and set up access control in step 7 of this section. Therefore, you have to retrieve a token to access the blob container. When the identity was created, an endpoint to a local token service was set up in the background by Azure. This is set as the MSI_ENDPOINT environment variable, and it's available to the function. Edit the code to call this using its Azure managed secret MSI_SECRET. Using these together enables you to obtain the access token for a given resource. (Note you can view these variables in Kudu Env Variables.) Delete from under `$status=` to above `#Associate` values and paste in the following code:

```
#Get the token for storage access from the MSI_ENDPOINT using the MSI_SECRET on
the header
$apiVersion = "2017-09-01"
$resourceURI = "https://storage.azure.com"
$tokenAuthURI = $env:MSI_ENDPOINT +
"?resource=$resourceURI&api-version=$apiVersion"
$tokenResponse = Invoke-RestMethod -Method Get -Headers @{"Secret"="$env:MSI_
SECRET"} -Uri $tokenAuthURI
$accessToken = $tokenResponse.access_token
$headers = @{}
$headers.Add("x-ms-version","2018-03-28")
$headers.Add("x-ms-client-request-id",[guid]::NewGuid())
$headers.Add("x-ms-date",(Get-Date).AddHours(1).ToString("ddd, dd MMM yyyy
HH:MM:ss G\MT"))
$headers.Add("Authorization","Bearer $($accessToken)")
$resp=Invoke-WebRequest -UseBasicParsing -Uri "https://<yourcontainername>.
blob.core.windows.net/msiblobcontainer/
<yourblobfilename>" -Method GET -Headers $headers
$resp.StatusCode
```

Execute the function in a test and then in a browser. The blob contents are displayed once more as shown in Figure 4-11.

FIGURE 4-11 Blob contents returned from the browser call

The process to retrieve the token for a VM is slightly different. You explore that in Skill 4.2 when you review Azure Key Vault.

User managed identity is currently in preview. A user managed identity is created as an identity in Azure AD, but it can be assigned to more than one Azure service. Therefore, you could have 100 VMs and assign the same user assigned managed identity to it. This would mean you could access multiple resources through the managed identity.

If you delete some of your VMs, the user managed identity is still available because it is a standalone resource. Assigning and granting access to the user managed identity is identical to the system managed as explored earlier; however, you need to know how to configure a user managed Identity:

```
az identity create -g myResourceGroup -n myUserIdentity
```

On the command line, it is a one-line command to create an identity that can be reused across resources. To view managed identities in the portal, search for the managed identities resource. This also has the ability to add and remove the managed identities.

Skill 4.2: Implement secure data solutions

Your customers' applications are now secured. You know what to recommend when architecting user-to-application and application-to-application authentication. That's just half the story, though. What about the data that is transported on premise or across the public internet—or even from private internet to the cloud? What happens to that data when it's stored for access at a later date? For this you need to understand the end-to-end encryption possibilities in Azure and which ones you should recommend based on the scenarios presented to you.

> **This skill covers how to:**
>
> - Create, read, update, delete keys, secrets, and certificates by using the key vault API
> - Encrypt and decrypt data at rest and in transit
> - Encrypt data with Always Encrypted
> - Implement Azure Confidential Compute and SSL/TLS communications

Create, read, update, delete keys, secrets, and certificates by using the key vault API

Before you start looking at encryption, you first need to think about the mechanisms used in encryption and secure transit and how these require an extra level of care. Your customers may have a web application, and it may need a connection string to a Redis Cache or perhaps a key to access some file storage. There could be a VM on the back end that cannot be called without some secure form of credentials.

In all of this, you have secrets and keys. Your customers' developers may have embedded some in the code or perhaps as plaintext in configuration files. Then there's infrastructure as code, and IT pros should be deploying this in a reusable manner, but usernames and passwords could have been accidentally left in scripts and templates. What happens to this infrastructure when embedded secrets and keys expire? How can you tell where they are being used and that they're being used for the correct purpose rather than being abused? What if these secrets end up in a public source code repository such as Github and a malicious party checks out your code and has access to your secrets? Even if the secrets don't get outside your customer's organization, how can they be sure a rogue employee hasn't managed to get access to secrets? Either way, your customer's infrastructure is now insecure, and their data is at risk. As a cloud architect, you need to ensure your customers know how to mitigate these risks, so how can you store these items securely? You need to use Azure Key Vault, a cloud-based security-enhanced secret store.

Key Vault gives your customers the ability to centrally store their secrets. These secrets are split into three groups:

- Keys
    - Symmetric and asymmetric (public/private key pair) keys. Private keys cannot be retrieved; they're used only in cryptographic operations.
    - They're generated by key vault or imported (bring your own key or BYOK).
    - They're used for Azure services like Always Encrypted and Transparent Data Encryption (TDE).
    - They're stored in a cryptographic key service. Keys are irretrievable.
- Secrets
    - For any sensitive information, database connection strings, Redis Cache connections, storage connections used in applications.
    - Other sensitive information you may need at runtime, if highly sensitive, should be encrypted before storing.
    - 25KB is the maximum size.
- Certificates
    - X509 certificates, used in HTTPS/SSL/TLS.
    - They can link to some external CAs for autorenewal.
    - They're stored as JSON wrapped secrets.

With centralized storage of secrets comes control of their distribution. You should be recommending that your customers secure access to the key vault to users via RBAC (currently only at the vault level) and access policies, creating three types of actors:

- SecOps
  - Create vaults, manage the keys and secrets in the vault. Revoke/delete.
  - Grant permissions to users and applications to perform cryptographic and management operations, read URIs, add keys, and so on.
  - Enable logging for auditors.
  - Can see some keys/secrets depending how they're stored.
- Developers
  - Add links to the keys and secrets into applications using URIs instead of actual values or keys.
  - Never see the keys or secrets.
- Auditors
  - Monitor the log files and review usage for compliance and security standards.
  - Never see keys or secrets.

With Azure Key Vault, Microsoft is unable to view or use the keys or secrets. This protection is by design and is a key component of a cryptographic vault.

Architects need to know how to create a key vault and secrets and then use this knowledge of key vault and secret creation to delve deeper into other key vault features.

> **NEED MORE REVIEW?** **AZURE KEY VAULT**
>
> To learn more about key vault, check out the article "What is Azure Key Vault" at *https://docs.microsoft.com/en-us/azure/key-vault/key-vault-overview*.

Creating a key vault, keys, secrets, and certificates

The introduction for this skill looked at the theory of key vaults, the secrets that can be stored within them, and how the actors within an organization would interact with the key vault. You now need to create a key vault to start storing your secrets. Follow these steps:

1. Select Create A Resource and search for Key Vault. Select Key Vault and click Create.

    Enter a name for the key vault. Choose something that's applicable to the key vault's use.

2. Select your Subscription, Resource Group, and Location.

3. For Pricing Tier, select Standard.

    - **Standard**   Software protected keys. Free to store, billed per transaction.
    - **Premium**   Hardware Security Module–stored keys certified to FIPS 140-2 (required by some regulated industries). Cost to store and per transaction.

4. Access Policies has one principal selected. If you click Access Policies, you can see your user as the security principle; click your user to view the permissions. The security principle has been given management access to all secret types but not cryptographic permissions; these are the defaults for a key vault creator. Leave everything as it is because you'll revisit this later. Click OK twice to return to the Key Vault creation blade.

5. Select Virtual Network Access to view the following options:

    ■ **All Networks**   Can be accessed from anywhere, including the public internet.

    ■ **Selected Networks**   Defaults to any trusted service, VMs, Disk Encryption, backup. Click the information next to Allow Trusted Microsoft Services To Bypass This Firewall? to see a full list. If you select No here, select the VNets and Public IP address ranges that require access.

    For this example, leave the setting on All Networks, and click Save.

6. Your key vault creation blade should look as shown in Figure 4-12. Click Create.

FIGURE 4-12 Create a key vault

Now that you have a key vault created, it's time to add some secrets. In the portal, navigate to the key vault you just added and use the following steps to add a secret to your newly created vault:

1. In the key vault plane, select Secrets.

2. Click Generate/Import at the top.

3. Under Upload Options, Certificate is deprecated, so you can only select Manual.

4. Enter a Name that identifies your secret appropriately.

5. In the Value field, enter the text string for the secret.

6. In Content Type – Optional, enter a description of the type of secret.

7. Activation and Expiration Date are for information only. They aren't enforced by Azure. For this example, you should leave them blank.

8. Your secret creation blade should look as shown in Figure 4-13. Click Create.

Create a secret

Upload options
Manual

* Name

myAppDbConnect

* Value

••••••••••••••••••••••••••••••••••

Content type (optional)

This is a simple database connection string

Set activation date? ☐

Set expiration date? ☐

Enabled?   Yes No

Create

FIGURE 4-13 Create a key vault secret

Your user was granted access to create secrets through the access policy created on the key vaults creation; therefore, the secret is created. Let's take a further look at access policies.

If List was not enabled for the secrets in the access policy, your user would not be able to list the secrets. You can see whether it's enabled by choosing Access Policies from the key vault plane. Click the access policy created for your user, and remove List against the Secrets. Log out of Azure and log in to force a permissions refresh. You can no longer see the secret you just added. Add List back in through the access policy.

List the secrets once more and click the secret name. You haven't updated this secret yet, so there's only one version displayed. Click this version to see the key details. Your user was granted Get permission on key vault creation, so when you click Show Secret Value at the bottom, you can view the secret. Go back to Access Policies on the key vault plane and remove Get Permission On The Secret by unchecking it, clicking OK, and then clicking Save. Now go back to the Secrets section of the blade; you can view the secrets list and see the versions, but on clicking on the version, you can no longer see the details of the secret or show the secret value. Reenable the Get permission for the secret in the access policy.

Finally, you'll need to turn on logging so that your customer's auditors can review how the secrets are being used. For this, you need a storage account so that key vault can have a container to write the logs into. You can do this in the portal, on the command-line interface (CLI), or in PowerShell, as shown here:

1. Open a PowerShell session and log in to Azure. Create a storage account named vaultLogs to house the logs container.

   ```
   $sa = New-AzStorageAccount -ResourceGroupName vaultRg -Name vaultLogs -Type
   Standard_LRS -Location 'northeurope'
   ```

2. Retrieve the key vault definition:

   ```
   $kv = Get-AzKeyVault -VaultName 'vaultExample'
   ```

3. Create a new diagnostic setting on the key vault which writes to the new storage container:

   ```
   Set-AzDiagnosticSetting -ResourceId $kv.ResolurceId -StorageAccountId $sa.Id
   -Enabled $true -Category AuditEvent
   ```

The logs can be read from the container insights-logs-auditevent.

> **NEED MORE REVIEW?**   **AZURE KEY VAULT SECURITY**
>
> To learn more about key vault Security through RBAC and access policies, read "Secure access to a key vault" at *https://docs.microsoft.com/en-us/azure/key-vault/key-vault-secure-your-key-vault*.

Throughout this section, the discussion has been predominantly about secrets. The processes to manage and use keys and certificates are similar and are covered in the sections "Encrypt and decrypt data at rest and in transit" (keys) and "SSL/TLS" (certificates).

Reading secrets, keys, and certificates

So far in this section, you've explored secrets using the portal. The portal when interacting with the key vault is a wrapper to the key vault REST APIs. The APIs we have touched on so far give you the ability to manage (management plane) the keys, secrets, and certificates. There is another set of APIs that allow you to get and use the secrets (data plane). You can see an example of the REST APIs when you view the secret created in the previous section. When you click the version number of the secret, the secret identifier appears as shown in Figure 4-14.

FIGURE 4-14 Secret identifier for a key vault secret

The identifier takes the following form:

```
https://<keyvaultname>.vault.azure.net/<secrets>/<secretName>/<version>?api-version7.0
```

Here you can replace <secrets> with <keys> or <certificates>, and their corresponding names and versions. The secret identifier make-up is still the same. You can try to access this directly with the URI as shown in the following, which is an example in PowerShell. Note that you need to use the URI from your secret identifier. Make sure you are logged into Azure in PowerShell to execute the following:

```
invoke-restmethod -Uri https://kvvaultexample.vault.azure.net/secrets/myAppDbConnect/
eeabaxxxxxxxxxxxxxxxxxxxxxxxxxxx31?api-version7.0
invoke-webrequest : The remote server returned an error: (401) Unauthorized.
```

Even though you're logged into Azure and therefore authenticated as the user the secret was created with, the API call cannot GET this secret due to the access and refresh OAuth 2.0 tokens not being present as part of the request. The (401) Unauthorized message is returned because the endpoint doesn't have the authorization yet.

Azure portal, Azure CLI, and PowerShell Az Module are all wrappers to Azure APIs, including the key vault REST API. Using the PowerShell command `Get-AzKeyVaultSecret` you can try to access the secret once more:

```
$secret=(get-azkeyvaultsecret -VaultName 'kvvaultexample' -secretName 'myAppDbConnect').
SecretValueText
$secret
kvdbexample.database.windows.net,1433
```

Here, you can see part of an Azure SQL Database connect string which was stored in the secret create in the key vault example. The command `Get-AzKeyVaultSecret` is substituting the given `VaultName` and `secretName` into the URI for you as part of the wrapping process, along with tokens required for access. Because you haven't specified the secret version, you will receive the current one.

> **NOTE   ON TOKENS, API USAGE, AND CLI/POWERSHELL**
> It's possible to retrieve the OAuth 2.0 tokens and access the secret in this way, but it's way beyond the knowledge required for the exam. This example is to explore what's happening on the back end.

Reading secrets, keys, and certificates with Managed Service Identity

The walkthroughs so far have looked at what you can do as a user (User Principal). However, as an architect, you need to be able to instruct on how to set up access for your applications to the key vault and its secrets. To grant access to an application or other Azure service, you need to create an access policy to an identity that has been assigned to the Azure service. This can be a Managed Service Identity (MSI) or a User Assigned Identity as explored in Skill 4.1. To see this in action, in the following example you deploy a Linux VM. You then access a key vault secret via MSI and check access from inside the VM. This simulates a developer using a software development kit (SDK) to access a secret.

The following steps break up a single Azure CLI script, describing the tasks each section performs. Execute each section in this script to explore accessing secrets through an MSI:

1. Initially set up some variables for multiple use throughout the script. Here you're setting resource group, location, and secret names. These should always be set as appropriate

for usage and follow naming conventions. Location should be as required by your customer:

```
rgName="kvrgexample"
rgLocation="northeurope"
kvName="kvvaultexample"
kvSecretName="kvsecretexample"
vmName="kvvmexample"
```

2. Create your resource group to house your resources:

```
az group create --name $rgName --location $rgLocation
```

3. Use the resource group to create a key vault. Key vaults need a resource group and a location. A key vault needs to be in the same location as the services accessing it:

```
az keyvault create --name $kvName --resource-group $rgName --location $rgLocation
```

4. Add a secret to your vault and record the ID return value for later use. That's your URI:

```
az keyvault secret set --vault-name $kvName --name $kvSecretName --value "Shhh
it's secret!"
```

5. Create a VM and set up for SSH:

```
az vm create --resource-group $rgName --name $vmName --image UbuntuLTS \
--admin-username sysadmin --generate-ssh-keys
```

6. Assign a managed identity to the VM, save the publicIpAddress return value for later use.

```
az vm identity assign --name $vmName --resource-group $rgName
```

7. Get the service principal ID of the managed identity for use in the key vault, vault policy addition:

```
spID=$(az vm show --resource-group $rgName --name $vmName --query identity.
principalId --out tsv)
```

8. Grant the VM identity access to the secret. The VM only needs list and get to retrieve the secret:

```
az keyvault set-policy --name $kvName --object-id $spID --secret-permissions
get list
```

> **NOTE AZURE KEY VAULT ACCESS**
>
> When access to secrets, keys, and certificates is given, it's for the entire vault. Therefore, it's part of best practice to separate key vaults across applications and then again across environments (dev, pre-prod, prod). This ensures that each environment's applications cannot use the other's keys. This separation also helps to make sure key vault transaction limits are not hit.

9. The VM is ready to test. Use SSH to get into the VM using the publicIpAddress saved in step 6. This will open up a secure shell where you can install CURL:

```
ssh publicIpAddress -l sysadmin
sudo apt-get update
sudo apt-get install -y curl
```

10. Staying in the secure shell, use Curl to grab an access token. This request calls the Azure Instance Metadata service endpoint; it returns metadata about a running VM and can only be accessed from inside the VM. To return the access token, you need to access the identity endpoint as shown here. Note the address of the Azure Instance Metadata service is static:

```
curl 'http://169.254.169.254/metadata/identity/oauth2/token?api-version=2018-02-
01&resource=https%3A%2F%2Fvault.azure.net' -H Metadata:true
```

sysadmin@kvvmexample:~$ curl 'http://169.254.169.254/metadata/identity/oauth2/token?api-version=2018-02-01&reso
urce=https%3A%2F%2Fvault.azure.net' -H Metadata:true
{"access_token":"eyJ0eXAiOiJKV1QiLCJhbGciOiJSUzI1NiIsIng1dCI6InU0T2ZOR1BId0VCb3NIanRyYXVPY1Y4NExuWSIsImtpZCI6In
U0T2ZOR1BId0VCb3NIanRyYXVPY1Y4NExuWSJ9.eyJhdWQiOiJodHRwczovL3ZhdWx0LmF6dXJlLm5ldCIsImlzcyI6Imh0dHBzOi8vc3RzLndp
bmRvd3MubmV0LzM5MmY3ZGM4LTAzYWQtNDJhY1yiZDA0LTd1Yzg1OGFiODgwOC8iLCJpYXQiOjE1NjM4MDA5NzUsIm5iZiI6MTU2MzgwMDk3NSw
iZXhwIjoxNTYzODMwMDc1LCJhaW8iOiI0MkZnWUpnOTQ2cGw4YUxuS1hQT25uNHpUZS9tQndBPSIsImFwcG1kIjoiMzM4MjVhZDktOTI1YS00Nj
Q5LThhZmUtYmI5NWYxYjI1MDE3IiwiYXBwaWRhY3IiOiIyIiwiaWRwIjoiaHR0cHM6Ly9zdHMud21uZG93cy5uZXQvMzkyZjdkYzgtMDNhZC00M
mFjLWJkMDQtN2VjODU4YWI4ODA4LyIsIm9pZCI6ImZlMGMwNDA4LTYyNWEtNDM1NS05YmY3LTEyYjYxZmE1Mjg5YyIsInN1Yi16ImZlMGMwNDA4
LTYyNWEtNDM1NS05YmY3LTEyYjYxZmE1Mjg5YyIsInRpZCI6IjM5MmY3ZGM4LTAzYWQtNDJhY1iyiZDA0LTd1Yzg1OGFiODgwOCIsInV0aSI6IjQ
1UTVCSTFyczBhTENhN1htLWhaQUEiLCJ2ZXIiOiIxLjAiLCJ4bXNfbWlyaWQiOiIvc3Vic2NyaXB0aW9ucy9jZjNkZmQ2ZC0zMzgwLTRhNTItOT
g0Yy11NGF1ODYzNjc4NDMvcmVzb3VyY2Vncm91cHMva3ZyZ2V4YW1wbGUvcHJvdm1kZXJzL01pY3Jvc29mdC5Db21wdXRlL3ZpcnR1YWxNYWNoa
1Jb8oyVEyUR0bsX6V1UaWYk8XR-jwHKWfznFvfuE5WtHmO3GSZo71ESUvayoDIiV8MnhnjQCnmeISmghziIfuJcsFCCF-xjS2u8etehSyfypQT4
dQOJF5CQhHTUx-WHOKoxkqRwP4--JoNavr-qYTJAzvYpNouYkeZfiguLpyRDCbLKy99nNV4GtDOZzth1J8fg8_1PIxOnt-WaUy0cyMhaae7VRgO
NtKOu6gBw7fIYm825dnSVRvvcRXu4HQvA","client_id":"33825ad9-925a-4649-8afe-bb95f1b25017","expires_in":"28800","exp
ires_on":"1563830075","ext_expires_in":"28800","not_before":"1563800975","resource":"https://vault.azure.net","
token_type":"Bearer"}sysadmin@kvvmexample:~$ ▌

FIGURE 4-15 Azure Instance Metadata service endpoint request and return from command line

11. Staying in the shell once more, copy the access token that has been output as in Figure 4-15, and use Curl again to grab the secret, substituting the ID from step 4 (URI), and the access token from the last step:

```
curl https://<YOUR-SECRET-URI>?api-version=2016-10-01 -H "Authorization: Bearer
<ACCESS TOKEN>"
curl https://kvvaultexample.vault.azure.net/secrets/kvsecretexample/
b8f1xxxxxxxxxxxxxxxx99c?api-version=2016-10-01 -H "Authorization: Bearer eyJxxxxx"
```

Once the Curl request is executed, you can view the secret as shown in Figure 4-16 to confirm you have the access directly from the VM. This confirms access via the identity and that the access policy is functioning correctly.

```
{"value":"Shhh it's secret!","id":"https://kvvaultexample.vault.azure.net/secrets
/kvsecretexample/ b8f1xxxxxxxxxxxxxxxx99c","attributes":{"enabled":true,
"created":1559775793,"updated":1559775793,"recoveryLevel":"Purgeable"},"tags":
{"file-encoding":"utf-8"}}
```

sysadmin@kvvmexample:~$ curl https://kvvaultexample.vault.azure.net/secrets/kvsecretexample/b8f188e9505f433694d
d6d69bab2999c?api-version=2016-10-01 -H "Authorization: Bearer eyJ0eXAiOiJKV1QiLCJhbGciOiJSUzI1NiIsIng1dCI6InU0
T2ZOR1BId0VCb3NIanRyYXVPY1Y4NExuWSIsImtpZCI6InU0T2ZOR1BId0VCb3NIanRyYXVPY1Y4NExuWSJ9.eyJhdWQiOiJodHRwczovL3ZhdW
x0LmF6dXJlLm5ldCIsImlzcyI6Imh0dHBzOi8vc3RzLndpbmRvd3MubmV0LzM5MmY3ZGM4LTAzYWQtNDJhY1iyiZDA0LTd1Yzg1OGFiODgwOC8iL
CJpYXQiOjE1NjM4MDA5NzUsIm5iZiI6MTU2MzgwMDk3NSwiZXhwIjoxNTYzODMwMDc1LCJhaW8iOiI0MkZnWUpnOTQ2cGw4YUxuS1hQT25uNHpU
ZS9tQndBPSIsImFwcG1kIjoiMzM4MjVhZDktOTI1YS00NjQ5LThhZmUtYmI5NWYxYjI1MDE3IiwiYXBwaWRhY3IiOiIyIiwiaWRwIjoiaHR0cHM
6Ly9zdHMud21uZG93cy5uZXQvMzkyZjdkYzgtMDNhZC00MmFjLWJkMDQtN2VjODU4YWI4ODA4LyIsIm9pZCI6ImZlMGMwNDA4LTYyNWEtNDM1NS
05YmY3LTEyYjYxZmE1Mjg5YyIsInN1Yi16ImZlMGMwNDA4LTYyNWEtNDM1NS05YmY3LTEyYjYxZmE1Mjg5YyIsInRpZCI6IjM5MmY3ZGM4LTAzY
WQtNDJhY1iyiZDA0LTd1Yzg1OGFiODgwOCIsInV0aSI6IjQ1UTVCSTFyczBhTENhN1htLWhaQUEiLCJ2ZXIiOiIxLjAiLCJ4bXNfbWlyaWQiOiIv
c3Vic2NyaXB0aW9ucy9jZjNkZmQ2ZC0zMzgwLTRhNTItOTg0Yy11NGF1ODYzNjc4NDMvcmVzb3VyY2Vncm91cHMva3ZyZ2V4YW1wbGUvcHJvdm1
kZXJzL01pY3Jvc29mdC5Db21wdXRlL3ZpcnR1YWxNYWNoaW5lcy9rdmJxZXhhbXBsZ...
5dGEEeM1BoebIt9kPJ150E8AqLusZ52ErEjHg2MgoBkGEY1Jb8oyVEyUR0bsX6V1UaWYk8XR-jwHKWfznFvfuE5WtHmO3GSZo71ESUvayoDIiV8
MnhnjQCnmeISmghziIfuJcsFCCF-xjS2u8etehSyfypQT4dQOJF5CQhHTUx-WHOKoxkqRwP4--JoNavr-qYTJAzvYpNouYkeZfiguLpyRDCbLKy
99nNV4GtDOZzth1J8fg8_1PIxOnt-WaUy0cyMhaae7VRgQNtKOu6gBw7fIYm825dnSVRvvcRXu4HQvA"
{"value":"Shhh it's secret!","id":"https://kvvaultexample.vault.azure.net/secrets/kvsecretexample/b8f188e9505f4
33694dd6d69bab2999c","attributes":{"enabled":true,"created":1559775793,"updated":1559775793,"recoveryLevel":"Pu
rgeable"},"tags":{"file-encoding":"utf-8"}}sysadmin@kvvmexample:~$ ▌

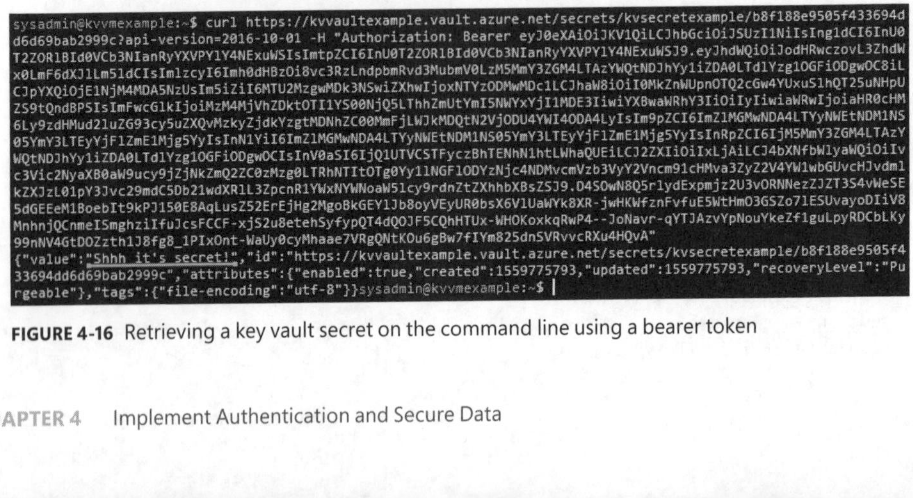

FIGURE 4-16 Retrieving a key vault secret on the command line using a bearer token

Updating and deleting secrets

Keys, secrets, and certificates can be updated within the key vault. It's possible to update the metadata or the secret itself. If the update is to the secret itself, a new version of the secret is created that can be referenced in the URI, either by its version number or by leaving the version number off the URI, which always returns the most recent version. Follow these steps in the portal to create a key and update this key to a new version to see versioning of keys in action:

1. Create a key in your key vault:

   A. Click Keys on the Key Vault blade, and select Generate/Import.

   B. Select Import and select any private key from your local machine in File Upload.

   C. Enter the password you used when creating the private key in Password. Note that you can only import an RSA Key.

   D. Enter a name for your key, and click Create.

2. The Key you have just created is listed in the Keys List. Now you can update it:

   A. Click on the key in the Keys list; select New Version.

   B. Select Import. The information required is identical to that above, except you don't need to supply a name. You may select the same private key here because it's a demo. Click Create.

   C. You are returned to the Keys version list, there are now Current and Older Versions listed. Both are enabled and can be used.

From an architect standpoint, you need to ensure your customers are updating their secrets regularly. This is called *rotation*, and for some secrets, such as keys, could be a regulatory requirement.

> *NOTE* **SECRET ROTATION**
>
> The example uses manual rotation. You either update the version after the rotate, or point your application at a new Key. This task can be automated using Azure Automation and Runbooks.

The deletion of a key or entire vault is a straightforward task in the portal. On the Vault blade, select Overview and Delete. You also can use PowerShell `remove-azKeyVault` and CLI `az keyvault delete` to perform vault deletion and associated commands for secret deletion.

The problem you need to be aware of as an architect is accidental deletion of a key vault or secret. In this scenario, unless you have a backup of the secret, you may no longer be able to communicate with your application or be unable to read encrypted data. You could place a resource lock on the key vault to stop it being deleted. However, key vault gives you two flags you can set at the vault level that are recommended for best practice. The following is an updated version of the CLI command used in the VM and key vault walkthrough from earlier in this section. You can execute this command to create a protected key vault:

```
kvName="ssekvexamplecli"
az keyvault create \
    --name $kvName \
    --resource-group $rgName \
    --location $rgLocation \
    --enable-soft-delete \
    --enable-purge-protection
```

Looking closely, you can see the following commands have been added at the bottom:

- **--enable-soft-delete**   If a secret or an entire vault is deleted, you can recover it for up to 90 days after deletion.

- **--enable-purge-protection**   If a secret or an entire vault is deleted and has gone into a soft-delete, it cannot be purged until the 90-day period because deletion has passed.

These options are not enabled by default and must be specified on creation or on an update to the Key Vault properties; updates must be performed on the command line. Here is an example in PowerShell of updating a key vault that has not been created with soft delete:

```
($vault = Get-AzResource -ResourceId (Get-AzKeyVault -VaultName $keyVaultName).
ResourceId).Properties `
 | Add-Member -MemberType NoteProperty -Name enableSoftDelete -Value 'True'
Set-AzResource -resourceid $vault.ResourceId -Properties $vault.Properties -Force
```

These two lines of PowerShell are retrieving the properties of the key vault, updating them to add the soft delete, and then setting the updated properties back to the vault.

> ***NEED MORE REVIEW?***   **SOFT DELETE FOR KEY VAULT**
>
> To learn more about configuring soft delete and purge protection on a key vault, read "Azure Key Vault soft-delete overview" at *https://docs.microsoft.com/en-us/azure/key-vault/key-vault-ovw-soft-delete*. Also review the other items listed under the section heading concepts from the same documentation page.

Encrypt and decrypt data at rest and in transit

As a solution architect, you need to be educating your customers in designing solutions that protect their data, taking into account all the possible states the data can occur in and the appropriate controls for those states. These data states are

- **At rest**   Data that is inactive and stored physically (persisted) in digital form—for example, databases, files, disks, and messages.

- **In transit**   Data that is being transferred. This could be between locations, over a network, or between programs or components.

Encryption at rest is designed to prevent a possible attacker from gaining easy access to data at rest on compromised physical media.

So, why use encryption at rest when there's a low chance of an attacker gaining access to Azure's physical media? Aside from encryption at rest being part of best practice for Data Security, our customers' data may have mandatory requirements for data protection from compliance and internal governance—for example, PCI DSS, HIPPA, or perhaps the new European data privacy laws, GDPR. Encryption at rest adds an additional layer of defense on top of Azure's already highly compliant platform, which is why it's enabled by default where possible.

By default, Azure resource providers (in this example, Azure Storage) use service-managed symmetric keys to encrypt the data as it is written to storage. This process is transparent to the user; the Azure resource provider manages the key and encryption process. The same key is then used to decrypt the data into memory before the data is accessible in an unencrypted format by the application, meaning that no code changes are required to use this feature. It also carries no cost to the customer. This is server-side encryption at rest and is shown in Figure 4-17.

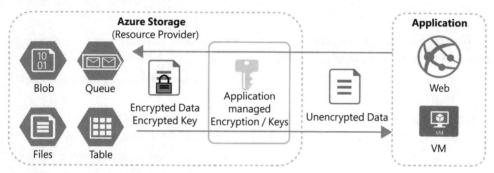

FIGURE 4-17 Server-side encryption at rest

The following services support encryption at rest with service-managed keys:

- Azure Storage (Storage Service Encryption or SSE)
- Azure SQL Database (Transparent Data Encryption or TDE)
- Azure Cosmos DB
- Azure Data Lake
- Managed disks (via SSE)

Encryption at rest also supports customer-managed keys on some services. With customer-managed keys, you can bring your own key (BYOK), importing a key into key vault, or you can create one directly within key vault. Customer-managed keys give your customers greater control over their key management process, including

- Import your own key or create one in key vault, which lets you decide when to rotate your keys. You can disable a key if compromised.
- Define access controls to your key.
- Audit of key usage.

Customer-managed keys are supported on Azure Storage (SSE) for blobs and files, Azure SQL Database (TDE), and Azure Disk Encryption for encryption at rest.

Enable customer-managed keys for Azure Storage encryption

As discussed above, Azure Storage uses Storage Service Encryption (SSE) for encryption at rest by default using service-managed keys. To use customer-managed keys, you need to specify your key for use. Follow these steps to configure a storage account to use customer-managed keys, using a new key vault and generating a new key:

1. Open a storage account you've already created. The one in this walkthrough is a Standard Gen Purpose V2 LRS Account.

2. In the Configuration blade, find the Encryption setting. Click this setting to see a description on how data is already encrypted at rest, but you can use your own key.

3. Check the box marked Use Your Own Key. Select A Key From Key Vault is selected by default.

4. Click Select Under key vault and select Create A New Vault. When you create a new key vault for use with SSE, the storage account and key vault must be in the same region. However, they can be in different subscriptions.

   Enter a name for the key vault and select the same resource group as the storage account for simple resource grouping. The location should be set to the same as the storage account. Leave the other options as default and click Create. Once the key vault is deployed, you're returned to the Use Your Own Key setup.

5. Click Select under Key and then select Create A New Key. This creates a new key in your new key vault. Enter a name for your key, and leave the other parameters as default. Once the key is added, you're returned to the Use Your Own Key setup.

6. Click Save at the top of the page. The change is submitted, and the Storage Service Encryption for this account will now be using your customer-managed key.

If you need to change the key used for encryption, go back to the same Encryption setting and select a new key in the key vault, or uncheck Use Your Own Key to revert to service-managed keys.

NEED MORE REVIEW? CONFIGURE CUSTOMER-MANAGED KEYS FOR AZURE STORAGE

To learn more about configuring customer-managed keys on SSE, visit the Microsoft Docs article "Azure Data Encryption-at-Rest" at *https://docs.microsoft.com/en-us/azure/storage/common/ storage-encryption-keys-portal.* Follow the linked articles for PowerShell and Azure CLI.

Azure Disk Encryption

Unmanaged Disks in Azure Storage are not encrypted at rest by Storage Service Encryption. Managed disks are automatically encrypted by SSE. As a solution architect, you need to be teaching your customers to encrypt at rest where possible because encryption at rest follows best practice in data security. To encrypt unmanaged disks, you must use a customer-managed key and Azure Disk Encryption. Like SSE, Azure Disk Encryption integrates with key vault for management of encryption keys.

NOTE AZURE DISK ENCRYPTION

Azure Security Center will flag unencrypted IaaS disks and recommend the disks be encrypted. This is listed as a High Severity alert.

Azure Disk Encryption uses the industry-standard features of BitLocker (Windows) and DM-crypt (Linux Kernel 2.6+) to encrypt the Data and operating system disks.

Now you configure Azure Disk Encryption on an existing VM image with a single unmanaged disk. Before you do anything, back up your VM! Then complete the following steps:

1. Navigate to your existing VM in the portal, select Disks from the Settings blade, and verify that the operating system disks and any data disks are unencrypted. In this case, the VM only has an operating system disk. See Figure 4-18.

FIGURE 4-18 Unencrypted operating system disk

2. To enable Azure Disk Encryption, you need to switch to the command line. For this example, you will work in Azure CLI. The existing VM is named "adevmexample." The VM in this example is Windows Server 2016 with unmanaged disks. You can verify that your existing VM isn't using encrypted disks in Azure CLI too. Execute the following set of Azure CLI commands. You'll see the message "Azure Disk Encryption is not enabled" returned to the console:

```
vmName="adevmexample"
rgName="diskEncryption"
rgLocation="northeurope"
az vm encryption show --name $vmName --resource-group $rgName
```

3. Staying in Azure CLI, execute the following to create the key vault. Note the `--enabled-for-disk-encryption`; you can't encrypt a disk with a key from the vault without it:

```
kvName="adekvexamplecli"
az keyvault create  --name $kvName  --resource-group $rgName --location
$rgLocation \
    --enabled-for-disk-encryption true
```

4. Staying in Azure CLI, execute the following to create a key using the new key vault. The protection setting here is only required if you have a premium tier key vault; you can then pick between hardware and software protection as required:

```
keyName="adekeyexamplecli"
az keyvault key create --vault-name $kvName --name $keyName --protection software
```

5. Staying in Azure CLI, execute the following to create a new service principle name, and then use this to create the service principle and store the ID and password. You need these to set up security on the key vault and then access the key for encryption:

```
spName="https://adespexample"
read spPassword <<< $(az ad sp create-for-rbac --name $spName --query password
--output tsv)
spId=$(az ad sp show --id $spName --query appId --output tsv)
```

6. Still staying in Azure CLI, execute the following to add a policy on the new key vault. This will allow the service principle to access keys from this key vault to encrypt the disk with the wrapKey permission:

```
az keyvault set-policy  --name $kvName --spn $spId --key-permissions wrapKey
--secret-permissions set
```

Now that the key vault, key, service principle, and key vault policy are in place, you can encrypt your VM disks using the service principle access to the key vault. Staying in Azure CLI, execute the following to encrypt the disks. In this command, `volume-type` of all is going to encrypt all your disks. If you add more data disks after encrypting a VM, use the same command with `--volume-type data`; otherwise your new disks won't be encrypted:

```
az vm encryption enable --resource-group $rgName --name $vmName --aad-client-id
$spId \
```

```
        --aad-client-secret $spPassword --disk-encryption-keyvault $kvName  --key-
encryption-key $keyName \
        --volume-type all
```

7. Depending on how many disks there are and their size, this command may take a while. It may also reboot the VM. The status can be periodically checked by issuing the following command:

```
az vm encryption show --resource-group $rgName --name $vmName --query [osDisk] -o
tsv
```

8. Now reissue the encryption status check `az vm encryption show` from step 2. If every-thing's working as planned, you see a JSON response with `"dataDisk": "Encrypted"`, `"osDisk": "Encrypted"` followed by the key vault and key details.

9. Switching back to the portal, follow the instructions in step 1 once more and check that the Disk Encryption is set to "Enabled." For belt and braces verification, you can look on the VM itself. RDP in, open an Explorer window, and select MyPC. The open padlock sign above the disk shows this is encrypted at rest by BitLocker, as shown in Figure 4-19.

FIGURE 4-19 BitLocker encryption at rest

> **NEED MORE REVIEW?** **AZURE DISK ENCRYPTION**
>
> To learn more about encrypting Azure Disks, including some important prerequisites and quickstarts, visit the Microsoft Docs article "Azure Data Encryption-at-Rest" at *https://docs. microsoft.com/en-us/azure/security/azure-security-disk-encryption-overview*.

Azure Storage client-side encryption

In the encryption examples, which in this skill have all been server-side so far, it's possible the data that has been in transit to Azure Storage has arrived through an unencrypted channel. Because the data has not been encrypted, it has been open to attack. When architecting a secure data solution, you need to address unencrypted data in transit because compliance and governance requirements may make encrypted in transit mandatory. Either way, it's best practice to encrypt in transit.

Client-side encryption for Azure Storage encrypts the data on the application side; there-fore, if the data is intercepted over an unencrypted communication channel, it's not as easily compromised. Figure 4-20 shows a diagram of Azure Storage Encryption reworked for client-side encryption. All data leaving the application is encrypted.

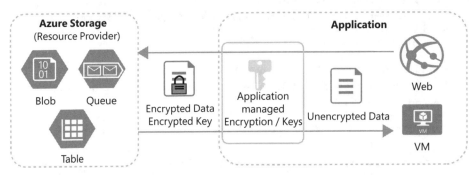

FIGURE 4-20 Client-side encryption process

Client-side encryption requires the Azure Storage Client Library to be called as part of an application. The encryption is performed using this process:

1. The Azure Storage client library generates a content encryption key (CEK), which is a one-time-use symmetric key.

2. The client library encrypts the data with the CEK.

3. The CEK is encrypted by a Key Encryption Key (KEK). The KEK has a key identifier, can be symmetric or asymmetric depending on the requirement, and can be stored locally or on Azure Key Vault. The client library doesn't have access to the KEK; it just uses the key wrapper it provides.

4. The encrypted data is loaded to Azure. The wrapped CEK is stored with the data for a blob or inserted (interpolated) into the data (queues and tables).

This process of wrapping the CEK key is called the envelope technique. During the decryption process, a key-resolver uses the key identifier to work out which key wrapped the CEK, meaning that again the Client Library has no need to access the KEK itself. Just call the KEK's unwrap algorithm.

EXAM TIP

You won't need to know how to invoke the client library in code as part of an application for the exam, but it's important to have a grasp of the process of encryption/decryption.

NEED MORE REVIEW? **CLIENT-SIDE ENCRYPTION FOR AZURE STORAGE**

To learn more about configuring client-side encryption for Azure Storage, visit the Microsoft Docs article "Configure customer-managed keys for Azure Storage encryption from Azure portal" at *https://docs.microsoft.com/en-us/azure/storage/common/ storage-encryption-keys-portal.*

Azure SQL encryption at rest—Transparent Data Encryption

Azure Storage is only one of the areas within Azure where data is at rest. The SQL family of products in Azure also stores data at rest in its data files and log files. This includes

- Azure SQL Database
- Azure SQL Managed Instance
- Azure SQL Data Warehouse
- SQL Server (within an IaaS VM on Azure)

The SQL Database family of products uses Transparent Data Encryption (TDE) to encrypt data at rest. When engaging with customers to design a storage solution on SQL in Azure, you need to ensure that they are aware only new Azure SQL Databases have TDE enabled by default when they're created. The other solutions and older versions of Azure SQL Database require TDE to be enabled manually.

TDE protects the data at rest by performing real-time I/O encryption of the data and log files at the page level. The pages are encrypted by a database encryption key (DEK), which is stored in the boot page (record on SQL Server) of the database, allowing startup and database operations within Azure including the following:

- Geo and Self Service Point in time Restore
- Restoration of a deleted database
- Geo-replication
- Database Copy

The now encrypted pages are then written to disk, and the same DEK is used to decrypt the page before it's read into memory for use. The master database holds the components required to encrypt or decrypt the pages using a DEK, which is why the master database is not encrypted by TDE. This all happens without interaction from the user or the application developers, and it happens with no extra cost.

TDE uses service-managed keys by default, with Azure managing the key rotation and so on and storing the keys in its own secure location. TDE also can be configured to use customer-managed keys just like Azure Storage Encryption, which gives your customers the data security implementation they may need for governance and compliance purposes, as described in the skill introduction. Using customer-managed keys is also called bring your own key (BYOK).

Unlike Azure Storage Encryption, the customer-managed key encrypts the DEK, not the data itself and is therefore known as a TDE protector. Once BYOK is enabled and the DEK is encrypted, it's stored at the boot page level, replacing the Azure-managed DEK if there was one. The customer-managed key used to encrypt the DEK must be stored in Azure Key Vault, where it can be imported to or created within the key vault. Storing the key in the vault gives your customers the same degree of management of the key as that described earlier in the discussion about Azure Storage Encryption.

> **NOTE EXPORTING AN ENCRYPTED AZURE SQL DATABASE TO BACPAC**
>
> When exporting an encrypted database to BACPAC, the data is first read into memory before it's sent as part of the BACPAC file. This means that the data in the BACPAC file is unencrypted as TDE unencrypts the data before writing to memory. Therefore, you need to ensure your customers are aware they must secure the BACPAC file by other means once exported.

Use the following steps to take a look at encrypting an existing Azure SQL Database using a customer-managed key. In this example, you need to use an already created Azure SQL Server/Database:

1. In Azure portal, navigate to the Azure SQL Server you have already created, click SQL Databases in the blade, and then select the database you created. On the Security section of the blade, select Transparent Data Encryption. Figure 4-21 shows that it's not possible to use your own key at the database level; therefore, a customer-managed key is applied at the server level. All databases with Data Encryption turned on will be encrypted by the same key. Switching the Data Encryption to off at this level will turn off encryption, just for this database.

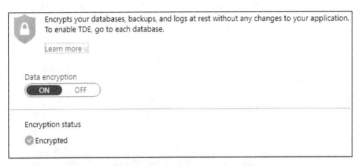

FIGURE 4-21 Transparent Data Encryption for Azure SQL Database

2. Switch back to the Security blade for the Azure SQL Server and select Transparent Data Encryption. Click Yes for Use Your Own Key. You have the option to Select a Key or Enter a Key Identifier. The Key Identifier can be copied off of the properties of a key stored in a key vault. In this example, you create a new key.

3. Click Select A Key Vault and select the key vault you would like to use. You need to select one with Soft Delete enabled. Once you've selected a key vault you're returned back to the Transparent Data Encryption page.

4. Select a Key, and then Create a new key. Leave the Options as Generate and enter a relevant name for your key. TDE only supports RSA, so leave the Key Type as RSA. If the compliance policies your customer needs to follow ask for a minimum RSA Key Size above 2,048 then select a different size. For this walkthrough, leave it at 2,048. If you don't want your new key to activate straight away, set an activation date. If your key needs to expire on a specific date or time, set the expiration date. Click Create.

5. The key is created in the key vault, and you're back to the TDE page. Click Save at the top, and save process will create a key vault access policy for the Azure SQL Server to the new key if possible, and then encrypt the DEK and complete the customer-managed key encryption process.

Encrypt data with Always Encrypted

You've made sure your customers know they need their data to be encrypted at rest, but what if there is some data that some users—even power users—should not be able to read? This is sensitive data.

Sensitive data could be personally identifiable information such as Social Security number (SSN), email address, date of birth, or perhaps financial data such as a credit card number. You should be ensuring your customers are protected from attackers with encryption for all sensitive data by encrypting at rest, but there are also times when power users—in this case database administrators—shouldn't be able to view sensitive information. Would you want the database administrator of your employer's human resource package to be able to view your SSN, data of birth, and so on? A solution architect needs to be able to advise how to prevent this, which is where Always Encrypted comes in.

Always Encrypted is a security feature within SQL products that is designed to protect sensitive data. This encryption happens on the client side, so it covers while the data is being used, when it is moving between client and server, and when it's at rest on the server. With Always Encrypted, the data is never viewable in the database in plain text, even in memory. Because the client is handling the encryption and decryption process, the application needs a driver to be installed for this to happen. This can be .Net, ODBC, JDBC, PHP, and so on, which opens up a variety of programming languages. However, unlike TDE, Always Encrypted means that there may be some code changes required in the application to use Always Encrypted.

Unlike TDE, which is database wide, Always Encrypted should be set against just the columns that are required to be encrypted. There's a slight performance hit with Always Encrypted; there also are limitations on types of columns that can be encrypted. It's important to define a set of rules with your customers as to which fields these should be, although this may be decided for you with compliance and governance requirements.

When Always Encrypted is set up, it requires two keys: the Column Encryption Key (CEK) and the Column Master Key (CMK). The CEK is used to encrypt the data, which is then encrypted by the CMK and stored in the column encryption key metadata in the database. The CMK is stored outside the database in a trusted key store such as Azure Key Vault, Windows Certificate Store, or Java Key Store. The database just stores metadata about where this key is. As in previous sections, by storing the CMK in a trusted key store, your customers have control of the key management, including rotation and revoking of keys.

To see how this all works theoretically in an application, follow a standard select statement as shown in Figure 4-22.

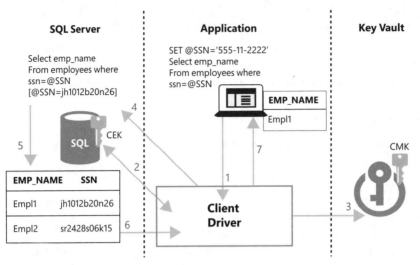

FIGURE 4-22 Always Encrypted encryption process

1. The Client Application executes a simple select. It creates a parameterized query and sends this to the Always Encrypted client driver.

2. The client driver checks against the SQL Server to see if the columns or parameters it's selecting against are encrypted. If so, the location of the CMK and the encrypted CEK are returned to the client driver.

3. The client driver uses the CMK location to retrieve the CMK and uses the CMK to decrypt the CEK.

4. The client driver uses the decrypted CEK to encrypt the parameters.

5. The client driver is now able to execute the SQL statement against the database.

6. The results are returned to the client driver.

7. The client driver decrypts the columns returned if required and returns the result set to the application.

In steps 4 and 5, the client library is executing the SQL statement using encrypted parameters in the where clause. The ability to do this depends on what column encryption type you select. There are two column encryption types. Here's how they differ:

Deterministic	Randomized
The same value is generated each time for the same piece of plain text.	A different value will be generated each time the same piece of plain text is encrypted.
This makes it easy to work out repeated data, in particular for small data sets, like Booleans or a handful of rows.	This is the more secure method as even in a small data set the values are hard to guess.
These are easier to use in SQL statements, can join, do lookups, group, and index on these columns.	You can't search on these columns, group, index, or join.
They're good for data that is searched, ID numbers, emails, dates of birth, and so on.	You should only use randomized on columns you display—never those you have to search or index.

In the example, the SSN column must have been using Deterministic as its Column Encryption Type; otherwise, SQL Server would have returned an error. It's not possible to search on a Randomized column.

It's time to set up a couple of encrypted columns and test this out. In this example, set up an empty key vault and a simple single Azure SQL Database with an employees table. Make this SQL Database accessible directly to your local IP on the Azure SQL Server Firewall. Use the following steps to set up Always Encrypted and encrypt two of the columns:

1. Open SQL Server Management Studio (SSMS), log in to your database, expand the Tables folder in the Object Explorer, and right-click on the Employees Table.

2. The Always Encrypted wizard opens. Click Next on the introduction page. On the Column Selection page, select SSN and Salary. You will want to search on SSN but just display Salary, so SSN is Deterministic encryption and Salary is Randomized, as shown in Figure 4-23. The wizard automatically sets the CEK name, the same Key is used for both columns. Click Next.

Name	State	Encryption Type	Encryption Key
⊟ dbo.employees			
☐ emp_name			
☑ ssn	⚠	Deterministic	▾ CEK_Auto1 (New)
☑ salary	✏	Randomized	▾ CEK_Auto1 (New)

FIGURE 4-23 Column selection and encryption type for Always Encrypted

3. Select where the CMK is so that the CEK can be protected. Select Azure Key Vault, log in to Azure, select the key vault created for this walkthrough, and click Next. Figure 4-24 shows the selection of the key vault to store the CMK.

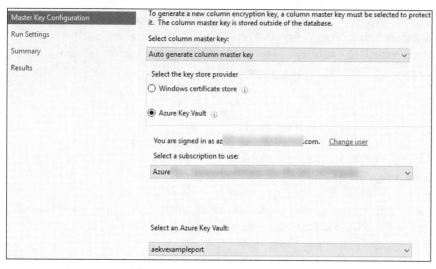

FIGURE 4-24 Azure Key Vault for Column Master Key store

4. You can select to generate a PowerShell Script for automation purposes later, or click Proceed to finish now. You see a summary of the choices you have made in the wizard to check against. Click Finish to encrypt the columns.

5. The wizard asks you to log in to Azure once more so that the CMK can be created in the chosen key vault. Once this shows each step as passed, the columns are encrypted. You can see the created CEK and CMK by navigating to Security > Always Encrypted Keys > Column Master Keys And Column Encryption Keys in the Object Explorer under the database. If you right-click the CMK and CEK and select Script To Query Window, you can see the URI to the key vault and the Encrypted Key value respectively. You also can see how the table definition has changed by scripting it to the query window.

> **NOTE PERMISSIONS FOR CREATING THE CMK IN THE KEY VAULT**
>
> At this point, if you've forgotten to set the permissions on the key vault, you see a wrapKey error, and you need to start the wizard again. The permissions required via an access-policy are create, get, list, sign, verify, wrapKey, and unwrapKey.

You can use SQL Server Management Studio to mimic an application that uses Always Encrypted by using some session settings. These settings are mandatory for an application that wants to use Always Encrypt. Follow these steps to set up the session settings and see Always Encrypt from an application perspective:

1. Open a new SSMS session to your Azure SQL database, but before you log in, select the Additional Connection Parameters tab, and enter the following command, and click Connect.

   ```
   Column Encryption Setting=enabled
   ```

2. In the menu, select Query; at the bottom of Query Options, click Advanced and check Enable Parameterization for Always Encrypted. Click OK. With these two settings, you can perform simple CRUD operations on the encrypted columns, as shown in Figure 4-25.

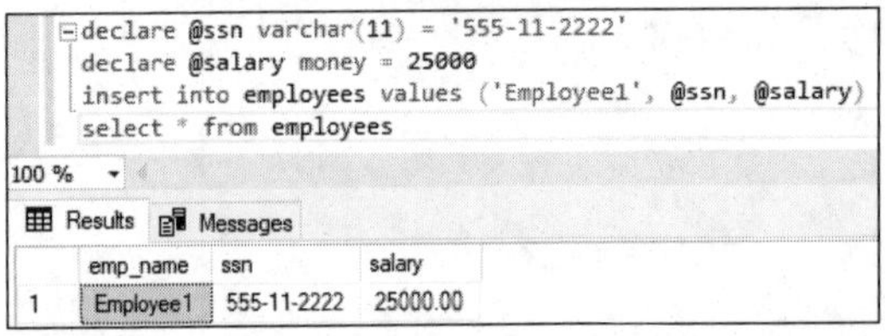

```
declare @ssn varchar(11) = '555-11-2222'
declare @salary money = 25000
insert into employees values ('Employee1', @ssn, @salary)
select * from employees
```

	emp_name	ssn	salary
1	Employee1	555-11-2222	25000.00

FIGURE 4-25 Select Always Encrypted columns with encryption setting disabled

However, if you reconnect and don't enable Column Encryption Setting, you can't read the data, as you can see in Figure 4-26, and Create/Update/Delete will error.

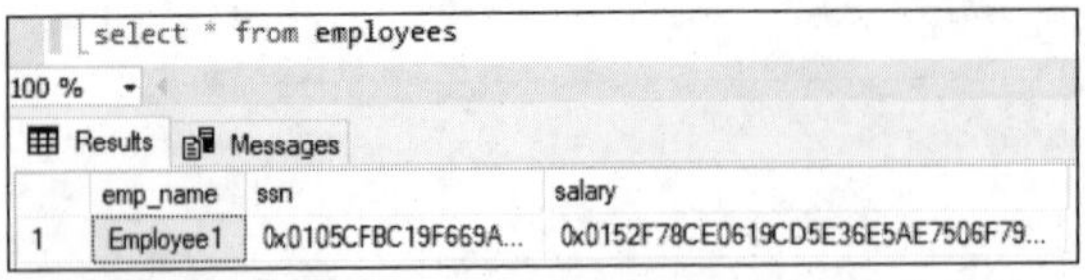

```
select * from employees
```

	emp_name	ssn	salary
1	Employee1	0x0105CFBC19F669A...	0x0152F78CE0619CD5E36E5AE7506F79...

FIGURE 4-26 Select Always Encrypted columns with encryption setting enabled

Implement Azure Confidential Compute and SSL/TLS communications

Beyond data at rest, there are further scenarios that we have not touched on so far, how to add
a secure layer to data in transit, and how data in use can be secured. These are covered in the
following sections, "SSL/TLS" and "Azure Confidential Compute."

SSL/TLS

Data in transit that isn't protected is more susceptible to attack, including session hijacking and
man-in-the-middle attacks, which allows malicious users to gain access to possibly confidential
data. Transport Layer Security (TLS) and Secure Sockets Layer (SSL) are both cryptographic
protocols that provide data encryption and communication between servers and applications
over a network, which protects the customer's data in transit.

SSL was the predecessor to TLS. With each new version of the SSL protocol, more secure
ciphers and algorithms were used; however, more and more vulnerabilities were discovered.
For this reason, all SSL protocols have been deprecated by the Internet Engineering Task Force
(IETF), along with TLS 1.0 and 1.1.

When recommending protocols for communication of data to customers, the current
best practice is TLS 1.2, with settings for SSL to be disabled. You may be thinking, "If SSL is
deprecated, why is it still available on many server configurations and often enabled by

default?" The answer is backwards compatibility. Some systems still do not support SSL or even the earlier versions of TLS. For example, on a recent project, a proxy server at one customer site did not support TLS 1.2. This meant the proxy server couldn't initiate the handshake with the Azure Application Gateway that had been configured for TLS 1.2 only. This meant traffic did not flow, and the application appeared to be down. Having configured the Application Gateway to only support TLS 1.2 as per best practice, the changes had to be backed out to TLS 1.0+.

You've already explored cross-premise connections using Azure VPN Gateway and Point-to-Site, Site-to-Site VPNs and ExpressRoute connections in Chapter 2, Skill 2.4 "Integrate an Azure virtual network and an on-premises network." Each of these resources leverage SSL/TLS for private tunnels/networks between on premise and Azure. Azure SQL Database and Azure Storage also leverage SSL/TLS for communication by default. This leaves traffic over the public internet—most commonly between a browser and webserver.

Use the following steps to create an Azure Web App service deploying with an app service SSL certificate for a custom domain, checking SSL/TLS 1.0/1.1 and HTTP support and verifying the SSL configuration as secure:

1. Using knowledge from previous chapters in this book, create a custom domain, if you no longer have one, and a web app service, making sure the tier is at least a B1. Select to publish a Docker Image of QuickStart and sample of Python Hello World on the app service. Note: On the lower App Service tiers, the container can take a while to pull down; enter container settings on the App blade to check the log for progress.

EXAM TIP

It's good to know which app service tiers support custom domains and SSL bindings and which do not.

2. Navigate to the web app you have just created within the portal, copy the URL from the Overview section of the blade, paste it into a browser address bar, but change https:// to http:// and press Enter to navigate to the page. Depending on the browser you're running from, you see either "Not secure" or an open padlock next to the address to verify that HTTP is not secure. Go back to the portal, and on the same blade, select SSL Settings, and change the HTTPS Only setting to On. Refresh the page with the HTTP link; you see that it is now redirected to an HTTPS page; it's no longer possible to access this page insecurely over HTTP.

3. To verify the current settings as secure, navigate to *https://ssllabs.com/ssltest* in a browser. Copy and paste the app service URL in for the test; it will take a few minutes. Once complete, you should see the configuration being presented with an A result. The implementation by default in Azure App Service under HTTPS is secure and well configured.

NOTE   SSLLABS.COM/SSLTEST

Ssllabs.com is a free service that analyzes the configuration of a public internet SSL web server. The resultant grade and report contain details on how to resolve SSL configuration issues, which could leave your server open to attack through vulnerabilities.

4. Go back to the portal and select SSL Configuration in the App Service blade. Downgrade the minimum TLS version to 1.0 for backward compatibility. Note that SSL versions are not configurable due to their deprecation. Rerun the SSL test from step 2. The SSL configuration is still A grade; however, there are now more orange warnings.

5. Navigate to Custom Domains in the App Service blade, select to Add Custom Domain, and enter the custom domain name from step 1. When you click OK, the custom domain is assigned to the Azure App Service, but as there is no SSL certificate for this domain, a warning displays. If you try the SSL test from step 3 with the newly assigned custom domain, the test errors because the SSL certificate doesn't exist, and the certificate chain points to the *.azurewebsites.net certificate.

6. Go back to the portal and select to create a new App Service Certificate in the marketplace. Then enter the following responses:

   A. **Name** A name for the app service certificate will be identified as this in Azure services.

   B. **Naked Host Domain** Enter the custom domain created for this walkthrough.

   C. **Certificate SKU** Standard (S1) is enough for this example. Wild Card (W1) certificate is only recommended if multiple subdomain use is required.

   Agree to the legal terms and click Create.

NOTE USING APP SERVICE CERTIFICATE

Even though the price for the SSL certificate is given per month, the entire year will be charged to your account when you click Create.

---

7. Navigate back to the App Service Certificate in the portal. Notice the key vault store warning message at the top of the Overview section. To use the certificate, you need to import it as a secret into a key vault and verify the domain.

   Click Configured Required Key Vault Store; create a new vault if required.

   Perform a Domain Verification by copying the Domain Verification Token displayed and creating a TXT record. Manage DNS Settings is held under App Service Domain on the App Service blade rather than Azure AD. Add a Record Set with the following details:

   A. **Name** The App Service name.

   B. **Type** TXT.

   C. **TTL** This is the Time To Live, speeds up DNS record update for the example as it is the time until cached address expires. Set to 5 minutes.

   D. **Value** Paste in the Domain Verification Token.

   Click OK. It shouldn't take more than 5 minutes for the DNS records to be updated. The domain can now be verified. Go back to App Service Certificate in the portal and select Domain Verification and verify the domain.

8. Navigate back to the app service that was created for this walkthrough; select SSL Settings in the blade. Now select the Private Certificates (.pfx) tab and Import an App Service Certificate. Select the certificate created in step 6 and click OK. The certificate is available to bind to the App Service. Note here you could upload your own certificates or import one already uploaded to key vault.

9. Click the Bindings tab and Add SSL Binding. Select the Custom Domain created in step 1, and then the private certificate imported in step 8. Because this is a B1 tier web app and SNI SSL type, click Add Binding.

10. Navigate back to the Overview section of the App Service blade. The URL should have changed to the custom domain. Paste the URL into a browser to check the app service is still responding on the new domain. Enter the URL on the SSL Test page from step 3 to verify the SSL settings for the new domain. Once again, you should see a grade A.

You can use the same process to add an App Service Domain and Certificate to secure a function app on a custom domain.

For connections coming in over the public internet, it's also likely you will be architecting solutions to a VM Scale Set or Azure App Service, which requires load balancing or features of the Web Application Firewall (or both). These requirements require placing the application gateway in front of the app service or VM scale set. You've already explored the application gateway configuration settings in Chapter 2, Skill 2.3 "Implement application load balancing," but let's take a look at the SSL/TLS options:

11. **SSL Termination (Offloading)** Traffic flows between the local client and application gateway using HTTPS. The traffic is unencrypted by the application gateway and travels between the application gateway and back-end applications in Azure in plaintext. This moves the overhead of decryption from the app server to the application gateway. To enable SSL Termination in the portal follow these steps. An example configuration is shown in Figure 4-27:

   A. On the Configuration section of Create An Application Gateway, select to add a Routing rule.

   B. Enter the Listener name. This should be appropriate to the route—in this case, SSL termination.

   C. Select Public for the Frontend IP, A Protocol of HTTPS, and a Port of 443.

   D. Upload the PFX certificate from your local machine. Note the domains must match, or it should be a wildcard subdomain certificate. Enter an appropriate name for the certificate and the password used when you created the private key.

   E. Leave the Listener type as basic for a single site. Click Add to add the route.

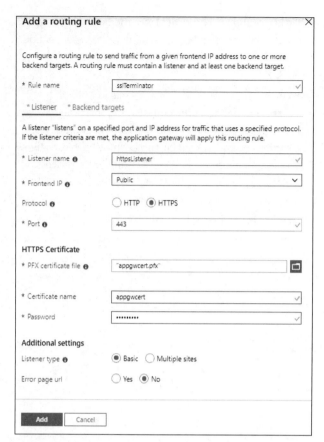

Add a routing rule

Configure a routing rule to send traffic from a given frontend IP address to one or more backend targets. A routing rule must contain a listener and at least one backend target.

* Rule name   sslTerminator

* Listener   * Backend targets

A listener "listens" on a specified port and IP address for traffic that uses a specified protocol. If the listener criteria are met, the application gateway will apply this routing rule.

* Listener name   httpsListener

* Frontend IP   Public

Protocol   ◯ HTTP ◉ HTTPS

* Port   443

HTTPS Certificate

* PFX certificate file   "appgwcert.pfx"

* Certificate name   appgwcert

* Password   •••••••••

Additional settings

Listener type   ◉ Basic ◯ Multiple sites

Error page url   ◯ Yes ◉ No

Add   Cancel

FIGURE 4-27 Azure Application Gateway SSL termination

EXAM TIP

Understanding that Application Gateway provides SSL termination, and knowing how to configure this on an existing app gateway is useful.

It's also possible to use a key vault certificate (in preview) if you're using an application gateway V2 SKU. This uses a managed identity to access and assign the certificate from the key vault.

12. **End-to-End SSL**   Traffic flowing between the local client, application gateway, and back-end applications in Azure is encrypted at all times. To communicate using SSL/TLS with the back end, root certificates (v2 SKU) must be trusted on the application gateway, or to communicate with an app service or other Azure Web Service, these are implicitly trusted (v2 SKU). To configure HTTPS on the back end for a v1 SKU application gateway in the portal, complete the following:

Open an existing application gateway in the portal. Select HTTP Settings on the blade, and then select the AppGatewayBackendHTTPSettings line. On Protocol select HTTPS.

You now need to upload the public key of the pfx certificate from the back-end server/ service by uploading it and adding it in the Backend Authentication Certificates section.

Azure Confidential Compute (ACC)

When data is in use, it is often required to be plaintext, or "in the clear," while loaded in memory. It's often a requirement for processing to happen efficiently. During this time the data is susceptible to attack from malicious power users, hackers, malicious software, or anyone (or anything) that could get access to read a server's memory. Your customers may have sensitive data, such as financial and medical information, that may require protection during process-ing in memory. This is particularly problematic in the cloud, where the customer may have less control over the underlying operating system and no control over the security of the hardware. Architects need to be able to advise a technology to address this requirement.

This is where Azure Confidential Compute comes in. It uses Trusted Execution Environments (TEE) to protect data and code while an application is running. Figure 4-28 shows a high-level overview of how TEEs work:

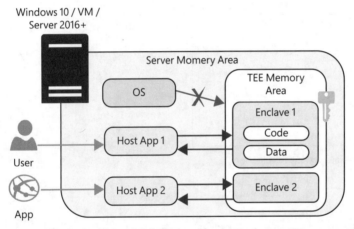

FIGURE 4-28 Trusted Execution Environment

A TEE can be at the hardware or software (hypervisor) level. In hardware, it's part of the CPU instruction set. A TEE implementation gives an application the possibility to execute sections of code within a protected area called an *enclave*. The enclave pretty much acts like a bubble, protecting the application from the host machine. As you can see from Figure 4-28, even the operating system cannot penetrate the bubble to access or tamper with the program or code. In the diagram, the TEE has created two enclaves. Enclave 1 is expanded just to show it has code and data within it.

An enclave has a trust relationship to a host application. Going back to Figure 4-28, only Host App 1 can access Enclave 1, and Host App 2 can access only Enclave 2. This trust relation-ship uses attestation, a protocol that ensures the code in the enclave is signed and trusted before sending protected data. The two enclaves have no visibility with each other; they can't access the other's data or code. This opens the possibility of running multiple workloads with different sources of protected data all on one server without compromising data security.

You may not have realized it, but it's likely you've encountered TEE/Enclave technology already on your smartphone, especially if it's storing your fingerprint/facial recognition (biometric data) for phone or app access. Use cases that can be fulfilled currently within Azure are

- DC-series VMs running Open Enclave SDK, TEE enabled applications.
- SQL Server (2019+ IaaS) Always Encrypted with secure enclaves running on a DC-series VM. (Brings complex SQL searching, not currently available in Azure SQL.)
- Multi-source machine learning.
- Confidential Consortium Blockchain, running the COCO framework.

This is an expanding area; future use cases will include IOT Edge for processing sensitive data before aggregating to the cloud.

EXAM TIP

Setting up an application to use Confidential Compute via Open Enclave SDK is beyond the scope of the exam. However, understanding the basic concepts and potential use cases will be beneficial.

To complete this section, follow these steps to provision a Ubuntu DC-series VM ready for confidential computing:

1. In the portal, navigate to the Search bar and search for confidential computing. Select Confidential Compute VM Deployment from the marketplace. On the overview screen, there are more links that may be useful. Click Create.

2. On the Basics blade, note the text at the top. There are only a handful of regions that support ACC. The values entered for this section are no different than a standard VM apart from four places, as shown in Figure 4-29:

    A. **Image**   Select a Ubuntu or Windows 2016 Datacenter image as required. For this example, select Ubuntu.

    B. **Include Open Enclave SDK**   Select yes to have this installed for you; however, it can be installed later.

    C. **Resource Group**   Must be an empty resource group.

    D. **Location**   Must be one of the regions listed at the top of the blade.

3. Click OK and enter the VM Settings blade. Once again, the settings are no different to a standard VM. You can configure a standard VNet with default subgroup. In this walkthrough, allow SSH so that installation of Open Enclave SDK can be verified. Note only DC size VMs are available to select as shown in Figure 4-29. Click OK to validate the configuration, and then click OK to create the VM.

4. Once the VM has been created, go to Overview on the VM blade and copy the SSH connect string into a console. SSH into the VM and verify the SDK is installed. If it is, you have an openenclave directory under /opt:

```
sysadmin@accsvmexample:/$ cd /opt/openenclave
sysadmin@accsvmexample:/opt/openenclave$
```

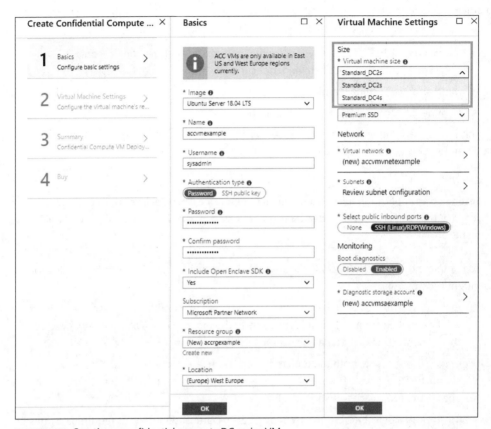

FIGURE 4-29 Creating a confidential compute DC series VM

NEED MORE REVIEW? **CONFIDENTIAL COMPUTING**

To learn more about Confidential Computing, visit the Solutions Overview "Azure confidential computing" at *https://azure.microsoft.com/en-gb/solutions/confidential-compute*. A further excellent resource is at *https://azure.microsoft.com/en-gb/blog/azure-confidential-computing*.

Chapter summary

- Windows-Integrated Authentication in a legacy application will leverage NTLM or Kerberos for SSO. In the cloud, this is accomplished using AD Connect and the single sign-on feature. AD Connect and single-sign on requires password or pass-through synchronization to be used. Microsoft recommends using conditional access policies for Multi-Factor Authentication using Azure AD.

- App-to-API and API-to-API security via OAuth authorization can be configured in the client application or using Azure API Management. The flow used is dependent on use case to determine how to retrieve the access token. OAuth 2.0 uses authorization and access tokens in the form of JSON Web Tokens (JWTs). JWTs should be validated; in API Management, you should use validate-jwt.

- Managed identities allow you to authenticate against services in Azure without having to use credentials or certificates. Authentication is performed through Azure AD. When a managed identity is created, a service principle is automatically created, registered against the Azure AD, and trusted. System-managed identities exist for the lifetime of a resource. User-managed identities can be reused on multiple resources.

- When enabling an identity on an app service/function app, the environment variables MSI_SECRET and MSI_ENDPOINT are created so that an access token can be obtained for use on a resource. VMs use the Azure Instance Metadata Service Endpoint to obtain an access token for use on a resource. This endpoint is only accessible from inside the VM.

- To secure secrets, keys, and certificates, use Key Vault. If you need HSM-backed keys for FIPS compliance, you need the premium tier. Microsoft can't read the keys, secrets, or certificates in your vault. The key vault APIs can be called directly or via wrappers using Azure portal, PowerShell, CLI, and code libraries. Key vaults should be protected from deletion by mistake.

- Storage Service Encryption (SSE) is data encryption at rest for Azure Storage. System-managed keys support all services; customer-managed keys are for blobs and files. Managed disks are automatically encrypted by SSE and do not support BYOK. Unmanaged disks must use BYOK. Azure security center flags unencrypted, unmanaged disks as a risk.

- Azure SQL supports encryption at rest by Transparent Data Encryption (TDE) and column-level encryption with Always Encrypted. Both technologies support BYOK. Always Encrypted requires code changes in the application; TDE does not.

- SSL is the predecessor to TLS. Both are protocols that enable encrypted transmission of data. TLS is the current best practice minimum to support. SSL protocols should be disabled. Application gateway supports SSL Termination (Offloading). Communication with the application gateway is over SSL, but on termination the communication between the application gateway and background services is not encrypted.

Thought experiment

In this thought experiment, demonstrate your skills and knowledge of the topics covered in this chapter. You can find answers to this thought experiment in the next section.

You have been hired as a consultant solutions architect by Contoso Stocks, a company managing investment portfolios. Contoso Stocks have decided to move their in-house software from an on-premises data center to Azure. Business and integration analysis of the current offering has identified the following key requirements:

■ Transactional data and user financial data (including bank details) are stored in a SQL Server 2012 Standard Edition database.

■ A front-end web application installed on a virtual machine uses HTML forms to authenticate using Windows Authentication (NTLM) against a single AD. The current implementation is Single Sign-On.

■ The front-end web application is ASP.Net running on IIS 7 on a Windows 2012 Server. It isn't published beyond the firewall, so it isn't deemed worth securing.

■ A back-end VM runs a bespoke mathematical algorithm to forecast portfolio growth and feedback into the portfolios on the SQL Database. This is Contoso Stock's own IP and major value add offering. The VM stores data locally to learn from historically after every run.

Current Azure/Cloud services being used are that all users are running Office 365 with AD Connect synchronizing domain users.

Contoso Stock leadership and SecOps requirements include the following:

■ All data should be encrypted at rest.

■ Data transmitted between users and the Web API should be encrypted.

■ Application administrators need to provide extra security for authentication when not in one of the organization's offices.

■ Bank details should not be visible to developers or SQL DBAs at any time.

■ SecOps require any encryption keys or secrets to be rotated regularly for compliance.

■ SecOps would like to see the current hard-coded database, VM, and storage account credentials removed and stored securely.

■ SecOps don't allow password hashes from Windows AD to be stored in the cloud.

■ The preference is to keep Single Sign-On if possible; however, the app must secure using the Windows AD credentials.

■ It's desirable to rearchitect the app away from IIS on a VM. However, it's not possible to make code changes to the mathematical algorithm on the VM until they're ready to leverage Machine Learning in Azure.

With this information in mind, please answer the following questions:

1. What solution(s) would you implement to ensure the user's financial and transactional information is secured at rest and personally identifiable information is protected?

2. How could Contoso Stocks meet the requirements of SecOps for the removal of hard-coded secrets and rotation of encryption keys for compliance?

3. What would you recommend to Contoso Stocks for the authentication of the web app users and administrators?

Thought experiment answers

This section contains the solution to the thought experiment. Each answer explains why the answer choice is correct.

1. Data is stored in two resources currently: SQL Server and the VM. These are the resources that need to be secure at rest on migration to the cloud. The data on SQL Server can be migrated to Azure SQL, where Azure SQL would enable Transparent Data Encryption by default. However, this contains financial information, so customer-managed keys should be used to further encrypt the TDE key as best practice.

   The personally identifiable information in the Azure SQL Database includes bank details. To secure this information from possibly malicious employees, you would recommend using Always Encrypted and encrypt the financial information columns. This requires code changes within the web app; however, code changes on the web app were marked as acceptable. You should recommend these changes happen as a rearchitecture to an Azure Web App.

   The data on the VM must also be encrypted at rest. As the VM stores historical financial information, you should be recommending that Contoso Stocks rotate encryption keys. The application code on the VM can't be altered at this stage; therefore, the recommendation to migrate this VM would be "lift and shift," utilizing unmanaged disks. By recommending unmanaged disks, Contoso Stocks can encrypt the VM disks with a customer-managed key and Azure Disk Encryption.

   Further encryption mechanisms on the VM cannot be used as they require code changes to implement.

2. The answer in question 1 requires access to customer-managed keys for all encryption scenarios. Couple this with the requirement for secret management, Azure Key Vault must be recommended as the first part of this solution. Azure Key Vault stores keys and secrets, which gives the Contoso Stocks SecOps team the ability to audit key and secret usage. Azure Key Vault facilitates key rotation either by manual rotation or automated rotation using Azure Automation. You should also recommend setting the soft delete and purge options on the key vault to stop accidental vault deletion, which could lead to loss of data.

Managed identities should be recommended for use on the VM and rearchitected Azure Web App. This will remove the necessity for credentials to be hard-coded, with access to these secrets granted to each Identity through Access Policies.

3. The requirements for this question call for using Windows AD credentials, but there is also a mention that Contoso Stock's users are already using Office 365 with AD Connect. This points to Azure AD already being available to use for authorization. It may even be possible that any Windows AD security groups for this application have already been synchronized for use in Azure. You should recommend that Contoso Stocks review the AD Connect settings to ensure that the Single Sign-On and Pass-Through Authentication are the chosen settings. This will satisfy the requirement of no password hashes in the cloud from Windows AD and to keep Single Sign-On where possible.

   The second part of this solution is for application administrators to provide further credentials when logging in from outside the offices. Your recommendation for this should be to upgrade Azure AD to a premium tier and implement location conditional access to an administrative Azure AD group created for this application.

Always be aware there will often be more information given in the requirements than needed to answer use-case style questions.

## CHAPTER 5

Develop for the cloud and for Azure Storage

Microsoft Azure platform provides a rich set of options for storage needs for microservices-based distributed application architecture and built-in capability to monitor and autoscale cloud-hosted applications.

As an Azure architect and for AZ-300 certification exam success, you need to understand the available storage solutions and messaging services options and know how to choose one over the other to fit for a given application scenario. You also need to understand design aspects to develop reliable and resilient cloud applications.

Skills covered in this chapter:

- Skill 5.1: Develop solutions that use Cosmos DB Storage
- Skill 5.2: Develop solutions that use a relational database
- Skill 5.3: Configure a message-based integration architecture
- Skill 5.4: Develop for autoscaling

Skill 5.1: Develop solutions that use Cosmos DB Storage

In today's world, many global businesses want to deploy globally distributed applications to achieve low latency, higher throughput, and high availability by putting application instances and databases close to the geographic location of their user base. The application deployment in multi-datacenter comes with deployment complexity. One example is the burden of upgrading databases without affecting production traffic.

To alleviate the complexity of database schema management during upgrades, the concept of NoSQL comes in. Additionally, for global applications, you need to consider the scalability and availability of the databases. Selecting the right database service based upon the nature of your application is a critical design decision.

Create and manage Azure Cosmos DB account

In this section, you learn how to set up an Azure Cosmos DB account and configure its advanced features such as security, business continuity, and disaster recovery.

What is Cosmos DB?

Azure Cosmos DB is Microsoft's globally distributed, multi-model database. Azure Cosmos DB enables you to elastically and independently scale throughput and storage across the globe with guaranteed throughput, latency, availability, and consistency.

The Cosmos DB offers the following benefits:

- **Guaranteed throughput**   Cosmos DB guarantees throughput and performance at peak load. The performance level of Cosmos DB can be scaled elastically by setting Request Units (RUs).

- **Global distribution and Always On**   With an ability to having multi-master replicas globally and built-in capability to programmatically (or manually) invoke failover, Cosmos DB enables 99.999% read/write availability around the world. The Cosmos DB *multi-homing API* is an additional feature to configure the application to point to the closest datacenter for low latency and better performance.

- **Multiple query model or API**   Cosmos DB supports many APIs to work with the data stored in your Cosmos database. By default, you can use SQL (the default API) for querying your Cosmos database. Cosmos DB also implements APIs for Cassandra, MongoDB, Gremlin, and Azure Table Storage.

- **Choices of consistency modes**   The Azure Cosmos DB replication protocol offers five well-defined, practical, and intuitive consistency models. Each model has a trade-off between consistency and performance.

- **No schema or index management**   The database engine is entirely schema agnostic. Cosmos DB automatically indexes all data for faster queries response.

Security and compliance in Azure Cosmos DB

Security has always been a shared responsibility between the customer and a cloud provider. In the case of a platform-as-a-service (PaaS) database offering such as Azure Cosmos DB, the customer's responsibility to keep the data secure shrinks to some extent as the cloud provider takes on more responsibility. In addition to keeping your data secure in the cloud, the cloud provider also helps customers meet their compliance obligations with the product offerings.

- **Security**   Azure Cosmos DB by default provides encryption at rest and in transit for documents and backups in all Azure regions without requiring any configuration from you. The AZ-300 exam expects you to know the ways to secure your data stored in Cosmos DB.

- **Inbound request filtering**   The first defense you can turn on is IP address-based access control. The default is allowed, provided a request is with a valid authorization token. You can add a single client IP or IP ranges in Classless Inter-Domain Routing (CIDR) or by subnet of the VNet to allow access to the Cosmos DB. Figure 5-1 shows the Azure portal Cosmos DB blade and how to configure IP-based security for Cosmos DB.

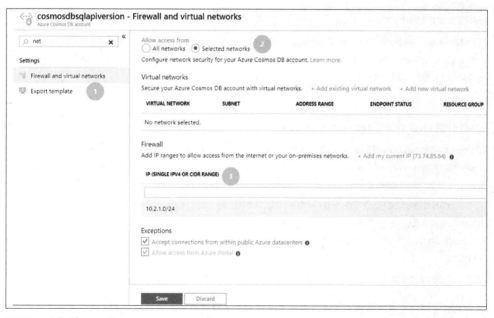

FIGURE 5-1 Setting up Cosmos account security

- **Fine-Grained Access** Azure Cosmos DB uses a *hash-based message authorization code* (HMAC) to authorize access at the account level or even at the resource level like database, container, or items. Access to the account and resources is granted by either the master key or a resource token. The master key is used for full administrative access; the resource token approach is based on the fine-grained Role-Based Access Code (RBAC) security principle.

> *NEED MORE REVIEW?* **DATA SECURITY IN AZURE COSMOS DB**
>
> To learn more about the options to set up secure access to Cosmos DB and secure your data, visit the Microsoft docs article "Security in Azure Cosmos DB - overview" at *https://docs.microsoft.com/en-us/azure/cosmos-db/database-security/*.

- **Compliance** Azure Cosmos DB has a major industry certification to help the customer meet their compliance obligations across regulated industries and markets worldwide.

> *NEED MORE REVIEW?* **COMPLIANCE CERTIFICATION**
>
> To learn more about the compliance certification of Cosmos DB, please visit the Microsoft docs "Compliance in Azure Cosmos DB" located at *https://docs.microsoft.com/en-us/azure/cosmos-db/compliance.*

Understand the Cosmos account

Azure Cosmos account is a logical construct that has a globally unique DNS name. For high availability, you can add or remove regions to your Cosmos account at any time. You also can set up multiple masters/write replicas across different regions in your Cosmos account.

You can manage your Cosmos account in an Azure subscription either by using Azure portal, Azure CLI, or AZ PowerShell module, or you can use different language-specific SDKs. This section describes the essential fundamental concepts and mechanics of an Azure Cosmos account.

As of writing this book, you can create 100 Azure Cosmos accounts under one Azure subscription. Under the Cosmos account, you can create one or more Cosmos DBs (Cosmos databases), and within the Cosmos DBs, you can create one or more containers. In the container, you put your massive data. Cosmos DB container is a fundamental unit of scalability—a logical resource composed of one or more partitions.

Figure 5-2 gives you the visual view of what we've shared about Cosmos account thus far.

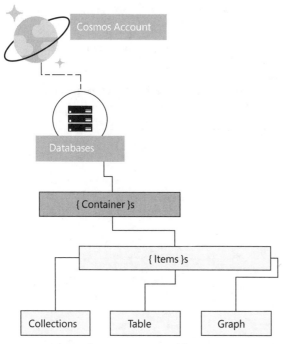

FIGURE 5-2 Azure Cosmos account entities

Create a Cosmos account

To set up a Cosmos account using the Azure portal, use the following steps:

1. Sign into Azure portal (*https://portal.azure.com*).

2. Under your subscription, on the upper-left corner, select Create A Resource and search for Cosmos DB.

3. Click Create (see Figure 5-3).

FIGURE 5-3 Creating an Azure Cosmos account

4. On the create Cosmos DB account page, supply the basic mandatory information, as shown in Figure 5-4.

- **Subscription** The Azure subscription you need to create an account under.
- **Resource Group** Select or create a resource group.
- **Account Name** Enter the name of the new Cosmos account. Azure appends documents.azure.com to the name you provide to construct a unique URI.

FIGURE 5-4 Create an Azure Cosmos Account wizard

- **API** The API determines the type of account to create. Azure Cosmos DB provides five APIs: Core (SQL) and MongoDB for document data, Gremlin for graph data, Azure Table, and Cassandra. *You must create a separate Cosmos account for each API.* The **Core (SQL)** is to create a document database and supports query by using SQL syntax.
- **Location** Choose the geographic location you need to host your Cosmos account.

5. You can skip the Network and TAG section and Click Review + Create. It takes a few minutes for the deployment to complete. You can see the Cosmos DB created under the resource group resources.

Global distribution and multiple write replicas

To set up the global distribution of your Cosmos DBs and enable multiple replicas across regions, please use the following steps:

6. Go to your Cosmos account and open up the Replicate Data Globally menu (see Figure 5-5). You have an option to either add region by selecting hexagon icon of your desired region on the map or choose from the drop-down menu after you click +Add Region on the right side.

7. To remove regions, clear one or more regions from the map by selecting the blue hexagons with check marks.

8. Click Save to commit the changes.

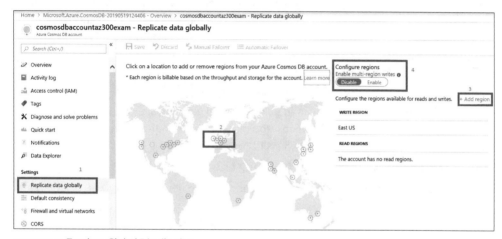

FIGURE 5-5 Turnkey, Global Distribution

> **IMPORTANT AZURE COSMOS DB—MULTI-WRITE REPLICAS**
> You cannot turn off or disable the multi-region writes after it's enabled.

Business continuity and disaster recovery

Business continuity and disaster recovery is one of the critical factors moving to the cloud. Cosmos DB global distribution with an ability to have multiple read/write replicas provides an option to either automate failover to the secondary database in case of a regional outage or do it manually when needed. Cosmos DB also automatically back up your database every four hours and stores it in the GRS blob storage for disaster recovery (DR). At any given time, at least last two backups are retained for 30 days.

Manage scalability and implementing partitioning schemes for Cosmos DB

Azure Cosmos DB uses horizontal partitioning to scale individual containers not only in terms of storage but also in terms of throughput. As the throughput and storage requirements of an application increase, Azure Cosmos DB transparently moves partitions to automatically spread the load across a larger number of physical servers to satisfy the need of scalability and performance need of a container in the database.

Azure Cosmos DB uses *hash-based partitioning* to spread logical partitions across physical partitions. Queries that access data within a single logical partition are more cost-effective than queries that access multiple partitions. You must be very mindful when choosing a partition key to query data efficiently and avoid "Hot Spots" within a partition.

Following are the key considerations for a partition key:

- As of the writing of this book, a single partition has an upper limit of 10 GB of storage.
- Azure Cosmos DB containers have a minimum throughput of 400 request units per second (RU/s). RUs are a blended measure of computational cost (CPU, memory, disk I/O, network I/O). 1RU corresponds to the throughput of reading of a 1 KB document. All requests on the partition are charged in the form of RUs. If the request exceeds the provisioned RUs on the partition, Cosmos DB throws RequestRateTooLargeException or HTTP Status code 429.
- Choose a partition key that has a wide range of values and access patterns that are evenly spread across logical partitions.
- Candidates for partition keys might include properties that frequently appear as a filter in your queries.

Cross-partition query

Azure Cosmos DB automatically handles the queries against the single partition that has a partition key in the header request. For example, the following pseudo query1 is routed to the *userID* partition, which holds all the documents corresponding to partition key value XMS-0001.

Query 1
```
IQueryable<DeviceReading> query = client.CreateDocumentQuery<Employee>(
    UriFactory.CreateDocumentCollectionUri("myDatabaseName", "myCollectionName"))
    .Where(m => m.name== "singh" && m.userID == "ID-1");
```

The second pseudo query doesn't have a filter on the partition key (userID). Azure Cosmos DB fans out the query across partitions. The fan-out is done by issuing individual queries to all the partitions, and it's not default behavior. You have to explicitly mention in the using Feed options by setting the EnableCrossPartitionQuery property to on.

Query 2
```
IQueryable<DeviceReading> crossPartitionQuery = client.CreateDocumentQuery<Employee>(
    UriFactory.CreateDocumentCollectionUri("myDatabaseName", "myCollectionName"),
    new FeedOptions { EnableCrossPartitionQuery = true })
    .Where(m => m.FirstName == "Guru" && m.LastName > "jot");
```

Setting Request Units (RUs), partition key for the containers using Azure portal

The throughput and performance of Cosmos DB depend on the Requests Units (RUs) and partition key you specify while creating a container. RUs are the blended measure of CPU, IOPS, and memory that's required to perform a database operation. Use the following steps to create a container with the required RUs and a partition key.

1. Log in to the Azure portal and navigate to your Cosmos account under the Resource Group.
2. On the Data Explorer pane, select New Container (see Figure 5-6).
3. The screen shown in Figure 5-7 appears; enter the container name and database name.
4. Check the box for Provision Database Throughput and specify RUs according to your scalability need.
5. Specify the Partition Key (for example, /state/city/zip).
6. Click OK.

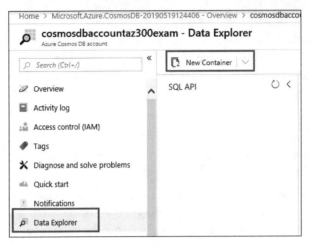

FIGURE 5-6 Cosmos DB Data Explorer blade

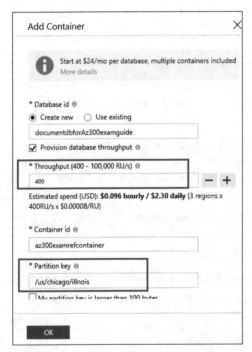

FIGURE 5-7 Create a new Cosmos DB wizard

> **NOTE DEFINE A PARTITION KEY FOR A CONTAINER**
>
> You can only define a partition key for a container during its creation; it cannot be changed after the container is created. So be very thoughtful while choosing a partition.

Set appropriate consistency level for operations

In geo-distributed databases, it's likely that you're reading the data that isn't the latest version, which is called a *dirty read*. The data consistency, latency, and performance don't seem to show much of a difference within a datacenter as data replication is much faster and takes only one millisecond. However, in the geo-distribution scenario, when data replication takes several hundred milliseconds, the story is different, which increases the chances of dirty reads. The Cosmos DB provides the following data consistency options to choose from with trade-offs between latency availability and performance:

- **Strong** A strong consistency level ensures no dirty reads, and the client always reads the latest version of committed data across the multiple read replicas in single or multi-regions. The trade-off going with the strong consistency option is the performance. When you write to a database, everyone waits for Cosmos DB to serve the latest writes after it has been saved across all read replicas.

- **Bounded Staleness** The bounded staleness option gives you an ability to decide how much staleness of data in terms of updates in a time interval an application can tolerate. You can specify the lag by an x version of updates of an item or by time interval T by which read lags behind by a write. The typical use case for you to go with bounded staleness is to guarantee low latency for writes for globally distributed applications.

- **Session** Session ensures that there are no dirty reads on the write regions. A session is scoped to a client session, and the client can read what they wrote instead having to wait for data to be globally committed.

- **Consistent Prefix** Consistent prefix guarantees that reads are never out of order of the writes. For example, if an item in the database was updated three times with versions V1, V2, and V3, the client would always see V1, V1V2, or V1V2V3. The client would never see out of order like V2, V1V3, or V2V1V3.

- **Eventual** You probably use eventual consistency when you're least worried about the freshness of data across the read replicas and the order of writes over time, but you need the highest level of availability and low latency.

To set up a desired consistency on the Cosmos DB, follow the following steps:

1. Log in to the Azure portal and navigate to your Cosmos account under the Resource Group.

2. On the Data Consistency pane (see Figure 5-8), select the desired consistency from the five consistency levels.

3. For bounded staleness, define the lag in time or operations an application can tolerate.

4. Click Save.

FIGURE 5-8 Setting Cosmos DB consistency

> **NOTE** **BUSINESS CONTINUITY AND DISASTER RECOVERY**
>
> For high availability, it's recommended that you configure Cosmos DB with multiregion writes (at least two regions). In the event of a regional disruption, the failover is instantaneous, and the application doesn't have to undergo any change; it transparently happens behind the scene. Also, if you're using the default consistency level of strong, there will not be any data loss before and after the failover. For bounded staleness, you may encounter a potential data loss up to the lag (time or operations) you've set up. For the Session, Consistent Prefix, and Eventual consistency options, the data loss could be up to a maximum of five seconds.

Create, read, update, and delete data by appropriate APIs

As said previously, Azure Cosmos DB currently provides five APIs (see Figure 5-9): Core (SQL) and MongoDB for document data, Cassandra, Azure Table API, and Gremlin (graph) API. As of the writing of this book, you can create only one API per Cosmos account.

The data stored in Cosmos DB is in the JSON format, and you can use multimodel APIs as shown in Table 5-1. The table shows the SDKs that are available for programming languages to interact with Cosmos DB and resources as of the writing of this book.

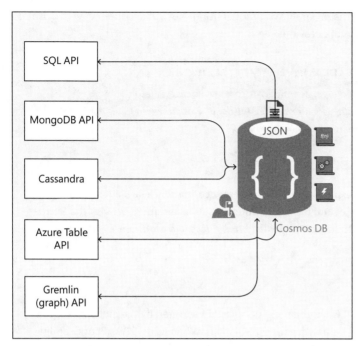

FIGURE 5-9 Cosmos DB APIs

TABLE 5-1 Supported language APIs for Azure Cosmos DB

	Java	.Net	Node.JS	Python	Go	Xamarin	Gremlin
SQL API	Available	Available	Available	Available		Available	
MongoDB API	Available	Available	Available	Available	Available	Available	
Gremlin	Available	Available	Available	Available			Available
Table API	Available	Available	Available	Available			
Cassandra API	Available	Available	Available	Available			

The choice of selecting which APIs to use ultimately depends on your use case. You're probably better off selecting SQL API if your team already has a skillset of T-SQL, and you're moving from a relational to a nonrelational database. If you're migrating an existing application that uses a MongoDB to Cosmos DB, you don't need to make any changes and can continue to use MongoDB API; the same is true for Cassandra API. Similarly, to take advantage of better performance, turnkey global distribution, and automatic indexing, use Table API if you're using Azure Table storage. The Gremlin API is used for graph modeling between entities.

The next section looks at the programming model using .Net SDKs to interact with Cosmos DB for SQL APIs mentioned in the previous section.

EXAM TIP

The AZ-300 exam doesn't expect you to know the service limits by heart. But it's worthwhile to know them in case you get into the weeds during solution design. Please visit the Microsoft docs "Azure Cosmos DB service quotas" at *https://docs.microsoft.com/en-us/azure/cosmos-db/concepts-limits*.

SQL API

Structured Query Language (SQL) is the most popular API adopted by the industry to access and interact with Cosmos DB data with existing SQL skills. When using SQL API or Gremlin API, Cosmos DB also gives you an ability to write server-side code using stored procedures, user-defined functions (UDFs), and triggers, as shown in Figure 5-10. These are essentially JavaScript functions written within the Cosmos DB database and scoped at the container level.

Following are the key considerations when you choose writing server-side code with Cosmos DB:

- Stored procedures and triggers are scoped at partition key and must be supplied with an input parameter for the partition key, whereas UDFs are scoped at the database level.

- Stored procedures and triggers guarantee atomicity (ACID) like in any relational database. Transactions are automatically rolled back by Cosmos DB in case of any exception; otherwise, they're committed to the database as a single unit of work.

- Queries using stored procedures and triggers are always executed on the primary replica as these are intended for write operations to guarantee strong consistency for secondary replicas, whereas UDFs can be written to the primary or secondary replica.

- The server-side code must complete within the specified timeout threshold limit, or you must implement a continuation batch model for long-running code. If the code doesn't complete within the time, Cosmos DB roll back the whole transaction automatically.

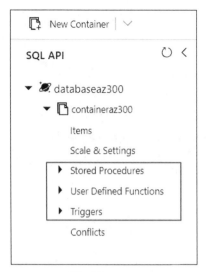

FIGURE 5-10 SQL API

- There are two types of triggers you can set up:
  - **Pre-triggers**   As the name defines, you can invoke some logic on the database containers before the items are created, updated, or deleted.
  - **Post-triggers**   Like pre-triggers, these are also tied to an operation on the database; however, post-triggers are run after the data is written or updated in the database.

Create, read, update, and delete data in Cosmos DB using .NET SQL API SDK

In this section, we programmatically interact with Cosmos DB and perform CRUD operations on it, using .NET SQL API SDK. You can use any of the supported languages or respective SDKs, as discussed previously.

For the example, we use Cosmos DB that we previously created using the Azure portal. Following are the prerequisites to get started:

- You need Visual Studio 2017 or later either licensed or community edition with Azure development kit installed.
- Azure subscription or free Cosmos DB trial account.
- If you would like to use local Cosmos DB emulator, install the local emulator as mentioned in the previous section.
- Under the Azure Cosmos account, create a database databaseaz300 and container FlightReservation using Azure portal.

After you have your environment ready, you can get right into the code. Use the following steps:

5. Create a Visual Studio project.

6. Select the Windows Application and Console .NET application template and name the project **AZ_300_Exam_Prep_Code**.

7. After you have named and created a project, open NuGet package manager.

8. Install Microsoft.Azure.DocumentDB from *https://www.nuget.org/packages/microsoft.azure.documentdb*

9. You need referencing to the following libraries in your code:

```
using System.Net;
using Microsoft.Azure.Documents;
using Microsoft.Azure.Documents.Client;
using Newtonsoft.Json;
```

10. Log in to the Azure portal and capture the Cosmos DB REST API endpoint and the keys from your Cosmos account as shown in Figure 5-11 to be referenced in the code. Here we take read-write keys as we will perform both read and write operations.

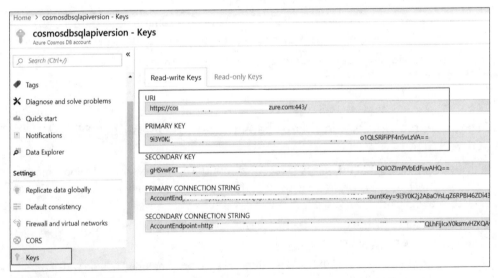

FIGURE 5-11 Cosmos DB keys

11. In your console application, under the namespace AZ_300_Exam_Prep_Code, replace Program.cs with FlightReservation.cs, as shown in the following code snippet.

In the following code, we have constant variables referencing Cosmos DB account keys and other constants representing database name, container name, and the partition you need to write to:

```
namespace AZ_300_Exam_Prep_Code {
    class FlightReservation    {
        private const string EndpointUrl = "https://cosmosdxxxxxx.documents.azure.
com:443/";
        private const string PrimaryKey =
"9i3Y0K2j2A8aOYxxxxxxxxxxxxxxxxxxxxxxxxxxxxQLSRiFiPF4n5vLzVA==";
        private DocumentClient client;
        private static string cbDatabaseName = "databasxxxxxeaz300";
        private static string cbContainerName = "FlightReservation";
        private static string PartitionKey = "AZ300ExamCod";
}
```

Add the following POCO (plain old CLR object) classes TravellerInfo, Itinerary, and Address under the namespace AZ_300_Exam_Prep_Code. The object is serialized when written to the Cosmos DB database. You want to make sure that all reservation data goes under the same partition for better performance and throughput, so here we're setting up a partition key value (PartitionKey) in the code logic. Cosmos DB automatically put the reservations that have a matching partition key property under the same partition of a container:

```
// TravellerInfo class , that holds properties of a traveler and itinerary
information
public class TravellerInfo    {
        [JsonProperty(PropertyName = "id")]
        public string Id { get; set; }
        public string LastName { get; set; }
        public string FirstName { get; set; }
        public string DOB { get; set; }
        public Itinerary[] TravelItinerary { get; set; }
        public Address { get; set; }
        public bool IsRegistered { get; set; }
        public override string ToString()           {
            return JsonConvert.SerializeObject(this);
        }
        public string PartitionKey { get; set; }
    }
    public class Itinerary    {
        public string SourceAirport  { get; set; }
        public string DestinationAirport { get; set; }
        public DateTime DepartureDate { get; set; }
        public DateTime? ReturnDate { get; set; }
        public bool IsRoundTrip { get; set; }
    }
    public class Address    {
        public string State { get; set; }
        public string County { get; set; }
        public string City { get; set; }
    }
```

12. To interact with Cosmos DB programmatically, initiate a connect with Cosmos DB RestAPIs using the DocumentClient library of the SDK as shown here with the main method:

```
static void Main(string[] args)        {
        client = new DocumentClient(new Uri(EndpointUrl), PrimaryKey);
   }
```

13. Now that you have a solution ready to make a connection with Cosmos DB, add a function CreateReservationDocumentIfNotExists in the FlightReservation class and call it from the main method as shown in the following code snippet. All you're doing here is initializing the connection to Cosmos DB using SQL API SDK. Then you create an object of a travelInfo class that holds information to a traveler and his or her itinerary. Next, you initialize a new object of FlightReservation class to call the function CreateReservationDocumentIfNotExists.

```
static void Main(string[] args)        {
client = new DocumentClient(new Uri(EndpointUrl), PrimaryKey);
 var travellerInfo = reservation.GetTravellerInfo(DateTime.Now.AddDays(10));
 FlightReservation reservation = new FlightReservation();
reservation.CreateReservationDocumentIfNotExists(cbDatabaseName, cbContainerName,
travellerInfo).Wait();
       }
// Function to create a reservation in Cosmsos DB
private async Task CreateReservationDocumentIfNotExists(string databaseName,
string collectionName, TravellerInfo Travellers)        {
        try {
              await client.ReadDocumentAsync(UriFactory.
CreateDocumentUri(databaseName, collectionName, travellers.Id),
                    new RequestOptions { PartitionKey = new
PartitionKey(PartitionKey) });
              WriteToConsole($"Found {travellers.Id}");
        }
        catch (DocumentClientException de)  {
            if (de.StatusCode == HttpStatusCode.NotFound)
            {
                await client.CreateDocumentAsync(UriFactory.CreateDocumentColl
ectionUri(databaseName, CollectionName), travellers);
                WriteToConsole($"Created reservation {travellers.Id}");
            }
            else
            {
                throw;
            }
        }
        catch(Exception) {
            WriteToConsole($"An Error in the reservation {travellers.Id}");
        }
      }
```

After compiling your solution, run it by pressing F5 or using the Start menu in Visual Studio, log in to Azure portal and navigate to your Cosmos DB. Click the Data Explorer properties and then an item in the database, as shown in the Figure 5-12.

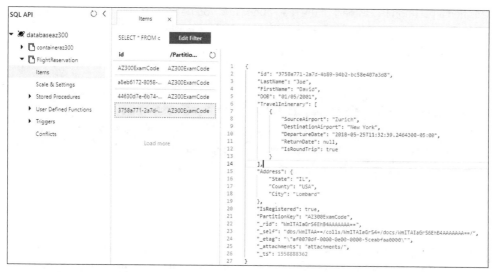

FIGURE 5-12 Cosmos DB Data Explorer

14. As shown in the following code snippet, to update or delete a specific document or reservation in the database, you use the ReplaceDocumentAsync or DeleteDocumentAsync functions that are part of SDK. The ReplaceDocumentAsync function requires an ID of the document or collection needed to be updated with a new object reference, and the DeleteDocumentAsync function requires you to supply the ID of the document to be deleted:

```
await client.ReplaceDocumentAsync(UriFactory.CreateDocumentUri(databaseName,
collectionName, documentID), traveller);
await client.DeleteDocumentAsync(UriFactory.CreateDocumentUri(databaseName,
collectionName, documentID));
```

15. The following code snippet shows an example of reading a query against the Cosmos DB database where are you searching the reservation database for a traveler with lastname= Joe within the partition you had created.

```
// Set some common query options.
        FeedOptions queryOptions = new FeedOptions {EnableCrossPartitionQuery
=false };
            IQueryable<TravellerInfo> travellers = client.CreateDocumentQuery
<TravellerInfo>(
            UriFactory.CreateDocumentCollectionUri(databaseName,
collectionName), queryOptions)
            .Where(r=>r.LastName== "Joe" && r.PartitionKey==PartitionKey);
```

Cross-partition query

Querying the document from Cosmos DB is not that complex. All you need is to specify the database name and the container name after you're authenticated and have a valid authorization token to read the data. As you can see in the following LINQ query, we haven't specified a partition key as part of the read query, and you need to enable cross-partition query. The default is OFF, otherwise you will receive an error asking to allow it to.

```
FeedOptions queryOptions = new FeedOptions {EnableCrossPartitionQuery=TRUE };
                    .Where(r=>r.LastName== "Joe");
```

> **NEED MORE REVIEW?**   **SQL QUERY REFERENCE GUIDE FOR COSMOS DB**
>
> To learn more about SQL Query examples and operators, visit the Microsoft doc "Getting started with SQL queries" at *https://docs.microsoft.com/en-us/azure/cosmos-db/sql-query-getting-started#GettingStarted*

EXAM TIP

Azure Cosmos DB was formerly known as Document DB; therefore, the commands in Azure CLI refer to the default SQL API as document DB. It's likely in the exam that you may get a question to check your knowledge of Azure CLI commands to create and manage Azure Cosmos account and resources. That said, it's recommended that you visit "Azure CLI samples for Azure Cosmos DB" at *https://docs.microsoft.com/bs-latn-ba/azure/cosmos-db/cli-samples*.

MongoDB API

You can switch from MongoDB to Cosmos DB and take advantage of excellent service features scalability, turnkey global distribution, various consistency levels, automatic backups, and indexing without having to change your application code. All you need to do is to create a Cosmos DB for MongoDB API (see Figure 5-13). As of the writing of this book, Cosmos DB's MongoDB API supports MongoDB server version 3.2, and you can use existing tooling, libraries, and open source client MongoDB drivers to interact with Cosmos DB.

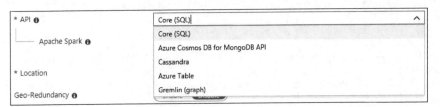

FIGURE 5-13 Cosmos supported APIs

Table API

Similar to MongoDB API, applications that are originally written for Azure Table storage can seamlessly be migrated to Cosmos DB without having to change the application code. In this case, you would create a Cosmos DB for Azure Table from the API options.

The client SDKs in.Net, Java, Python, and Node.js are available for Table API. Migrating from Azure Table storage to Cosmos DB provides you the service's premium capabilities, as we've been discussing since the start of this chapter.

Cassandra API

You can switch from Apache Cassandra and migrate to Cosmos DB and take advantage of enterprise-grade features scalability, turnkey global distribution, various consistency levels, automatic backups, and indexing without having to change your application code. As of the writing of this book, Cosmos DB's Cassandra API supports Cassandra Query language V4, and you can use existing tooling, libraries, and open source client Cassandra drivers to communicate with Cosmos DB.

Gremlin API

The Gremlin API is used for generating and visualizing a graph between data entities. The Cosmos DB fully supports an open-source graph computing framework called Apache TinkerPOP. You use this API when you would like to present complex relationships between entities in graphical form. The underlying mechanics of data storage are similar to what you have learned in the previous sections for other APIs, such as SQL or Table. That being said, your Graph data gets the same level of

- Scalability
- Performance and throughput
- Auto-indexing
- Global distribution and guaranteed high availability.

The critical components of any Graph database are the following:

- **Vertices** Vertices denote a discrete object such as a person, a place, or an event. If you take the analogy of an airline reservation system that we discussed in the SQL API example, a traveler is a vertex.

- **Edges** Edges denote a relationship between vertices. The relationship could be uni- or bidirectional. For example, in our analogy, an airline carrier is a vertex and the relationship between the traveler and the airline that defines which airline you traveled within a given year is considered an edge.

- **Properties** Properties include the information between vertices and edges—for example, the properties for a traveler, comprised of his or her name, date of birth, address, and so on. The properties for the edge (airline) could be airline name, travel routes, and so on.

Gremlin API is widely used in solving problems in a complex business relationship model like social networking, the geospatial, or scientific recommendation in retail and other businesses.

Here's a quick look at the airline reservation analogy and how to create vertices and edges using the Azure portal. You can do this programmatically as well using SDKs available in .NET and other languages.

CREATING VERTICES

Use the following steps to create a vertex traveler in the Graph database:

1. Log in to Azure portal and navigate to your Cosmos DB account that you created for Gremlin API.

2. On the Data Explorer blade, create a New Graph database by specifying the name, storage capacity, the throughput, and a partition key for the database. You have to provide the value for the partition key that you define. In our example, the partition key is graphdb and its value is az300 while creating vertices.

3. After the database is created, navigate to the Graph Query window, as shown in Figure 5-14, and run the following commands to create vertices, edges, and several properties for travelers and airlines:

```
g.addV('traveller').property('id', 'thomas').property('firstName', 'Thomas').
property('LastName', 'Joe').property('Address', 'Ohio').property('Travel Year',
2018).property('graphdb', 'az300')
g.addV('traveller').property('id', 'Gurvinder').property('FirstName',
'Gurvinder').property('LastName', 'Singh').property('Address', 'Chicago').
property('Travel Year', 2018).property('graphdb', 'az300')
g.addV('Airline Company').property('id', 'United Airlines').
property('CompanyName', 'United Airlines').property('Route 1', 'Chicago').
property('Route 2', 'Ohio').property('graphdb', 'az300')
g.addV('Airline Company').property('id', 'American Airlines').
property('CompanyName', 'American Airlines').property('Route 1', 'California').
property('Route 2', 'Chicago').property('graphdb', 'az300')
g.addV('Airline Company').property('id', 'Southwest Airlines').
property('CompanyName', 'Southwest Airlines').property('Route 1', 'Chicago').
property('Route 2', 'California').property('graphdb', 'az300')
g.addV('Airline Company').property('id', 'Delta Airlines').property('CompanyName',
'Delta Airlines').property('Route 1', 'Chicago').property('Route 2', 'Ohio').
property('graphdb', 'az300')
```

In the preceding Gremlin commands, "g" represents your graph database and g.addV() is used to add vertices. Properties() is used to associate properties with vertices.

CREATING EDGES

Now that you've added vertices for travelers and airlines, you need to define the relationship in a way that explains which airline a traveler has traveled with in a given year and if travelers know each other.

Create an edge on the vertex 'traveler' that you created previously. As you created vertices in step 3 in the preceding section, follow the same method and run the following commands on the graph window to create edges (see Figure 5-14):

```
g.V('thomas').addE('travelyear').to(g.V('Delta Airlines'))
g.V('thomas').addE('travelyear').to(g.V('American Airlines'))
g.V('thomas').addE('travelyear').to(g.V('United Airlines'))
g.V('Gurvinder').addE('travelyear').to(g.V('Delta Airlines'))
g.V('Gurvinder').addE('travelyear').to(g.V('United Airlines'))
g.V('thomas').addE('know').to(g.V('Gurvinder'))
```

FIGURE 5-14 Gremlin API

In this example, addE() is used to define a relationship with vertex traveler and an airline using g.V(). After you run the preceding commands, you can see the relationship between entities on the graph using Azure portal, as shown in Figure 5-15.

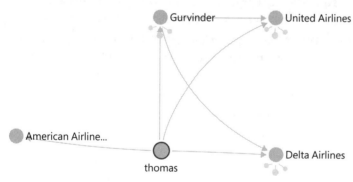

FIGURE 5-15 Gremlin API Graph

Skill 5.2: Develop solutions that use a relational database

Small, medium, and large enterprise companies have been using the relational databases for decades as a preferred way to store data for their small- or large-scale applications. In a relational database, the data is stored as a collection of data items with a predefined relationship between them. The data in any relational database is stored in rows and columns. Each row of the table has a unique key and represents a collection of values associated with an entity and can be associated with rows of other tables in the database that defines the relationship between entities. Each column of a row holds the values of an entity or object. In addition to it, the relational databases come with built-in capability of managing data integrity, transactional consistency, and ACID (Atomicity, Consistency, Isolation, and Durability) compliance.

Microsoft, as part of Azure platform PaaS suite of relational database offerings, provides the following databases to choose from for your application need:

- **Azure SQL database** Azure SQL database is a Microsoft core product and the most popular relational database in the cloud. It's meant to be replacement of SQL server on premises.

- **Azure SQL Data Warehouse** A relational database for big data solutions with an ability to massively process data parallelly.

- **Azure database for MySQL** Azure database for MySQL is a fully managed database as a service where Microsoft runs and manages all mechanics of MySQL Community Edition database in the cloud.

- **Azure database for PostgreSQL** Like MySQL, this is a fully managed database-as-a-service offering based on the opensource Postgres database engine.

- **Azure database for MariaDB** Azure database for MariaDB is also a managed highly available and scalable database as a service based on the opensource MariaDB server engine.

Regardless of the database you select for your application needs, Microsoft manages the following key characteristics of any cloud-based service offerings:

- High availability and on-demand scale
- Business continuity
- Automatic backups
- Enterprise-grade security and compliance

Provision and configure relational databases

In this section, we dive into the critical aspects of how you set up a relational database in the cloud and configure the cloud-native features that come with the service offering.

Azure SQL database

Azure SQL database is the Microsoft core and most popular relational database. The service has the following flavors of database offerings.

■ **Single database** With a single database, you assign preallocated compute and storage to the database.

■ **Elastic pools** With elastic pools, you create a database inside of the pool of databases, and they share the same resources to meet unpredictable usage demand.

■ **Managed Instance** Microsoft recently launched a Managed Instance flavor of the service that gives close to 100% compatibility with SQL Server Enterprise Edition with additional security features.

> ***NOTE* REGIONAL AVAILABILITY OF SQL AZURE SERVICE TYPES**
>
> Although Exam AZ-300 does not expect you to get into the weeds of regional availability of the Azure SQL database service, as an architect, it is crucial that you know this part. Please visit Microsoft docs "Products available by region" at *https://azure.microsoft.com/en-us/global-infrastructure/services/?products=sql-database&regions=all.*

Now that we looked at different types of databases that you can create with Azure SQL database offering, it is crucial that you understand the available purchasing model that helps you choose the right service tier that meets your application needs. Azure SQL database comes with the following two options of purchasing model:

■ **DTUs (Database Transaction Units) model** DTUs are the blend of compute, storage, and IO resource that you preallocate when you create a database on the logical server. For a single database, the capacity is measured in terms of DTUs; for elastic databases, capacity is measured in eDTUs. Microsoft offers three service tiers, Basic, Standard and Premium for single and elastic pool databases. Each of the tiers has its own differentiated range of compute, storage, fixed retention, backup options, and pricing levels.

- **vCore (Virtual Core) model**   The vCore-based model is the Microsoft recommended purchasing model where you get the flexibility of independently choosing compute and storage to meet your application needs. Additionally, you get an option to use your existing SQL Server license to save up to 55% of the cost. The vCore purchasing model provides three service tiers—General Purpose, Hyperscale, and Business Critical. Each of them has its own range of compute sizes, types and size of storage, latency, and I/O ranges. In the vCore model, you can create a single, elastic, or managed instance database.

EXAM TIP

Database migration is a crucial part of any cloud migration project. It's likely that in the Exam AZ-300, Microsoft checks your knowledge of different database migration strategies and options available. Please check the Microsoft docs Azure Database Migration Guide at *https://datamigration.microsoft.com/*.

Create a SQL Azure single database using Azure portal

The databases (single or pooled) reside on a logical SQL database server, and the server must exist before you can create a database on it. The security firewall setting, auditing, and other threat protection policies on the server automatically apply to all the databases on the server. The databases are always in the same region as their logical server. Use the following steps to create a database server and database:

1. Log in to Azure portal.

2. On the Navigation blade on the left side of the portal, click Create A Resource and search for SQL Database.

3. Select the SQL Database as shown in Figure 5-16.

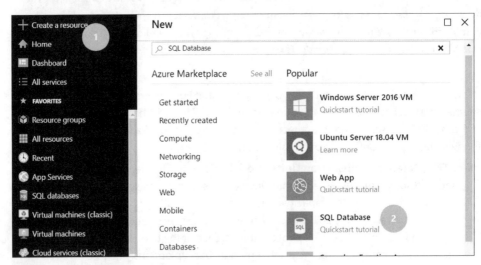

FIGURE 5-16 Search for a new resource

4. On the Create Database screen (see Figure 5-17), provide the database name, select subscription, resource group, and server. Make sure Want To Use Elastic Database is selected as No. If the SQL Server doesn't exist, you have to provide the detail for the new server along with the database request (see Figure 5-18).

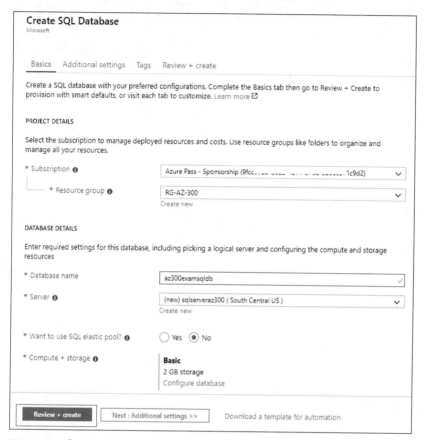

FIGURE 5-17 Create a SQL database

The Allow Azure services to access server option, as shown in Figure 5-18, is checked by default; it enables other Azure IP addresses and subnets to be able to connect to the SQL Azure server.

New server ✕

* Server name

```
sqlserveraz300
```
.database.windows.net

* Server admin login

```
az300examadmin
```

* Password

```
•••••••••
```

* Confirm password

```
•••••••••
```

* Location

```
South Central US                    ⌄
```

☑ Allow Azure services to access server
ⓘ

Select

FIGURE 5-18 Create a SQL Server

5. Ignore the Next Additional Settings and Click Review +Create. In this example, we're creating a single blank database for demonstration purposes.

6. On the review screen, you can review your configuration and click Create to initiate database deployment, as shown in Figure 5-19.

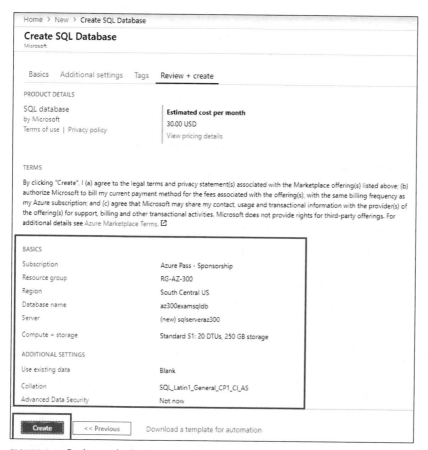

Home > New > Create SQL Database

Create SQL Database
Microsoft

Basics   Additional settings   Tags   **Review + create**

PRODUCT DETAILS

SQL database
by Microsoft
Terms of use | Privacy policy

Estimated cost per month
30.00 USD
View pricing details

TERMS

By clicking "Create", I (a) agree to the legal terms and privacy statement(s) associated with the Marketplace offering(s) listed above; (b) authorize Microsoft to bill my current payment method for the fees associated with the offering(s), with the same billing frequency as my Azure subscription; and (c) agree that Microsoft may share my contact, usage and transactional information with the provider(s) of the offering(s) for support, billing and other transactional activities. Microsoft does not provide rights for third-party offerings. For additional details see Azure Marketplace Terms.

BASICS

Subscription	Azure Pass - Sponsorship
Resource group	RG-AZ-300
Region	South Central US
Database name	az300examsqldb
Server	(new) sqlserveraz300
Compute + storage	Standard S1: 20 DTUs, 250 GB storage

ADDITIONAL SETTINGS

Use existing data	Blank
Collation	SQL_Latin1_General_CP1_CI_AS
Advanced Data Security	Not now

Create   << Previous   Download a template for automation

FIGURE 5-19 Review and submit a request

After the database is created, you need to set up firewall rules (see Figure 5-20) to allow inbound connections to the database. The rule can be set up for a single IP address or ranges in CIDR for clients to be able to connect to the SQL Azure database from outside of Azure. By default, all inbound connections from the internet are blocked by the SQL database firewall. The firewall rules can be at the server level or the individual database level. The server-level rules apply to all the databases on the server.

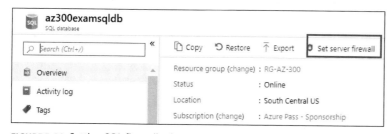

FIGURE 5-20 Setting SQL firewall rules

az300examsqldb
SQL database

Search (Ctrl+/)   Copy   Restore   Export   Set server firewall

Overview   Resource group (change) : RG-AZ-300
Activity log   Status   : Online
                      Location   : South Central US
Tags   Subscription (change) : Azure Pass - Sponsorship

Another option to control access to the SQL Azure database is to use virtual network rules. This is specifically to implement a fine-grained granular control as opposed to the Allow Access to Azure Services option, which allows access to the database from all Azure IP addresses or Azure subnets that may not be owned by you.

EXAM TIP

Unlike a single or pooled database, the managed instance of a SQL Azure database doesn't have a public endpoint. Microsoft provides two ways to connect to the Managed Instance databases securely. Please visit Microsoft docs at *https://docs.microsoft.com/en-us/azure/sql-database/sql-database-managed-instance-quickstart-guide* to check out options.

Geo-replication and automatic backups

One of the appealing features of Azure SQL database (single or pooled) is an ability to spin up four read-only copies of secondary databases in the same or different regions. The feature is specially designed for a business continuity solution where you have an option to failover (manually or via some automation) to the secondary database in the event of a regional disruption or large-scale outages. In an active geo-replication, the data is replicated to secondary databases immediately after the transactions are committed on the primary database. The replication happens automatically and asynchronously. If you're using SQL Azure Managed Instance, you use the auto-failover group feature for business continuity. You can initiate or create a geo-replication and create up to four copies of the secondary read-only database from the pane, as shown in Figure 5-21.

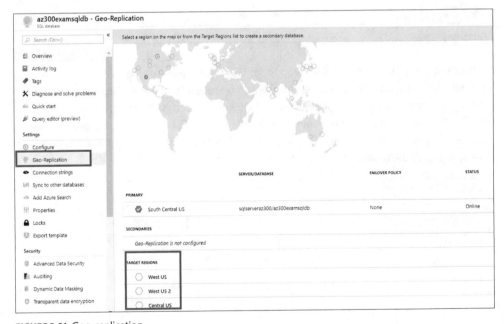

FIGURE 5-21 Geo-replication

Regardless of the service tiers you choose, Azure automatically takes a backup of your databases as part of a disaster recovery solution. The backups are retained automatically between 7 and 35 days based on your service tier (basic or higher) and do not incur any cost. If your application needs require you to maintain the backups beyond 35 days, Azure provides an option to set up a long-term backup retention option to keep the backups up to 10 years.

Create elastic pools for Azure SQL databases

As said previously, the elastic database pools are best suited for the applications that have predictable usage patterns. Choosing a flexible database pool is the best bet to save cost when you have many databases, and overall average utilization of DTUs or vCores is low. The more databases you add in the pool, the more cost it saves you because of efficiently unused shared DTUs and vCores across the databases.

The following steps show how you can create an elastic database pool for databases:

1. Log in to Azure portal.

2. On the navigation pane on the left side of the portal, click Create A Resource.

3. Search for SQL Elastic Database pool from the marketplace; the screen appears (see Figure 5-22).

4. Click Create.

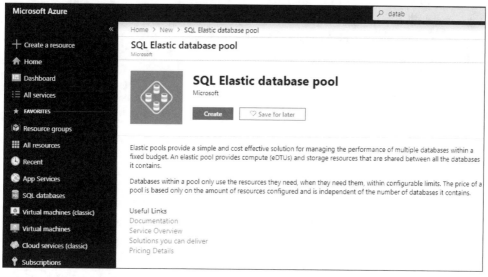

FIGURE 5-22 Elastic database resource

5. After you have clicked Create, you will be navigated to another screen called Elastic Pool (see Figure 5-23). Provide the pool name, choose the resource group, service tiers, and SQL server, and click Create.

FIGURE 5-23 Elastic Pool create form

After the pool is created, you can create a new database and add it to the pool. You can also add an existing database on the same server to the pool or remove databases from the pool.

6. To add a new database to the pool, navigate to the elastic database pool you created in step 5, and click Create A Database (see Figure 5-24).

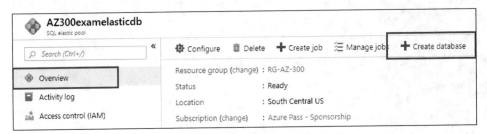

FIGURE 5-24 Create a database in the pool

7. The screen to create a database appears (see Figure 5-25). Provide the database name and click OK.

8. To add an existing database from the same server in the pool or remove the database from the pool, go to the Configure tab on the left pane of the screen shown in Figure 5-26.

FIGURE 5-25 Create new database form

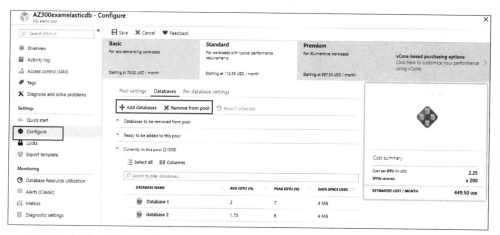

FIGURE 5-26 Elastic database scale setting

Create, read, update, and delete data tables by using code

In this section, we look at some programming aspects to interact with Azure SQL database and perform CRUD operation on the database tables using ADO.NET and Visual Studio IDE. Before we jump into the code, there are few prerequisites you must ensure exist:

- You have created a database server and a database.
- You have set up firewall rules on the server to allow your client computer to connect to the database.

- You have Visual Studio 2017 or higher installed. You need the community or licensed version.

In the previous section, we already explained the process of creating and enabling a connection with the SQL Azure database, so we leverage the same database in this section. Figure 5-27 shows the Entity Relationship (ER) diagram that we use to demonstrate our goal of this section. Here we are creating two tables called tblcustomer and tblOrder, where the parent table tblcustomer has one-to-many relationships with its child table, tblorder.

You need to open Visual Studio and create a new console application (.NET framework).

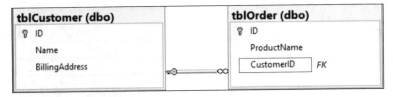

FIGURE 5-27 ER diagram

After you have created a Console App using Visual Studio, in the program.cs file, add the following code snippet in the Main method. In the following code, you have to refer to your SQL Azure database and its credentials:

```
//.NET Framework
// create a new instance of the SQLConnectionStringBuilder to populate database
endpoints and credentials for SQL connection.
                var cb = new SqlConnectionStringBuilder();
                cb.DataSource = "sqxxxxxxaz300.database.windows.net";
                cb.UserID = "az300exxxxxxxn";
                cb.Password = "gxxxxxxxxx";
                cb.InitialCatalog = "az300exaxxxxxxb";
```

The next step is to write TSQL commands to create database tables and perform CRUD (create, read, update, and delete) operation on the tables. The next code snippet shows the functions and their respective TSQL commands statements.

Static class TSQL encapsulates all the TSQL operations that you'll execute on the database. The class has a total of seven methods:

- **TSQL_CreateTables**   Returns the TSQL to drop and create tables in the database
- **TSQL_InsertCustomerandOrder**   Returns the TSQL to sample records for the customer and their order history
- **TSQL_UpdateCustomerBillingAddress**   Has responsibility for returning TSQL to perform update operation on the tables
- **TSQL_DeleteCustomerByID()**   Returns the TSQL to execute the delete statement on the tables to remove a customer and its order history by customer ID

- **TSQL_SelectCustomerandItsOrder**   Returns TSQL to perform the read operation on the tables and displays all customers and their related orders

- **ExecuteCommand**   Creates the connection to the database and runs commands on the database to create update and delete operations

- **ExecuteQuery**   Runs the read command on the database and displays all customers and their orders on the GUI

```
/// <summary>
/// static class that exposes various methods to perform database operation
/// </summary>
public class TSQLS {
    /// <summary>
    /// A Function that return TSQL to drop and create table
    /// </summary>
    /// <returns></returns>
    public static string TSQL_CreateTables()  {
        return @"
                DROP TABLE IF EXISTS tblOrder;
                DROP TABLE IF EXISTS tblCustomer;
                CREATE TABLE tblCustomer
                (
                    ID   int not null identity (1,1) primary key,
                    [Name]  nvarchar(50)           null    ,
                    BillingAddress  nvarchar(255) null
                )

                CREATE TABLE tblOrder
                (
                    ID   int not null identity (1,1) primary key,
                    ProductName     nvarchar(128)      not null,
                    CustomerID  int                null
                    REFERENCES tblCustomer (ID)
                );
";
    }
    /// <summary>
    /// A Function that returns a TSQL to create sample customer and their orders
    /// </summary>
    /// <returns></returns>
    public static string TSQL_InsertCustomerandOrder() {
        return @"
-- Three customer exist for your online business  .
INSERT INTO tblCustomer (Name, BillingAddress)
VALUES
    ('Gurvinder', 'chicago, IL lombard'),
    ('Mike', 'Phoenix'),
    ('Amit', 'San Jose');
--Each customer have bought some product from your online store.
INSERT INTO tblOrder (ProductName, CustomerID)
VALUES
    ('Apple Phone case'  , 1),
    ('Google Pixel Phone case'  , 2),
    ('Google PixelXL Phone case'  , 3) ";
    }
```

```
/// <summary>
/// A Function that returns a TSQL to update Customer billing address by name
/// </summary>
/// <returns></returns>
public static string TSQL_UpdateCustmerBillingAddress() {
    return @"
            DECLARE @CustomerName  nvarchar(128) = @paramCustomerName; -- for
example Gurvinder;
            -- upsate the billing address of customer by name
            UPDATE c
            SET
                c.BillingAddress ='lombard'
            FROM
                tblCustomer   as c
            WHERE
                c.Name = @CustomerName; ";
}
/// <summary>
/// A function that returns a TSQL to delete customer and his/her order history
by customerID
/// </summary>
/// <returns></returns>
public static string TSQL_DeleteCustomerByID() {
    return @"
            DECLARE @cusID  int;
            SET @cusID = @paramCusID;
            DELETE o
            FROM
                tblOrder   as o
            INNER JOIN
                tblCustomer as c ON o.id = c.id
            WHERE
                c.id = @cusID
            DELETE tblCustomer
                WHERE ID = @cusID; ";
}
/// <summary>
/// A Function that Returns the list of customers and their order history from
the database
/// </summary>
/// <returns></returns>
public static string TSQL_SelectCustomerandItsOrder() {
    return @"
-- Look at all the customer and their order history
        SELECT
            c.*,o.*
        FROM
            tblCustomer   as c
            JOIN
            tblOrder as o ON c.id = o.CustomerID
        ORDER BY
            c.name; ";
}
/// <summary>
/// A Function to run creates tables and CRUD operation on the database tables
/// </summary>
```

```
/// <param name="sqlConnection"></param>
/// <param name="databaseOperationName"></param>
/// <param name="sqlCommand"></param>
/// <param name="parameterName"></param>
/// <param name="parameterValue"></param>
public static void ExecuteCommand(SqlConnection, string
databaseOperationName,string sqlCommand, string parameterName = null,string
parameterValue = null) {
        Console.WriteLine();
        Console.WriteLine("=================================");
        Console.WriteLine("DB Operation to {0}...", databaseOperationName);
        using (var command = new SqlCommand(sqlCommand, sqlConnection))
        {
            if (parameterName != null)
            {
                command.Parameters.AddWithValue(
                parameterName,
                parameterValue);
            }
            int rowsAffected = command.ExecuteNonQuery();
            Console.WriteLine(rowsAffected + " = rows affected.");
        }
    }
/// <summary>
///  A Function that runs the read operation on the database.
/// </summary>
/// <param name="sqlConnection"></param>
/// <param name="tSQLquery"></param>
public static void ExecutQuery(SqlConnection sqlConnection, string tSQLquery) {
    Console.WriteLine();
    Console.WriteLine("=================================");
    Console.ForegroundColor = ConsoleColor.Green;
    Console.WriteLine("Displaying, Customers and their order history...");
    Console.ForegroundColor = ConsoleColor.White;
    Console.WriteLine();
    Console.WriteLine("=================================");

    using (var query = new SqlCommand(tSQLquery,sqlConnection))
    {
        using (SqlDataReader reader = query.ExecuteReader())
        {

            while (reader.Read())
            {
                    Console.WriteLine("{0} , {1} , {2} , {3} , {4},{5}",
                     reader.GetInt32(0),
                     reader.GetString(1),
                     reader.GetString(2),
                     reader.GetInt32(3),
                     reader.GetString(4),
                     reader.GetInt32(5));
            }


        }
    }
    Console.WriteLine();
```

```
            Console.WriteLine("===================================");
        }
    }
```

Now that we've looked at a TSQL class and its various encapsulated methods, it's time to call them and see all the operations in action. In the Main method of your Program.cs class, place the following code snippet, and compile the complete solution. After you have compiled the solution, press F5, or click Start on the top menu of Visual Studio. The output of the program is shown in Figure 5-28.

```
using (var connection = new SqlConnection(cb.ConnectionString)) {
                    connection.Open();
                    TSQLS.ExecuteCommand(connection, "1 - Create-Tables", TSQLS.
TSQL_CreateTables());
                    TSQLS.ExecuteCommand(connection, "2 - Insert Customer and Orders",
TSQLS.TSQL_InsertCustomerandOrder());
                    TSQLS.ExecuteCommand(connection, "3- Update Customers", TSQLS.TSQL_
UpdateCustmerBillingAddress(), "@paramCustomerName","Gurvinder");
                    TSQLS.ExecuteCommand(connection, "3- Delete Customer and Its Order
history ", TSQLS.TSQL_DeleteCustomerByID(), "@paramCusID", "1");
                    TSQLS.ExecutQuery(connection,TSQLS.
TSQL_SelectCustomerandItsOrder());
                }
```

Finally, you can clean up the resource you have created in the Azure portal by deleting a resource group.

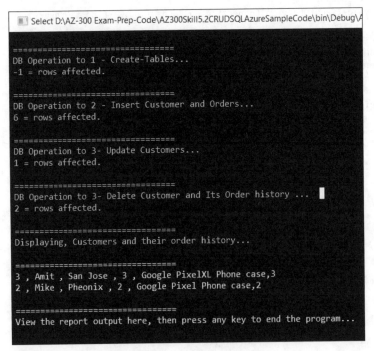

FIGURE 5-28 The console window

Skill 5.3: Configure a message-based integration architecture

In today's world of distributed application development that embraces microservices architecture, messaging systems play a vital role in designing a reliable, resilient, and scalable application. Creating a successful distributed microservices-based application involves lots of complexity and requires you think of a robust way of establishing communication and networking between autonomous, loosely coupled components of the application.

To address this problem, you have to have some messaging-based architecture that orchestrates applications to communicate in a loosely coupled manner. Microsoft provides the Azure Integration suite of services to leverage in your microservice-based solution, which we will discuss in detail later in this chapter.

The messaging solution provides the following key benefits for developing loosely coupled distributed applications:

- Messaging allows loosely coupled applications to communicate with each other without direct integration.

- Messaging allows applications to scale independently. The compute-intensive tasks of the application can be asynchronously handled by a background job that can scale independently of the lightweight client or GUI. You can trigger the job by a message in the queue.

- Messaging allows several types of communication protocols that cater to a variety of business use cases, like one-to-one, one-to-many, or many-to-many.

- Advanced messaging technologies facilitate designing a solution when the order of workflows between discrete application components is critical and duplication is unaffordable.

This skill covers how to:

- Configure an app or service to send emails, Event Grid, and the Azure Relay Service
- Create and configure Notification Hubs, Event Hub, and Service Bus
- Configure queries across multiple products

Configure an app or service to send emails, Event Grid, and the Azure Relay Service

Integrating the distributed application often requires you to orchestrate workflow and automate business processes. For example, if you're creating a resource group in Azure subscription and adding a contributor to manage resources, you may want to have some governance in place to let the Resource Group Owner or a Subscription Owner know via email or SMS when new resources are created or updated in the resource group. Azure Logic Apps, one of the services from the Azure Integration suite of services, allows automating such workflows.

Azure Logic Apps

Logic Apps allows you to define workflows and processes without having to write any code and facilitate application and services integration across enterprises and organizations. Logic Apps are also called a designer-first serverless integration service that allows you to use Azure portal and visually see and design workflows.

As of the writing of this book, Logic Apps support more than 200 managed connectors that provide triggers and actions to access cloud-based SaaS Services, Azure native suite of services, and on-premises services using a Logic App gateway agent. The overview of Logic Apps is shown in Figure 5-29.

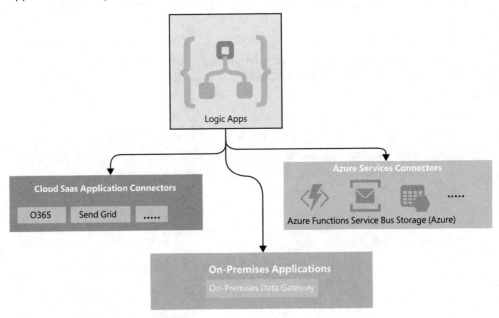

FIGURE 5-29 Azure Logic Apps overview

Azure Event Grid

Some integration scenarios require you to respond to events in real time as opposed to the standard message polling mechanism. In this scenario, the source system where some condition or state change happens may need the subscribers to be notified to take some action. As an example, one use case that we briefly discussed previously is sending an email notification to Azure subscription owner or Azure Resource Group Owner when a new resource is updated (the event happened) by resource group contributors.

The Azure Event Grid service is best suited for use cases that act as a message broker to tie one or more subscribers to discrete event notifications coming from event publishers. The service is fully managed and uses a serverless computing model. It's massively scalable.

Figure 5-30 shows that Event Grid has built-in support to integrate Azure services, where you can define your event publisher and event handlers. Event publishers emit events and send them to Event Grid using an endpoint called Topics; you also can create custom topics for your custom events. Event Grid then pushes those events instantaneously to Event Handlers, and it guarantees at least one delivery of the event messages for each subscription.

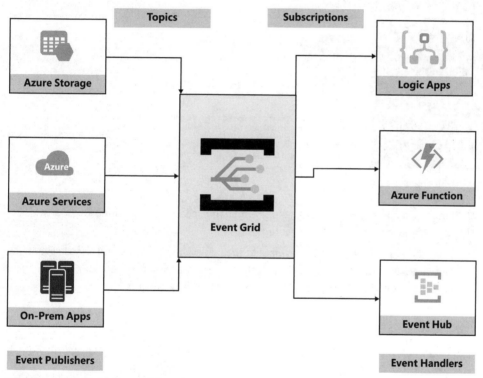

FIGURE 5-30 The Azure Event Grid service

To receive an event and act on it, you define an event handler on the other hand and tell Event Grid which event on the Topic should be routed to which handler. This is done using Event Subscription.

Send an email using SendGrid and Logic Apps and Azure Event Grid

SendGrid is a third-party SaaS application that allows sending emails. With Azure logic app, Event Grid, and SendGrid connector, you can define a workflow to send an email. Event Grid here acts as a trigger for Azure Logic App to invoke the email workflow.

The following steps describe how to set up a workflow to send email using SendGrid connector. The following section assumes you have an Azure Storage account and SendGrid account already created. In this example, we create a logic app and set up a workflow to send an email notification on changes to the Azure Storage account.

1. Log into Azure portal and go to the Create Resource blade to search for Logic App. Click Create (see Figure 5-31).

FIGURE 5-31 Create a logic app

2. On the Create screen, provide the logic app name, choose a subscription, resource group, and location, and click Create.

3. After the logic app is created, navigate to the Logic Apps Designer and choose Event Grid as your trigger (see Figure 5-32). You're prompted to sign in with your Azure credential for Logic Apps to be able to connect to the Event Grid.

FIGURE 5-32 Logic Apps Designer

4. Set up an event publisher for your logic app. In this example, we select the Resource Type as Microsoft.Resources.ResourceGroups and Event Type as Microsoft.Resources. ResourceActionSuccess (see Figure 5-33).

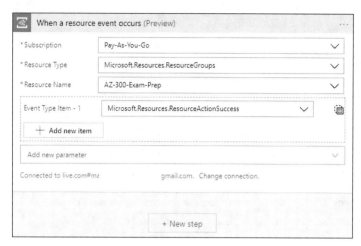

FIGURE 5-33 Logic app event publisher

5. The next step is to Add Condition and Action to the Logic App workflow (see Figure 5-34). On the expression editor on the left side of the condition add, **triggerBody()?['data']['operationName']** and click OK. Keep the middle box operator IsEqual To. On the right side of the equation, add **Microsoft.Storage/ storageAccounts/write**.

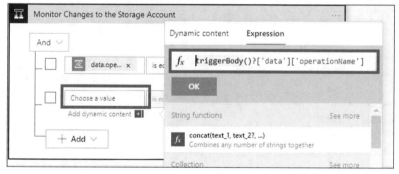

FIGURE 5-34 Logic app condition dialog box

6. Add an action to send an email using SendGrid. On the Add Action dialog box, search for SendGrid (see Figure 5-35). You have to provide the SendGrid account key for Logic Apps to connect to it.

FIGURE 5-35 A logic app action dialog box

7. Define the email template and add a recipient to receive an email, as shown in Figure 5-36.

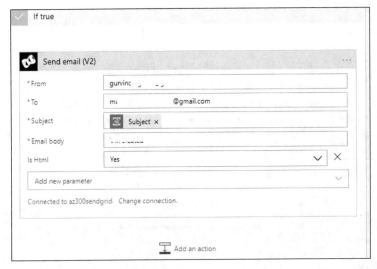

FIGURE 5-36 Set up an email recipient

After you've added conditions and actions to the Logic Apps Designer, it looks like Figure 5-37.

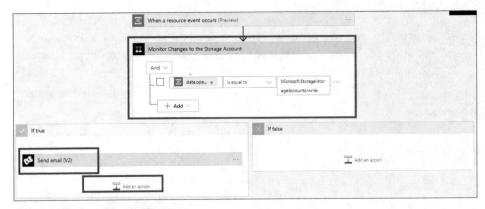

FIGURE 5-37 A logic app workflow

8. To see this in action, go to your storage account and make some updates. You will see that an email is sent to the recipient after the changes are successful.

EXAM TIP

There is a very high likelihood of you getting a use case where you need a logic app workflow to be able to react to the changes to the on-premises data source—for example, data updates in the on-premises SQL server database. Azure Logic Apps gives you the ability to connect to a variety of data sources sitting behind the organization firewall using a gateway installer. Please check out Microsoft documents for supported on-premises connectors at *https://docs.microsoft.com/en-us/azure/logic-apps/logic-apps-gateway-install.*

Azure Relay services

Azure Relay services allows establishing a secure connection to the services running behind the corporate network without opening any firewall ports. The Relay service has two types:

- **Hybrid Connections** Hybrid connection is based on standard Http and Web Socket protocols and hence can be used in any platform and languages.

- **WCF Relay** WCFRelay is A legacy Relay offering that works only for .NET framework Windows Communication Foundation endpoints.

Use the following steps to create a Relay Service namespace and configure Hybrid Connections or WCFRelay on the Azure portal:

1. Log in to the Azure portal and navigate to create a resource from the left pane. Search for Relay.

2. Click Create (see Figure 5-38).

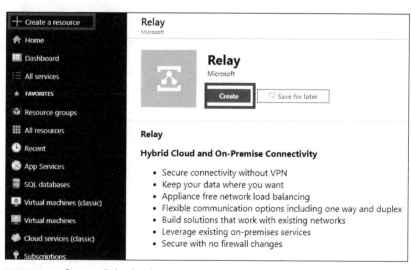

FIGURE 5-38 Create a Relay Service

3. Create a namespace, providing the name and selecting the subscription, resource group, and location as shown in Figure 5-39. Click Create.

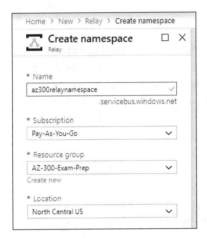

FIGURE 5-39 Create a Relay Service namespace

4. After the namespace has been created, navigate to the resource. On the overview tab, you see an option to configure a Hybrid Connection or a WCFRelay (see Figure 5-40).

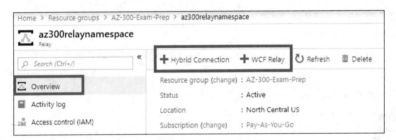

FIGURE 5-40 Configure a Hybrid Connection or a WCF Relay

Create and configure Notification Hubs, Event Hubs, and Service Bus

Microsoft Azure platform provides a variety of options for applications that are based on messaging-based architecture and require an optimal way to process or consume messages or push notifications to other services. The following sections look at the use cases to help you choose the service that is the best fit.

Azure Notification Hubs

In today's digital world, the use of mobile and handheld devices is growing faster than ever. One of the critical factors that help you grow your business is to keep the customer engaged and be notified of the offers and the latest event as soon as they come. The diversity of the customers, their choices of what they should be notified on, and the types of mobile device platforms they use are vast. This is where Azure Notification Hubs comes in.

Azure Notification Hubs allow you to send massively scaled push notification to devices from backed services either running on the cloud or on premises. Notification Hubs are platform agnostic and can send push notification to any platform (iOS, Android, Windows, Kindle, Baidu).

Use the following steps to create and configure Azure Notification Hubs:

1. Log in to the Azure portal and navigate to create a resource on the left pane. Search for Notification Hub. You can create the namespace first or create it at the same time as you create the hub.

2. Click Create as shown in Figure 5-41.

FIGURE 5-41 Create an Azure Notification Hub

3. On the Create screen as shown in Figure 5-42, provide the name for the Notification Hub and Notification Hub namespace and select the location, subscription, resource group, and pricing tier and click Create.

FIGURE 5-42 Create a Notification Hub

4. After the Notification Hub is created, you can set up a push notification service using any one of the supported providers (see Figure 5-43).

FIGURE 5-43 Setting up push notification service

> **NEED MORE REVIEW?**   **AZURE NOTIFICATION HUBS AND GOOGLE FIREBASE CLOUD MESSAGING (FCM)**
>
> Microsoft has very comprehensive documentation to register push notification providers (PNS) with Notification Hubs. For detailed information, please visit Microsoft docs "Push notifications to Android devices by using Azure Notification Hubs and Google Firebase Cloud Messaging" at *https://docs.microsoft.com/en-us/azure/notification-hubs/notification-hubs-android-push-notification-google-fcm-get-started.*

EXAM TIP

It's very likely that if you're using some existing push notification mechanism, you may wonder how you switch to use to Azure Notification Hubs seamlessly. Azure Notification Hubs supports bulk import of device registration. Please take a look at the implementation of export and import Azure Notification Hubs registrations in bulk at *https://azure.microsoft.com/en-us/pricing/details/app-service/plans.*

Azure Event Hubs

Event Hubs is a big-data pipeline meant to take a massive real-time stream of event data from various event producers. Unlike Event Grid, Event Hubs allows capture, retain, and replay of event data to a variety of stream processing systems and analytic services, as shown in Figure 5-44.

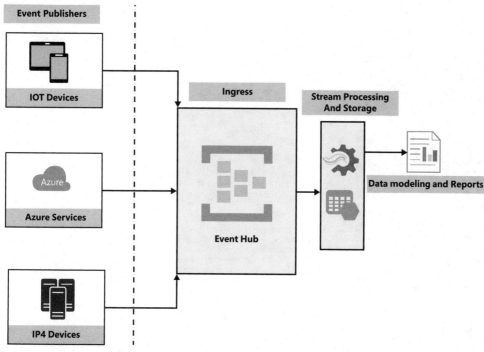

FIGURE 5-44 Azure Event Hubs

Event Hubs provides a distributed stream-processing platform with low latency and seamless integration with other ecosystems like Apache Kafka to publish events to Event Hubs without intrusive configuration or code changes. It has a support for advanced messaging protocol like HTTP, AMQP 1.0, Kafka 1.0, and major industry languages (.NET, Java, Python, Go, Node.js). The partition consumer model of the Event Hub makes it massively scalable. It allows you to partition the big data stream of events among the different partitions and enable parallel processing with an ability to give consumers its own partitioned event stream.

Create an event hub

To create an event hub, you need to create a container called the namespace, as we previously created for Event Grid.

Use the following steps to create and configure Event Hubs:

5. Log in to the Azure portal and navigate to create a resource on the left pane. Search for Event Hubs. Click Create as shown in Figure 5-45.

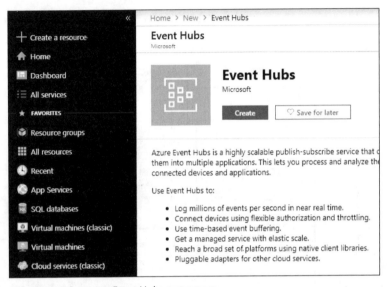

FIGURE 5-45 Create an Event Hubs namespace

6. The next screen that opens is shown in Figure 5-46. On the screen, do the following:

    A. Enter a name for the namespace.

    B. Choose the pricing tier (Basic or Standard). If you need message retention customization, choose Standard.

    C. Select the subscription, resource group, and a location.

    D. Choose the desired throughput.

    E. Click Create.

FIGURE 5-46 The Event Hubs namespace Create form

7. After the namespace has been created, navigate to the resource. Now you can click the +Event Hub icon to create an event hub under it (see Figure 5-47).

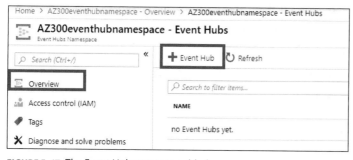

FIGURE 5-47 The Event Hub namespace blade

8. Provide the name of the event hub and choose the retention and partition as needed. Click Create. (See Figure 5-48.)

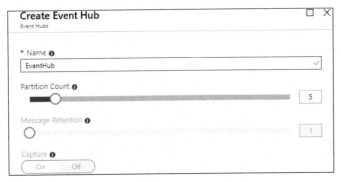

FIGURE 5-48 The Create Event Hub screen

> **NOTE EVENT GRID VERSUS EVENT HUBS**
>
> Event Grid and Event Hubs both offer some similar capabilities, but each is designed to address a specific business scenario. Event Grid isn't meant for queuing the data or storing it for later use. Instead, because of its nature of integration with Function Apps and Logic Apps, it's meant for distributing events instantaneously and trigging application logic to react to application metrics to take some actions.

Azure Service Bus

Like Event Hubs and Event Grid, Azure Service Bus also offers messaging capability at an enterprise scale, enabling the loosely coupled application to connect asynchronously and scale independently.

Service Bus provides enterprise messaging capabilities, including queuing, publish/subscribe, and an advanced integration patterns model for an application hosted on the cloud or on-premises. It has the following key features:

- Message persistence and duplicate detection
- First-in-first-out order of message delivery
- Poison message handling
- High availability, geo-replication, and built-in disaster recovery
- Transactional integrity, an ability to have queued read or write messages as part of a single transaction
- Supports advanced messaging protocol like HTTP, AMQP 1.0, and significant industry languages (.NET, Java, Python, Go, Node.js, and Ruby)

Service Bus allows you to implement a publish/subscribe model using topics and subscriptions. One or more topics in the service bus queue enable you to send messages to these topics and have subscribers receive these messages on the topics they have subscribed for. See Figure 5-49.

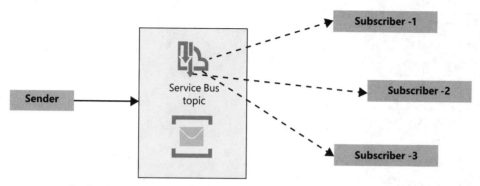

FIGURE 5-49 Service Bus topics and subscriptions

Use the following steps to create and configure the Azure Service Bus, topics, and subscriptions. Like any other messaging service, you have to create a container called namespace first.

1. Log in to the Azure portal and navigate to create a resource on the left pane. Search for Service Bus. Click Create (see Figure 5-50).

FIGURE 5-50 Service Bus resource

2. The next screen that opens is shown in Figure 5-51. On the screen, you see the following:

   A. Enter a name for the namespace.

   B. Choose the pricing tier (Basic or Standard). Select at least Standard pricing tiers if you need topics.

   C. Select the subscription and resource group in which you want to create the namespace.

   D. Select a location for the namespace.

   E. Select Create.

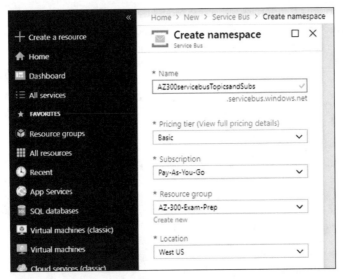

FIGURE 5-51 Create a Service Bus namespace

3. After the namespace has been created, navigate to the resource. Here you can create queues or topics under the namespace. See Figure 5-52.

FIGURE 5-52 The Service Bus Resource blade

EXAM TIP

As an architect, the AZ-300 exam expects that you take the right decisions to solve complex problems and choose appropriate services among the variety of different messaging options. Please take a look at advanced features that are available in the service bus queue offering listed in the Microsoft documentation located at *https://docs.microsoft.com/en-us/azure/service-bus-messaging/service-bus-messaging-overview#advanced-features*.

Configure queries across multiple products

Monitoring and collecting telemetry data and analyzing across the products and services is a crucial part of any platform to maximize performance and high availability by identifying issues and correcting them before they affect the production users. This is where the role of Azure Monitor comes in.

Azure Log Analytics is a primary data store for telemetry data that we emit from a variety of data sources, including Azure services, on-premises datacenters, and Application Insights custom tracing, that helps you to emit application metric data as part of performance and health monitoring. Azure Monitor now has an integration with Log Analytics and Application Insights that enables you to query and analyze data across multiple log analytics workspaces within or across Azure subscriptions.

Querying telemetry and log data across Log Analytic workspace and Application Insights

To query across the Log analytics workspace, the Identifier "workspace" is used. To query across Application Insights, the identifier "app" is used.

The following example (see Figure 5-53) queries records across two separate Application Insights—'AZ300appinsights-1' and 'AZ300appinsights-2'—against the requests table in two different apps. It counts the total number of records, regardless of the application that holds each record.

```
union app('AZ300appinsights-1').requests, app('AZ300appinsights-2').requests, requests
| summarize count() by bin(timestamp, 1h)
```

FIGURE 5-53 Queries across Application Insights using Azure Monitor

In a similar way, the following query shows an example of querying the data between two Log Analytics workspaces. It counts total records of Heartbeat, regardless of the workspace that holds each record:

```
union Heartbeat, workspace("AZ300ExamRefLAWorkspace"). Heartbeat, Heartbeat
```

Skill 5.4: Develop for autoscaling

The key benefit with cloud computing is agility and elasticity to provision resources on demand to keep the desired performance of the application intact as load grows at any given time. When the load goes down, or there is no need for additional resources, you can remove them or deallocate them to minimize the cost.

Azure provides you with built-in capability for most of its services to dynamically scale them as the need arises.

Scaling can be achieved in the following two ways:

- **Horizontal Scaling** (also called a Scale out or Scale In)   In this, you add or remove resources dynamically without affecting the availability of your application or workload. An example of horizontal scaling is virtual machine scale set. You're running two instances of VM behind the load balancer. When load increases, you add two instances to spread the load among four VM instances instead of two. The scaling out approach doesn't require downtime or impact availability because the load balancer automatically routes traffic to new instances when they are in a ready state. Conversely, additional instances are gracefully removed automatically as load stabilizes.

- **Vertical Scaling**   You add or remove capacity to the existing resources in terms of compute and storage. For example, you move the existing VM from one tier (say general purpose) to another compute-optimized tier. Vertical scaling often requires VMs to be redeployed; hence, it may cause temporary unavailability to the service while an upgrade is happening. Therefore, it's a less conventional approach to scaling.

> **This skill covers how to:**
> - Implement autoscaling rules and patterns
> - Implement code that addresses transient state

Implement autoscaling rules and patterns

Azure provides a built-in feature for the majority of platform services to achieve autoscaling based on demand or metrics. The Azure monitor gives you a common platform to schedule and configure the autoscaling for supported services as mentioned later. Following are the list of the services that use Azure autoscaling:

- **Azure Virtual Machines** Azure VMs use virtual machines scale sets, a set of identical virtual machines grouped together for autoscaling. Scaling rules can be configured either based on metrics, such as CPU usage, memory usage, and disk I/O, or based on a schedule to trigger scale out to meet a service level agreement (SLA) on the performance.

- **Azure App Services** Azure App services come with a built-in mechanism to configure autoscaling rules based on resource metrics such as CPU usage, memory demand, and HTTP queue length or on specific schedules. The rules are set to an app service plan and apply to all apps hosted on it.

- **Service Fabric** Likewise, virtual machine scaling, service fabric also supports autoscaling using virtual machine scale sets.

- **Cloud Services** These are Microsoft legacy PaaS offerings, but they do support autoscaling at the individual roles level (Web or Worker).

- **Azure Functions** Azure functions are a Microsoft serverless compute option. The autoscaling options depend on the hosting plan you choose. If you select the App Service plan, the scaling then works the same as we discussed for Azure App Service. However, if you decide to have the on-demand consumption plan, you don't have to configure any autoscaling rules because of the nature of the service; it allocates the required compute-on-demand as your code runs.

In addition to configuring the autoscaling rules using Azure Monitor, you can set up custom metrics using Application Insights and define a custom autoscaling solution on top of it. The custom autoscaling solution might require you think through carefully if none of the platforms provided rules meet your application scaling requirements.

> **NOTE SERVICE LIMITS, QUOTAS, AND CONSTRAINTS**
>
> You must pay careful attention when designing a scalable solution on Azure. There are some constraints and limits on the services regionwise and at the subscription level. Please visit the article "Azure subscription and service limits, quotas, and restrictions" at *https://docs.microsoft.com/en-us/azure/azure-subscription-service-limits*.

Code design considerations and best practices for autoscaling

The Azure platform-level capabilities to configure resource autoscaling may not be fruitful if the application isn't designed to scale. Consider the following points to make the best of autoscaling features:

The application must be designed to support horizontal scaling. Always develop services to be stateless so that requests can be evenly spread across healthy instances. Avoid using session affinity or sticky session. Consider using a queue-based load leveling pattern where the application can post the requests as a message in the queue, and messages can be picked up by any background worker instances to process.

For better resource utilization and cost-effectiveness, avoid long-running tasks in a single monolithic application and break them to run on separate instances using a queue-based mechanism. This approach facilitates scaling application components independently that requires high compute power as opposed to scaling everything.

Since autoscaling (Scale out and Scale in) is not an immediate process, it takes time for the system to react to the autoscaling rules and make additional instances in a ready state. Consider a throttling pattern to reject the requests if they are beyond the defined threshold limit.

Ensure the configuring scale-in rule in combination with the scale-out rule. Having only one rule will end up scaling only in one direction (Out or In) until it reaches a maximum or minimum value, which is not an optimal approach.

Always have a different and adequate margin between the minimum and maximum values of instance count. For example, if your rule set is minimum instance count =2, maximum is also =2, and default is also =2, autoscaling will never be triggered.

Consider an adequate margin between threshold values of autoscale metrics with a legitimate cool-down period. For example, the ideal desired scale-out and scale-in values for the following metrics would be

- Increase instances by two counts when CPU% >= 90 over 10 minutes
- Decrease instances by two counts when CPU% <= 60 over 15 minutes

Setting the metrics values close to each other would result in undesired results.

Common autoscaling metrics

As said in the previous section, Azure monitor allows you to set up autoscaling rules based on the built-in platform metrics for Azure App Services, virtual machine scale sets, Cloud Services, and API management services.

- **Scale based on metrics** The standard metrics used for autoscaling are built-in host metrics that are available in VM instances like the following:
  - CPU usage
  - Memory Demand
  - Disk read/writes

  Autoscaling rules also use the metrics from one of the following sources:
  - Application Insights
  - Service Bus Queue
  - Storage account

- **Scale based on schedule** Sometimes you may want to have scaling configuration (In or Out) based on a schedule that makes sense when you have predictable usage patterns, and you want to have the system ready to meet the on-demand scaling need as opposed to reactive scaling based on metrics.

- **Custom metrics** Custom metrics enables you to leverage application insights to meet the scaling demand of a complex scenario when none of the platforms provided scaling options to meet your requirements.

NEED MORE REVIEW? **AUTOSCALING GUIDANCE AND BEST PRACTICES**

You can find additional information about the autoscaling options and best practices at *https://docs.microsoft.com/en-us/azure/azure-monitor/platform/autoscale-best-practices.*

To set up autoscaling rules based on metrics for Azure App Service plan, use the following steps. This section assumes you have an app service plan already created:

1. Log in to the Azure portal and navigate to Azure Monitor.

2. On the left menu, click Autoscale, as shown in Figure 5-54.

3. On the right side, filter and select the required resource for autoscaling configuration.

4. Set up autoscale rules (Scale out and Scale In), as shown in Figure 5-55.

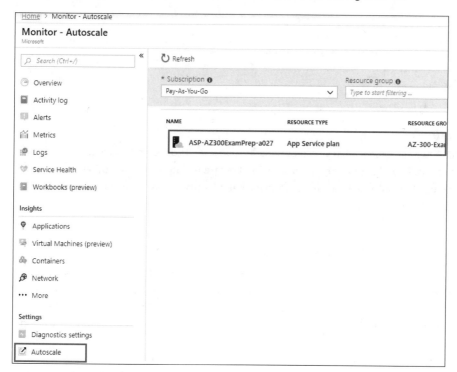

FIGURE 5-54 Azure Monitor

⊟ Save   ✗ Discard   ⊘ Disable autoscale   ⟳ Refresh

Configure   Run history   JSON   Notify   Diagnostics logs

* Autoscale setting name	ASP-AZ300ExamPrep-a027-Autoscale-836
Resource group	AZ-300-Exam-Prep ⌄

Default Auto created scale condition ✎   ⊘

Delete warning	ⓘ The very last or default recurrence rule cannot be deleted. Instead, you can disable autoscale to turn off autoscale.
Scale mode	◉ Scale based on a metric ○ Scale to a specific instance count

Rules	**Scale out**			
	When	ASP-AZ300Exam...	(Average) CpuPercentage > 70	Increase instance count by 2
	Scale in			
	When	ASP-AZ300Exam...	(Average) CpuPercentage <= 40	Decrease instance count by 2

＋ Add a rule

Instance limits	Minimum ⓘ	Maximum ⓘ	Default ⓘ
	2 ✓	6 ✓	2 ✓

Schedule   **This scale condition is executed when none of the other scale condition(s) match**

FIGURE 5-55 Autoscaling rules

EXAM TIP

The AZ-300 exam expects that you know what is supported in different tiers of the app service plans. To understand what is supported in regard to autoscaling and other features, please look at the Microsoft documentation located at *https://azure.microsoft.com/en-us/pricing/details/app-service/plans/*.

Autoscaling and singleton application

Azure platform offerings such as Azure WebJobs and Azure Functions enable you to run your code as a background job and leverage the on-demand horizontal autoscaling capability of the platform. By default, your code runs on all the instances of the WebJobs or Azure Functions. For Azure WebJobs, you configure your code to run on the single instance by using the key is_singleton:true either in the configuration file settings.job or adding an attribute programmatically that comes as part of Azure WebJob SDK as shown in the following code snippet:

```
[Singleton]
public static async Task ProcessJob([BlobTrigger("file")] Stream bytearray)
{
    // Process the file.
}
```

Similarly, with Durable Azure Functions, you have an ability to configure a singleton background job orchestration by specifying the instance ID to an orchestrator when you create it.

Singleton Implementation for session persistence

A singleton pattern allows only one instance of the class created and shared among all callers. The following code snippet shows a straightforward implementation of a singleton class where the instance of a singleton class is created and stored at local memory of the VM. That creates a bottleneck for scalability because the state will not be persisted when you create a new instance of the VM, unless you store it at some external system like Azure Storage, an external database, or in some caching mechanism using Redis cache.

```
public sealed class SingletonAz300 {
        private static SingletonAz300 GUID = null;
        private static readonly object threadlock = new object();
        public static SingletonAz300 GUID  {
   get {
                lock (threadlock) {
                    if (GUID == null {
                        GUID = new SingletonAz300();
                    }
                    return instance;
                }
            }
        }
```

Storing the state using external providers requires additional development efforts and may not be best suited for your performance requirements because you would have to interact with an external service to save and retrieve state, and that comes with latency and throughput cost.

Azure Service Fabric Stateful Service allows you to maintain the state reliably across the nodes of the service instance locally. Stateful service comes with a built-in state manager called Reliable Collections that enables you to write highly scalable, low-latency applications.

When you create a stateful service using the Visual Studio (2017 or later) Service Fabric Application template, it uses the availability of state provider by default in its entry point method RunAsync as shown in the following code snippet:

```
protected override async Task RunAsync(CancellationToken cancellationToken)  {
            var myDictionary = await this.StateManager.GetOrAddAsync<IReliableDictionary
<string, long>>("myDictionary");
            while (true)  {
                cancellationToken.ThrowIfCancellationRequested();
                using (var tx = this.StateManager.CreateTransaction())  {
                    var result = await myDictionary.TryGetValueAsync(tx, "Counter");
                    ServiceEventSource.Current.ServiceMessage(this.Context, "Current
Counter Value: {0}",
                        result.HasValue ? result.Value.ToString() : "Value does not
exist.");
                    await myDictionary.AddOrUpdateAsync(tx, "Counter", 0, (key, value)
=> ++value);
```

```
                    // If an exception is thrown before calling CommitAsync, the
transaction aborts, all changes are
                    // discarded, and nothing is saved to the secondary replicas.
                    await tx.CommitAsync();      }

            await Task.Delay(TimeSpan.FromSeconds(1), cancellationToken);

        }
    }
```

Reliable collections can store any .NET type or custom types. The data stored in the reliable collections must be serializable because the data is stored on the local disk of service fabric replicas.

Implement code that addresses the transient state

When you're designing an application for the cloud, the recommended design approach is to design to handle failure and errors gracefully. It's obvious that you can't prevent failure to happen, and things could go wrong—for example, temporary network outage in the datacenter or any temporary service interruption. A transient state that could lead the service in the temporarily unstable state is not uncommon in any distributed application. Here are some of the examples of the transient state:

- Service temporary unavailable because of network connectivity issues.
- Service is busy and returns a timeout error.
- Degraded performance of the service.

The following design patterns are recommended for handling transient faults:

- **Retry Pattern**   In this pattern, when the remote service is temporarily unavailable, the following strategies are considered to handle failure.

  - **Cancel**   When the calls to remote service are not of type transient and likely to fail. The application immediately returns exceptions instead of trying to call a remote service. An example of such a fault could be authentication failure because of incorrect credentials.

  - **Retry**   If the nature of the error is not standard or rare, the application could retry the failed request because it may be successful. An example of such a fault is a database timeout error that could be caused by prolonged running queries on the database or deadlocks on the tables.

  - **Retry-After Delay**   Using a back-off logic to add a delay in the subsequent retry attempts is recommended when you know the fault is likely to happen again and could be successful at a later point in time.

NOTE **DESIGN GUIDANCE AND BEST PRACTICES FOR RETRY**

Microsoft provides in-build functionality as part of services SDKs to implement a Retry mechanism for transient fault. For more information, please visit the Microsoft documentation "Retry guidance for specific services" at *https://docs.microsoft.com/en-us/azure/architecture/best-practices/retry-service-specific.*

The following code snippet shows the custom C# program to handle transient faults using a retry logic with delay. The transient errors vary based on the service you're using. RemoteServiceCall function calls the remote service; if exceptions happen, the catch block in the following code checks whether the error type is transient. If the error is temporary in nature, the program retries it gracefully.

```
public class RetryAZ300   {
private int retryCount = 3;

    private readonly TimeSpan delay = TimeSpan.FromSeconds(5);
    public async Task RetryWithDelay()       {
      int currentRetry = 0;
      try
      {
        // Call remote service.
        await RemoteServiceCall();
        // Return or break.
        break;
      }
      catch (Exception ex)   {
        currentRetry++;
        // Check if the exception thrown was a transient exception
        // based on the logic in the error detection strategy.
        // Determine whether to retry the operation, as well as how
        // long to wait, based on the retry strategy.
        if (currentRetry > retryCount || !IsTransientInNature(ex))   {
          // If this is not transient, do not retry and throw,
          // rethrow the exception.
                  throw;
      }
      }
      // Wait to retry the operation.
      await Task.Delay(delay);
    }
}
```

■ **Circuit Breaker Pattern** The Circuit Breaker pattern is used for a transient fault that is long lasting, and it's not worthwhile to retry an operation that's most likely to fail. The Circuit Breaker pattern is different from the Retry in the sense that a Retry attempt assumes it will succeed, whereas, in contrast, the Circuit Breaker pattern prevents the application from making an attempt that is likely to fail. The pattern is called Circuit Breaker because it resembles the electrical circuit breaker. There are three states of a Circuit Breaker Pattern:

- **Closed** In a closed state, which is the default state, the requests to services are successful. If there is a transient failure, the Circuit Breaker increments the Failure count, and as soon it exceeds the threshold value within a given period, the circuit breaker changes its state from Closed to Open State.

- **Open** In Open state, an exception is returned immediately before a connection request is made to a remote service.

- **Half-Open** In the Half-Open state, the Circuit Breaker starts the timer as soon as state changes from Closed to Open. When it expires based on the value we define, it makes a limited number of requests to remote service to see if it has been restored. If the request is successful, the Circuit Breaker switches to Closed state; otherwise, it goes back to the Open state and restarts the timer.

The following pseudocode shows an example of a Circuit Breaker implementation using C#:

```
/// <summary>
/// A sample code for Circuit Breaker Pattern
/// </summary>
public class CircuitBreakerForAZ300    {
// CircuitBreakerStateEnum enum, used for three flags of a circuit breaker
    enum CircuitBreakerStateEnum {
        Closed = 0,      Open = 1,     HalfOpen = 2
    }
    private CircuitBreakerStateEnum State { get; set; }
    private readonly object halfOpenSyncObject = new object();
    private bool IsClosed { get; set; }
    private bool IsOpen { get; set; }
// The default constructor of a  CircuitBreakerForAZ300 class to set the default state
and configuration.
    public CircuitBreakerForAZ300(Action remoteServiceCall)          {
        IsClosed = true;
        State = CircuitBreakerStateEnum.Closed;
        TimerForHalfOpenWaitTime = TimeSpan.FromMinutes(3);
        Action = remoteServiceCall;
    }
// The Action denotes the remote service API Call .
    private Action { get; set; } // Call to Remote Service
    private DateTime LastStateChangedDateTimeUTC { get; set; }
    // Threshold Configuration to Switch States
// The following properties are used for timer and threshold values that we will use to
switch from one to another state in the circuit breaker.
    private TimeSpan OpenToHalfOpenWaitTime { get; set; }
    private Exception LastKnownException { get; set; }
    private int MaxAllowedFailedAttempts { get; set; }
    private int FailedAttempts { get; set; }
    private int SuccessfulAttempts { get; set; }
// The following Public RemoteServiceCall function is invoked from the client.
```

```
// It checks whether the state is open and if the timer for the Open state has expired,
it switches to HalfOpen() and makes an attempt to remote service.
        public void RemoteServiceCall (Action action)   {
            if (IsOpen)  {
                if (LastStateChangedDateTimeUTC + OpenToHalfOpenWaitTime < DateTime.
UtcNow)   {
                    try   {
                        Monitor.TryEnter(halfOpenSyncObject, ref lockTaken);
                        if (lockTaken)   {
            // Set the circuit breaker state to HalfOpen.
                            HalfOpen();
            // Attempt the operation.
                            action();
                            // If this action succeeds, close the state and allow other
operations.
                            // In an ideal case, instead of immediately returning to the Closed
state, a counter
                            //  is recommended to check the number of successful attempts and
then switch
                            // circuit breaker to the Closed state.
                            CloseState()

                            return;
}
                        }
                    catch(Exception ex)  {
                            // if there is an exception in the request that was made in
the Half-open state, switch to OpenState immediately.
                            OpenState(ex);
throw;
                        }
                    finally   {
// The HalfOpen state did not return any exceptions, you can Switch the circuit breaker
to ClosedState();
        ClosedState();
                        }
                    }
// The Open timeout hasn't yet expired. Throw a lastKnownException
                throw new CircuitBreakerOpenException(lastKnownException);
                }
//  if the state is in the closed already, this code executes, and state is closed, and
remote service is healthy.
            try {
                action();
            }
            catch (Exception ex) {
                // Log exception
            }
        }
    }
```

Chapter summary

- Azure has massively scaled Cosmos DB NoSQL database with an ability to turnkey global distribution for high availability and disaster recovery.

- Azure Cosmos DB automatically protects your data using encryption at rest or transit and has a different way to set restricted access to the database resources using network firewall or user and permissions.

- Azure Cosmos DB has major industry certifications to comply with compliance obligations.

- Azure Cosmos DB has five ways of setting up the consistency level for data read and write operations to meet your business scenarios.

- Azure Cosmos DB supports native SQL API, MongoDB API, TableAPI, Cassandra API, and Gremlin API, making it easy to migrate to Cosmos DB.

- Azure has a variety of options to run your relational database workload using Azure Platform core product SQL Azure, Azure SQL Data warehouse, Azure database for MySQL, Azure database for PostgreSQL, and Azure database for MariaDB.

- Azure SQL database has three types of database offerings: Single, Elastic, and Managed Instance. Each offering has its own security, performance, and redundancy options.

- Azure SQL databases come with two purchasing models: DTU and vCores. Each has its own scalability, performance, backup, and restore abilities for business continuity and disaster recovery.

- Azure SQL database allows you to create four secondary read-only copies of databases on the same or different datacenters.

- Elastic databases in Azure SQL allow you to efficiently achieve high performance cost-effectively by sharing the unused DTUs among the databases in the pool.

- Azure Integration suite of services provides massively scalable, performant, and highly resilient services for messaging- and events-based architectures.

- Azure Logic Apps, which is a designer-first serverless service, allows defining workflows to trigger an action based on some event by connecting services using more than 200 connectors and custom connectors.

- Azure Event Grid is an event routing service that allows the publisher to send an event to deliver it to one or more event handlerr in real time.

- Azure Relay provides an ability to expose services running on-premises or services behind the corporate network securely to services running on the cloud.

- Azure Notification Hubs gives an ability to send push notifications to a variety of devices on different platforms at massive scale.

- Azure Event Hubs is a big data pipeline solution that ingests a real-time stream of data from different devices and platforms. It then performs aggregation and exposes it to different stream analytic services or storage services for data modeling and reporting.

- The Azure Service Bus is a scalable and highly available message broker service that provides enterprise messaging capabilities. It gives a queueing mechanism with unique ability to deliver the messages in the order they are received or provide a publish/subscribe mechanism to send a message to one or many subscribers.

- Azure monitor provides one common platform to monitor application telemetry data for performance and availability and gives an ability to query data across services.

- Azure provides built-in options to scale an application horizontally automatically. The scaling methods vary from services to services.

- Azure App services has a built-in scaling mechanism. Azure VMs and Service Fabric can be scaled using virtual machine scale sets.

- Azure Functions can be configured to scale automatically using a consumption plan with no configuration or can be scaled using an app service plan with specific scaling configuration.

- Horizontal scaling rules can be either configured based on metrics like CPU or memory consumption or on a schedule.

- Azure Service Fabric allows you to configure an application as either stateless or stateful. The stateful service automatically manages the state using Reliable Collection locally on each fabric cluster.

- Retry and Circuit Breaker patterns allows you to handle transient state across Azure services elegantly.

Thought experiment

In this thought experiment, demonstrate your knowledge and skills that you have acquired throughout the chapter. The answers to the thought experiment are given in the next section.

You're an architect of an online education institution. The institution has its own IT and software development department. The institution has its student base across the world and provides online study courses on various subjects and conducts exams and provides degrees upon successful completion of the course. The course content is made available online during the weekdays, and instructor-led training is held over the weekend. The online applications of the institution have a NoSQL back end and are hosted in the United States. The institution is facing several challenges. First, they are getting feedback from students around the world that applications for online courses and practical exams crash and work slowly at times. Also, machines that are given to them on the weekend for hands-on work run very slow. Second, the students are not notified at times about the class schedule changes. The management of the institution wants to leverage cloud technologies to address these challenges and approaches you to answer the following questions:

1. How can the web application be made available close to the geo-location of the students and scaled based on the unique concurrent student login during exams?

2. How can students be notified of any changes in the courses and exam schedules in real time?

3. How can administrators of the institution be notified when new VMs are created and torn down during weekend classes?

Thought experiment answers

This section contains solutions to the thought experiment.

1. You would consider an application using Azure Web Apps and its back-end database Cosmos DB. The application can be hosted in different datacenters behind the traffic manager, and the back-end Cosmos DB can be configured with geo-distribution based on the need for regional requirements. The Cosmos database and the application can be configured with desired throughput and autoscaling to meet the demand of unique concurrent user login.

2. Use Azure Notification Hubs to send push notification in real time for any changes in the exam schedules or courses. Notification Hubs can facilitate send platform-agnostics notification across different mobile platforms.

3. Using Azure Logic App, a workflow can be configured to send emails to administrators when VMs are created during weekend classes and shut down after off-hours.

Index

A

C

W

X–Y–Z

Plug into learning at

MicrosoftPressStore.com

The Microsoft Press Store by Pearson offers:

- Free U.S. shipping

- Buy an eBook, get three formats – Includes PDF, EPUB, and MOBI to use with your computer, tablet, and mobile devices

- Print & eBook Best Value Packs

- eBook Deal of the Week – Save up to 50% on featured title

- Newsletter – Be the first to hear about new releases, announcements, special offers, and more

- Register your book – Find companion files, errata, and product updates, plus receive a special coupon* to save on your next purchase

 Pearson